Coming of Age:
URBAN AMERICA,
1915–1945

Coming of Age:
URBAN AMERICA,
1915-1945

WILLIAM H. WILSON
North Texas State University

JOHN WILEY & SONS, INC.

New York London Sydney Toronto

Library of Congress Cataloging in Publication Data:

Wilson, William Henry, 1935–
   Coming of age: Urban America, 1915–1945.

   Bibliography: p.
   1. Cities and towns—United States—History.
I. Title.
HT123.W485   301.36′0973   74-2033
ISBN 0-471-94962-0
ISBN 0-471-94963-9 (pbk.)

Printed in the United States of America

10 9 8 7 6 5 4 3 2 1

To Kitty

Preface

American cities matured from 1915 to 1945. Their physical maturity is reflected in a rapid change from the low-profile skylines of 1915 to the cluster of skyscrapers marking even the smaller cities at the end of World War II. Physical maturity involved much more than changes in the city as an environment or container. Black rural-to-urban migrations of the 1910s, 1920s, and 1930s produced the northern black ghettoes and their desperate problems. The fast, comfortable private car seriously competed with mass transit and forced extensive street reform in the interwar years.

As cities matured, they changed in the eyes of their observers. In 1915 few urban analysts thought of urban problems as national problems. By 1945 most analysts thought urban and national problems were inseparable. In 1915 proposals for radically altering cities received little attention. By 1945 calls to abandon the cities found respectable if skeptical audiences. In 1915 cities were thought to be mere creatures of the state governments. By 1945 there was a closer bond between the cities and the federal government than between the cities and the states in which they were located. At the end of World War II it appeared certain, for better or worse, that the national destiny would be played out in cities.

Chapter One describes the physical changes that occurred between 1915 and 1945. Chapter Two discusses the great migration of southern blacks to northern cities and problems of ethnic assimilation. Suburbanization and its consequences are the subjects of Chapter Three. Chapter Four analyzes the successes and failures of urban political reform. Chapter Five discusses the viewpoints of sociologists, novelists, and others who examined the cities between the world wars. Chapter Six deals with varieties of city planning, while the growth of federal-urban relationships is described in Chapter Seven.

vii

Several persons helped to improve this book, although they have no responsibility for the final product. Dwight Hoover, Henry Binford, Richard C. Wade, and Lyle W. Dorsett read the manuscript and made pertinent criticisms. Gustav L. Seligmann, Jr., Richard O. Davies, and Clifford L. Snyder offered help and encouragement. The dedication is an inadequate thanks to my wife for her patience and assistance.

WILLIAM H. WILSON

Contents

Coming of Age:
URBAN AMERICA,
1915–1945

CHAPTER ONE

The Cities Grow Up

American cities grew up in the years from 1915 to 1945.

One way to measure that growth is to see the city of 1915, then the city of 1945, through our own eyes. A contemporary American shot back in time would find a city of 1915 quaint and a bit disconcerting. Were he to land in the same place in 1945, he would experience a city dated in some respects but entirely comprehensible. The difference marks the cities' coming of age.

THE 1915 CITY

The 1915 city was low and squat. Except in lower Manhattan, Chicago's Loop, and a handful of streets elsewhere, buildings were rarely 20 stories above the pavement. Seattle's newly completed L. C. Smith tower soared 500 feet and 42 stories in splendid isolation. In Philadelphia and Milwaukee, nineteenth-century city halls dominated the skyline. Buildings lower than 20 stories could create the illusion of canyonlike streets, if they were densely packed and the streets sufficiently narrow. But few cities had enough buildings for more than the briefest illusions.

This provincial backwardness was not because the United States lacked the know-how. All the contemporary building techniques existed, save for air conditioning and the minor wrinkles born of advancing technology. Ground rents in many cities still were low enough for small buildings to survive downtown. Costs had not yet required placing the growing private bureaucracy in tall vertical files. Nor had many cities or their businessmen, yet succumbed to egotistical skyscrapermania.

Those short downtown streets characterized the compactness of 1915 cities. In Dallas, residential settlement had reached the shores of White Rock Lake, a mere six miles northwest of the commercial

1

district. Dallas' northern city limits would later lie 12 miles and more from downtown, and the contiguous suburbs would stretch settlement even farther. In 1915 the towns of Berkeley, San Mateo, Palo Alto, and San Jose were independent communities with discernible limits. Later they would merge into the urbanized ring around San Francisco Bay. Still later they would all but lose their identities in the "San San" megalopolis, 500 miles of continuous urbanization from north of Sacramento to south of San Diego.

The immediate sights, sounds, and smells of the 1915 city would be more compelling for the traveler from the late twentieth century. Trolleys growled as they picked up speed from passenger stops, clanged bells at intersections, screeched around curves. There were cars, of course, almost two and one half million in the whole country, concentrated in cities and towns. Nearly 900,000 would be produced in 1915, more than a third of them Model T Fords.

But what cars! They were high, narrow, squarish, painted black or dark colors, and most of them sported awkward cloth tops. There were a few closed models, some of them dignified electrics. But the typical driver and his passengers chugged along exposed to the weather unless they fiddled with side curtains, an option rivaling the top for awkwardness. Their engines—hand cranked on the Model T and other cheap cars—started with a splutter and ran with a clackety sound.

The horse and wagon were still important in drayage and delivery. Many were parked along downtown streets and were jammed hub to hub in wholesale and market districts. Here the air was redolent with excrement. Sparrows in flocks, sometimes clouds, descended in quiet moments to feed on the manure. Yet the motor intruded into this nineteenth-century scene. Every year more ungainly, chain-driven, hard-rubber tired trucks replaced the drays.

The streets on which this assortment of vehicles screeched, bounced, and clattered were brick or stone (and many still are, beneath layers of macadam). Brick thoroughfares stretched for miles from the commercial districts, but many side streets were covered with a kind of rolled chat or left unpaved. Cement curbs and sidewalks were common, but traffic control was almost nonexistent, and unstandardized where it did exist. The usual control was an arm-waving policeman, shrill whistle in his mouth, stationed at busy intersections during peak traffic hours.

The attire of people strolling the streets seemed as conducive to discomfort as the crowded trolleys and the bouncy cars. Even on broiling days many men appeared in hats and jackets. Women's styles had just begun their dramatic change from the Gibson Girl days. Full blouses were still the fashion, but hobble skirts were climbing. In the 1915 season the "ultra-fashionable" woman displayed a daring three or four inches of leg above her ankle. Fashion writers counseled the conservative to keep their dresses farther down. The sidewalk crowds trod past display windows unexciting by later standards. Thick black festoons of wires swayed overhead; utilities undergrounding was for the future.

An observer from the late twentieth century would sense something not just quaint, but vaguely disquieting in the scene. Then it would strike him: almost all of the people were white! Blacks were there, to be sure, but identified by uniform or task as menials, not as shoppers or clerks. Blacks could and did shop downtown but had to face so much covert and overt discrimination that most preferred shopping near Negro residential areas.

In middle-class residential areas the visitor from the future would find a rapidly changing scene but one almost light-years from his own time. Although the days of rambling frame and brick houses with big rooms were about over, middle-class dwellings were often cavernous by later standards. Some still included servants' quarters in a wing, near the back stairs, or over the garage. A few electric appliances such as the vacuum sweeper, range, coffee percolator, and "El Radio," a radiant heater, were available. Earnest advertisements explained to the housewifely *avant garde* that "any near-by electric light socket furnishes the power." Entertainment consisted of visiting, railroad excursions, trips to amusement parks, watching crude nickleodeon shows, or joy riding in the car. All in all, it was a narrowly circumscribed, uncomplicated world, about as sophisticated to the late twentieth-century American as the cities of the post-Civil War era. The forms of contemporary machines were there but, like the jerky cars and movies, they seemed closer to amusing caricatures than the real thing.

Hardly anybody thought of the United States as a nation of cities. The nationalizing forces were economic, not anything distinctively urban. Almost anyone with the price of a railroad or interurban ticket could reach the countryside in a few minutes. That was the reality. Cars, which would do so much to weld the urban centers together, were then strictly for short trips. Only someone with a few days' time and a compelling urge to drive over hundreds of miles of muddy lanes could travel between distant cities by car. People who were not trying to prove something took the train.

THE 1945 CITY

Contrast all this with the city of 1945 as seen by our late twentieth-century traveler. By 1945 skyscrapers had sprouted in cities entirely or nearly innocent of them 30 years before. Cities already well supplied had grown a new crop, as in New York, where the Grand Central area was transformed from its apartments, tenements, and lofts of 1915 into a forest of steel and cement. Most of the skyscrapers would appear dated, with much less glass than later models. There were a few glass cages. The Philadelphia Savings Fund Society building was the most prescient, but almost every metropolis had a glassy, boxy, "International Style" tower, its solar heating diminished by that new marvel, air conditioning.

Urban dimensions had changed too. In almost every city of a quarter million or so there were miles of residential areas built in the booming twenties. Even the not-so-booming thirties added their share, especially late in the decade after increasing prosperity and the Federal Housing Administration mortage guarantees made their impact. Cities had sprawled so much that in 1937 the Urbanism Committee of the National Resources Committee could plot a conurbanized band of settlement from New York to Philadelphia.

The houses in these later subdivisions had furniture, appliances, and heating systems essentially like contemporary models. Gadgety ranges (even garbage disposals in a few homes) shared kitchens with electric refrigerators, successors to the ice box. The mildly hideous, starkly functional bathroom had become a place of luxury and style. Oil and gas heating were rapidly replacing sooty coal. The living room held a radio, usually a phonograph, too. No television was there yet, but commercial TV was known to be just around the corner.

Downtown was still vital, indeed would witness a postwar skyscraper boom. Yet downtown businesses were already worried about the planned shopping centers developing in suburbia since the twenties. Branch stores in the centers were a partial solution to the problem. The shopping centers of 1945 lacked enclosed malls and acres of parking, but they were often well done and certainly recognizable for what they were.

The traffic had changed, too. Brick streets and trolleys survived, but in diminished numbers. Buses and trolley buses (trackless trolleys) of nearly contemporary design were much more numerous than the railcars that they were rapidly replacing. Cars and trucks recognizable as twentieth-century vehicles jammed the streets. They were still high and narrow, with long, decklike hoods and small windows, but they were rounded and curved on the outside, comfortable on the inside. Most cars were closed, and had efficient hot water heaters and radios. Here and there a boxy relic from the twenties or early thirties clattered along, but these anomalies survived only because civilian auto production halted during World War II.

The horse by 1945 was relegated to parades. Pedestrians remained, but what pedestrians! Men strolled the streets hatless, jacketless, even tieless. Women had been transformed. To save cloth during wartime many of them, especially young women, followed the prevailing short skirt style. The style decreed that hems should end at the knees, a patriotic sacrifice much appreciated by healthy men. This was not the only concession to war economy, male esthetics, and female comfort, for dresses were lighter, undergarments briefer. Increasing numbers of black shoppers on the streets reflected both the great cityward migration of blacks and the fair success of campaigns to reduce overt racial hostility in downtown stores.

Within and without the cities, thousands of miles of concrete and macadam carried the streamlined traffic. Most highways were two lanes, 18 or 20 feet wide, engineered for the construction techniques and traffic speeds of the twenties. By 1945 they were dated and dangerous. Around large cities there were suggestions of the future: four-lane, divided parkways with limited access; expressways with grade separations; and bypass highways. But these—the Merritt and Wilbur Cross Parkways in Connecticut, the Pennsylvania Turnpike, and the Pasadena Freeway—were hints only. The interstate highway system was more than a generation in the future. Within cities, streets widened to the sidewalks carried an overburden of cars. There were few wide viaducts or other devices for traffic relief. The jam was regulated, however, by thousands of standardized signals and signs. In sum, the city was a bit old-fashioned but in no way strange to the visitor from the late twentieth century.

The physical revolution of 30 years betokened a revolution in thinking about cities. In 1915 most students of urban affairs, the city-watchers, would have agreed that cities not only could, but should, solve their own problems. By 1945, few argued that position. Instead, they said, the United States was an urbanized nation. There was no longer any difference between urban and national problems. Furthermore, the problems of race, rural migration, bad housing, unemployment, crime, traffic, and commercial decay were interrelated and must be solved by coordinated effort. The effort required federal funds and varying degrees of federal direction; the states, by their indifference and obstruction, had counted themselves out long ago.

Boiled down, the 30-year debate was between the people who argued that problems should be met where they fall from local resources, *versus* those who believed in some sort of national formula for solutions. For a few years neither side could be certain of victory.

The political reforms of the late teens and after appeared to prepare cities for coping with their own problems through revamped administration and higher ideals of public service. Streamlined administration helped, sometimes, in some cities. It did not help Chicago and other cities deal with the great black migration beginning in 1915. Nor was suburbanization made more rational by good administration.

Students of the urban scene, whether novelists or social scientists, long cherished the belief that cities possessed the psychic and economic resources to solve their problems. They simply assumed urban survival, turning their attention instead to urban conditions. Planners, however, soon had to face the realities of growth and costs. They had to struggle against suburban dread of the central city, and to convince the overbonded cities to spend still more. The problems of finance overshadowed the philosophical and tactical fights that the planners waged among themselves.

The Great Depression destroyed the idea of metropolitan self-sufficiency. While urban budgets sagged, the New Deal moved beyond traditional federal aids to pump billions of relief and construction dollars into the cities. World War II ended illusions of federal ability to intervene in some urban situations while ignoring others. Deteriorating urban race relations and grossly inadequate housing forced the Roosevelt administration to act. Its actions were often reluctant and inadequate, but actions they were. There would be no turning back. From that time forward a crisis in urban America was a crisis for all America.

CHAPTER TWO

Out of Egypt

About the time of World War I, blacks began moving into the neighborhood of Chicago's Hull House settlement, once a polyglot European immigrant district. The latest arrivals differed in race, life-style, and interests from the old residents, but Jane Addams, the kindly founder of Hull House, ministered to them as she had to the others. "A club of colored women," Miss Addams wrote, "obliged to meet in the evening because they were all wage earners by day were so absorbed in the housing situation and so determined to find out why their own housing conditions were so wretched that it was impossible for the first year to interest them in anything else." [1]

Two or three years later a black carpenter, newly arrived in Chicago, described his circumstances to a friend in Hattiesburg, Mississippi. "I just begin to feel like a man," he wrote. "It's a great deal of pleasure knowing that you have got some privilege[.] My children are going to the same school with the whites and I dont have to umble to no one. I have registered—Will vote the next election and there isnt any 'yes sir and no sir'—its all yes and no and Sam and Bill." [2]

Jane Addams and the black carpenter stood at different points along the spectrum of urban experience. Yet their reactions were symptoms of the ethnic changes in migration from farm to city. In 1915 there was a temporary end to the migrations from Europe, a part of the vast rural-to-urban population shift of the nineteenth and twentieth centuries. Governed by wars and depressions, European immigration broke over the United States in roller waves, each peak

[1] Jane Addams, *The Second Twenty Years at Hull House*, Macmillan, New York, 1930, p. 97.

[2] "Additional Letters of Negro Migrants of 1916–1918: Letters from South to Friends North and from North to Friends South," *J. Negro History, 4,* 459 (1919).

higher than the last, each trough above the previous low. In 1905 immigrants from all sources—mostly European—topped one million, and did so again during four of the next eight years. In 1914, more than 1,218,000 newcomers arrived, but the European war, beginning in August of that year, impeded travel and forced 1915's total down to less than 327,000. The numbers would rise again—more immigrants arrived in 1921 than in 1908 or 1909—but the rise would be temporary.

RESTRICTIONS ON IMMIGRATION

A disparate coalition of nativists, labor leaders, and manufacturers fought for the restriction of European immigrants. They enjoyed one more success in 1917 with a literacy test passed over President Wilson's veto. (Asiatic immigration already had been severely restricted.) After the Great War foreigners filled with what one nativist supposed was "latent deviltry"[3] turned once more to America. Congress responded with the first quota law in 1921, reduced and shifted existing quotas to the disadvantage of Southern and Eastern Europeans in 1924, and established the "national origins" system in 1929. This system admitted an immigrant on the basis of the ratio between inhabitants of the United States claiming his country as their country of origin and the total United States population, as of 1920. It had little practical application because the worldwide depression drastically reduced immigration. A heavy return flow of immigrants, "reverse migration," frequently swelled larger than the number of newcomers. War further reduced immigration until after 1945.

All this had profound effects on the cities, effects not always apparent to the city-watchers of the day. With varying degrees of alarm, sympathy, and understanding they commented on slums and overcrowding, welfare costs and social disorganization, centrifugal growth and neighborhood decay, assimilation and the continuing ghetto. Some of them noticed that the city and its residents picked up the economic and psychic checks, both for the European immigration and for its ending.

THE GREAT MIGRATION

The "great migration" of southern blacks began in 1915 and continued into 1920. It was even more traumatic and disruptive to the

[3] Francis Butler Simkins, *Pitchfork Ben Tillman: South Carolinian*, Louisiana State University Press, 1944, p. 517.

cities than the European immigration it replaced. Its dynamics were similar, for it was a rural-to-urban movement. As with the European migration, in individual cases it was more than a simple trip from farm to city. It could involve several moves to scattered cities, and a lot of geographical crisscrossing before the migrant reached his destination. The point is, his destination was a city.

Black migration to cities, North and South, was nothing new in 1915. The patterns differed, because black urbanization below Mason-Dixon slowed after Reconstruction. When at last twentieth-century blacks turned to southern cities, they did so only at about the same rate as whites. In cities north of Mason-Dixon black migration maintained a steady momentum until the spurt of 1915. Although the absolute urban black increase was about the same in both regions, the relative increase differed significantly. Figures reflect that difference. Urban blacks in the South numbered 1,365,000 in 1900, almost three million in 1930. In the North during those years the number of city blacks shot from 637,000 to more than two and a quarter million. Reckoning the numbers in the 1915–1920 migration is largely guesswork, but about half a million blacks left the rural South during those years, some 75 percent destined for the large cities of the North and West.

As the migration patterns differed in the North and South, so did the white response. In the urban South the relatively fewer migrants could be assimilated within existing caste arrangements. There was some "trouble" here and there when crowded blacks expanded into neighborhoods previously white. In other cities, Winston-Salem and Dallas for instance, blacks and whites cooperated in staking out new expansion areas for both races.

The North felt the tremors of the black migration much more keenly. The shock first registered in the grimy industrial city of East St. Louis, Illinois, on July 2, 1917. On that grisly day a mob of whites, its feigned fury masking careful deliberation, set fire to Negro residences, then coolly shot the fleeing occupants. Other mobs beat and hanged blacks. During the bloody year of 1919 riots broke out in Chicago, Washington, D.C., Omaha, and elsewhere. A sharp depression, not the riots, checked the migration in 1920–1921, but the blacks resumed their trek late in 1922. The movement continued through the twenties and, at a slower pace, through the economically dismal thirties.

Much has been written about the black migration and the resulting urban condition that is culture-bound or racist in varying degrees, or plainly nonsensical. There is also much (often in the same studies) that is insightful and valid. The highly personal task of disentangling

authenticity from invalidity in the recorded black experience, plus
the heterogeneity of the black race itself, limits any discussion to
staking out some general propositions about the great migration and
its aftermath. First, expanding job opportunities in the North were
the prime movers of blacks from southern agriculture to northern
cities. Declining prospects or agricultural mechanization in the
South had little effect. It was true that cotton prices were low during
some years, that there were poor yields during others, and that the
boll weevil damaged crops year in and year out. Yet these influences
are easy to exaggerate, for conditions were by no means uniform over
the entire South. For instance, while cotton prices were about the
same everywhere, costs of production were lower in Texas than in
Georgia or South Carolina. The boll weevil had been chewing on
southern bolls since 1892, when it invaded Texas from Mexico. By
1915 it had advanced to the eastern edge of the cotton belt, while
farmers in weevil-infested regions were learning to reconcile themselves to the pest and to defend their crops against it. The argument
that low cotton prices helped the migration cannot be reversed, for
the soaring prices of 1919–1920 failed to produce a back-to-the-land
movement. Nor did the sickening slump of 1920–1921, 37½ cents to
less than 10 cents per pound, drive blacks to the cities in the face of
serious industrial unemployment. Mechanization's great impact on
southern agriculture came later, in the thirties.

Blacks learned of industrial opportunity from many sources. When
industrialists discovered that the World War had dried up immigration, they turned to the internal peasantry—southern blacks—using
the labor-recruiting techniques that had lured the European peasant
to northern industrial cities. Labor agents operated briefly in the
South before local ordinances stopped them. Race newspapers such
as the militant *Chicago Defender* carried advertisements and editorial exhortations to come north, where high wages and greater freedom replaced poor pay and quasi slavery. Letters from earlier migrants to friends "down home" helped to spread the word. "Never
pay less than $3.00 per day. . . . Remember this is the very lowest
wages. . . . Nothing here but money and it is not hard to get," wrote
a newly established black in East Chicago, Indiana.[4]

All this probably counted for little. The brief labor agent activity
aside, the written word had tough sledding indeed in the southern
black culture. Most southern blacks were truly peasants, whether or
not they lived in rural areas. White southerners had successfully
excluded them from most of what the white world called opportu-

[4] "Additional Letters," 464.

nities. The blacks knew little beyond the confines of their neighborhood, and what they did know was not very specific. Their illiter-
acy rate was appallingly high, between 30 and 35 percent, and it is
probable that some of the people classed as literate were functionally
illiterate. Granting that many copies of the *Defender* passed through
several black hands and that the paper's readership was larger than
its circulation, black poverty limited written appeals. In a day when
10 cents bought a dozen eggs, a dime for the *Defender* was a lot of
money.

Word of mouth was the likely way for news to travel. The literate
ones told the others what the *Defender* contained, but really big
news needed no literate population. (A friend had gone to Detroit. It
was colder longer there, he said on a return visit to Alabama, but he
hadn't frozen to death and didn't intend to. He could vote, and did.
People from all over the South were arriving, he told the skeptics,
and finding jobs, and making it. The city contained sights and activities really indescribable. And the wages! At least $2.72 per day at
Ford's, with raises to the fabled five dollars. What were daily wages
in Alabama? Seventy-five cents?) The wage differential was not all
gravy, for higher prices and costs accompanied the North's higher
wages. ". . . they give you big money for what you do but they
charge you big things for what you get," was the way one Pittsburgh
migrant put it.[5] Yet the migrants enjoyed real gains ranging from
about 50 to 100 percent.

The second proposition about the black migration and its consequences involves the question of black culture, a question generat-
ing large amounts of heat but less of light. It is false to argue, as do
some well-meaning whites, that blacks had no culture because the
slaveowner stripped them of their African heritage and permitted
them only a hand-me-down white culture, much as he allowed them
to wear his cast-off clothes. Culture consists of nongenetic characteristics transferred from generation to generation, and white-black relations in the United States did not extend to this kind of cultural
supervision. Far from being an imitation of white culture, the black
culture was rich in African survivals and American innovations. It
enriched the white culture, especially white music and slang, much
more than most whites imagined. When whites spoke of the lack of a
black culture, what they really meant was that most blacks lacked a
westernized, urbanized middle-class outlook including competition
for long-range social and material goals, deferred gratification, and
the like. There was little in blacks' African background to encourage

[5] "Additional Letters," 459.

such views and even less in American society—north or south—to encourage them. Whites did not directly control black culture, but they rigidly confined black opportunities. Black culture turned away from push-and-shove nineteenth-century individualism to develop distinctive forms of rhythm, language, religious worship, and self-help. The "Harlem Renaissance" and ghetto artistic flowerings elsewhere were products of black determination to preserve and enhance that culture.

The third conditioner of the black experience in great cities was the fact that blacks were Negroid, not Caucasoid. A chasm divided the races, a chasm deeper and wider than the Caucasians' intraracial divisions of religion, nationality, and ethnicity. There were white migrants to cities, too, and resident whites resented their rural peasant ways. The difference was that some white migrants could adapt, infiltrate established white neighborhoods, and become accepted into the dominant culture. Blacks could not. Whites had long since institutionalized their antipathy toward blacks to insure that blacks would not have even the circumscribed opportunities of the despised "micks," "dagos," "wops," and "hunkies."

Blacks were held to "Negro jobs," a misleading designation. With the exception of Pullman porters, "Negro jobs" were not exclusively black, although an institutionalized "job ceiling" was responsible for keeping blacks in mostly menial tasks. On the lower rungs of the job ladder blacks competed with whites for economic survival. In Chicago, in 1910, close to half of all working Afro-American males were porters, or servants, or waiters, or janitors. More than 80 percent of the women were seamstresses, laundresses, servants, and waitresses. Twenty years later things had not changed. The proper percentage of blacks in all occupations based on their percentage of the whole population, was eight percent. Yet blacks held but two percent of the jobs in "clean work," white collar, and skilled labor. Nine percent of blacks were manual laborers, while 34 percent were servants. Some men, and after 1915, some women, held industrial jobs, but jealous white unions and callous managers kept them out of semiskilled and skilled employment. A disproportionate number of black professionals were clergymen or music and dancing teachers, while a relatively small group found jobs in government civil service.

The "job ceiling" operated to keep most blacks out of prestigious jobs, too. Policymaking positions in white-owned businesses were closed to them. Except in government, supervisory jobs went to whites exclusively. Even in government blacks were limited to lower-rung supervisory posts. In banks, savings and loan associations, and stock brokerages blacks were hired—to run errands and sweep out.

A handful of able blacks rose to serve the needs and build the hopes of the race. The careers of Robert S. Abbott, Georgia-born publisher of the *Defender*, Jesse Binga, flamboyant real estate operator and banker, and Edward H. Wright, a rising politician, provided some vicarious fulfillment for other blacks. They provided little proof of anyone's ability to "make it" in Chicago's black ghetto. They were a better demonstration of how few opportunities were available to men of talent and ability.

Publisher Abbott suffered years of penury and virtual failure before launching his weekly *Defender* in 1905. For 10 years it hovered near collapse while Abbott relied on volunteer and poorly paid labor, and on handouts from black friends. He combined a burning desire to vindicate blacks with a talent for picking, usually, able writers and editors. Unusually dark himself, he had suffered scarifying slights from white people and from light-skinned Negroes wherever he went. After the *Defender* went into the black, Abbott, although a celebrity, was tormented in ways that whites in similar circumstances would have escaped. He found blatant discrimination in public accommodations, including, sometimes, those in South America and Europe. His marriage at age 50 to a much younger woman occurred largely because he was prominent and she was light-skinned and highly ornamental. The union ended in divorce. Scores of poor relations expected Abbott to assist them. He did so, even after the Great Depression and the defalcations of trusted subordinates added to his financial woes. Even in success Abbott found no respite from the burdens of his race.

Therefore the argument frequently advanced about Negroes, that they were simply another ethnic group beginning at the bottom of the economic ladder, will not wash. Blacks felt discrimination not only in jobs, but in housing as well. Black housing was inferior to white, and the relative lack of it forced blacks into greater densities than whites. Rents were higher. How much higher depended on the circumstances, as little as 10 or 20 percent, as much as 100 percent or more. As late as the thirties rents in Chicago jumped from 20 to 50 percent when blacks moved into a previously all-white neighborhood. Discrimination also occurred in amusement and recreational facilities and even in retail stores. The Chicago pattern repeated itself over all Northern cities.

The fourth premise about the migration is that newcomers fresh from the South altered, even disrupted, the established Negro sections in northern cities. Pressure from migrating blacks forced whites from the interstices of mixed neighborhoods. It caused many premigration blacks to flee established neighborhoods to escape Deep South "undesirables." The disruption carried a special poignancy for the old, settled black families of northern cities. They cherished family traditions and lived in comfortable, commodious houses in areas such as Chicago's Woodlawn section. They maintained their business and professional memberships, as in Washington's Cosmas Club, and their cultural groups, such as the Treble Clef Club in the same city. Although they felt sympathy for and kinship with the new migrants, they no more wished to live near those often strange, uncouth beings than did most whites. When the migrants spread toward the established, "nice" black neighborhoods, the old black families moved away. Whenever they tried to penetrate a previously all-white district they met a growing white militancy and exclusiveness that rarely respected persons. Whites usually refused to recognize class distinctions in the black community; "niggers" were "niggers" and had to be kept out. Occupation, length of family residence in the city, or status meant little when blacks sought to cross established race residence lines. Such difficulty was not new, of course, but it bore heavily on respectable, old-family blacks who should have received a measure of accommodation and respect. Their situation was especially desperate from about 1918, when migrants had taken up the slack in vacant or underoccupied housing in undesirable neighborhoods.

White hostility ranging from calculated aloofness to the bombing of houses newly occupied by blacks was not the only burden that old-family blacks had to bear. Many had to leave a neighborhood, perhaps a long-cherished house, and settle in another place, only to see the new neighborhodd deteriorate within a few years. A black professional man who had lived on Chicago's near South Side, in a residential pocket in the "bright lights" district, complained of

> *Negroes passing by at all times of the night [who] used the vilest language and engaged in fights. . . . At any time during the night you would hear a shot and the worst kind of cursing. My wife had a young baby and could not stand the nervous strain. We moved out to 51st and Michigan Avenue. It was beautiful out there, the lawn well kept and everything inviting. But the same thing is happening out there. The same class of Negroes who ran us away from 37th Street are moving out there. They creep along slowly like a disease.*[6]

Such a man might move only once during the great migration itself, and he might never meet white hostility directly, but he could

[6] E. Franklin Frazier, *The Negro Family in Chicago*, University of Chicago Press, Chicago, 1932, pp. 111–12.

not escape the impact. Just what psychic toll the great migration took on established black families will never be known. Most had the financial and emotional resources to ease the strain. And there were compensations. The migration was a windfall for black doctors, dentists, and lawyers, especially after race pride quickened among the migrants and the "New Negro" movement swept Northern cities. Then blacks sought out professionals of their own race, for solidarity was one expression of the "New Negro." Black entrepreneurs—real estate ôperators, newspapermen, politicians, morticians—also benefited. On the other hand, the extent of the benefits may easily be overexaggerated. The black upper class, corresponding roughly to the white middle class, was no more, and probably a good deal less, than five percent of the Negro population. The black middle class—teachers, social workers, clerks, Pullman porters—received few direct benefits.

The migrants themselves paid the heaviest price. That is the fifth proposition about the migration. If established blacks moved once or twice from the midteens to the late twenties, some migrants were urban vagabonds, moving from one run-down flat to another. A fourteen-year-old girl migrant whose child was conceived out of wedlock recounted four moves in Chicago within seven years. The moves were counterpoint to family quarrels, a kaleidoscope of relatives coming and going, degraded companions and parental neglect. Another young unmarried mother remembered eight addresses in six years; she had forgotten others.

Urban rootlessness was merely one symptom of a migrant social disorganization approaching chaos. The collapse of family structure reached almost epidemic proportions. This was so, largely because of the profound environmental changes the migrants experienced. Southern blacks of the pre-World War I vintage were what contemporary sociologists said they were—rural peasants. The sun and the seasons set their hours of labor, not the factory time clock. The expression "peasant," then as now, described only a cultural and status situation and was never intended to denigrate the culture or the status. Indeed the black's culture helped him, in the long run, to adjust to an urban milieu in which he remained, despite measurable economic improvement, a second-class citizen. Scarcely anything helped him in the short run.

Urban blacks suffered higher rates of divorce, desertion, illegitimacy, and juvenile delinquency than whites. The rates for migrant neighborhoods were higher in most categories than for blacks in established neighborhoods. A little qualification is needed here. Some of the statistics demonstrating these differences were gathered under conditions of migrant mobility and were doubtless inaccurate. Others masked social biases; for instance, higher migrant juvenile delinquency resulted partly from the greater propensity of the police to arrest footloose young blacks. Some statistical categories reflected white experience well enough but failed to allow for black modes of family organization or the etymological shifts in categories from one culture to the other. The high proportion of widows and widowers among blacks, more than one of every four aged 15 or older in some areas of Chicago, resulted partly from a higher death rate. Death ratios in Harlem were high too, 42 percent more than the whole of New York City, but that was not the only explanation. Women whose husbands had deserted them or who had ended a less formal alliance with a man often called themselves widows. Whether the percentages were a precisely accurate reflection of reality, their message was clear: social disorganization was endemic to the migrants' way of life.

The disorganization was the more painful because of the radical shift away from the stable, extended family of Southern tradition. Family ·stability through slavery, the war itself, Reconstruction, and the nineteenth century was typical of the black experience in the South, just as stability typified the settled black families in northern cities. Many families could not stand the strains of the migration, however, and family disintegration sharpened the sufferings of the migrants.

The southern peasant family had accommodated the illegitimate children of young mothers, attaching little or no stigma to such evidence of premarital sexual intercourse. It was assumed that the mother would form a permanent attachment someday, either with the father or with another man. Meanwhile there were grannies and aunties aplenty to care for the child. In northern cities, social workers reacted primly to stories of illegitimate birth (Negro women reacted in turn by claiming to be "married" or "widowed.") Fewer grannies or aunties went along in the migration or the weary moves to one dreary urban apartment after the other. One index of family disorganization was the rapidly declining number of children per family. Whites believed that newly arrived migrant families included swarms of children, and many did. The number of children in the families of more settled migrants fell, however, both from the ravages of disease and from separations. Negro family size for Chicago as a whole was lower than that of whites, while many migrants to Harlem were childless.

Small families and large tried to meet their financial problems by renting capacious houses or apartments and subrenting the surplus space to roomers. Roomers, or "lodgers," contributed to the family's monthly income, true, but they also contributed to what social surveys called the "lodger evil." In migrant neighborhoods roomers were the rootless ones. Sometimes they were stable, upright people; in other cases they introduced families to disease, crime, and vice. The lodger practice was too widespread to be simply a response to economic necessity. Black families who did not need the money sometimes took in newly arrived friends or relatives until the newcomers found homes of their own. In other cases landlords completely commercialized their homes and in extreme instances exploited the roomers, forcing them to sleep in shifts on the same bed. Whatever his individual circumstances, the roomer was one more evidence of rapid social change and maladjustment.

The migrant, in the midst of his pain and travail, received abundant good intentions from several black or interracial social services. Settlement houses, middle-class churches, urban leagues, YMCAs, and various kinds of self-help organizations tried to ease his transition. They claimed success, but it is doubtful whether they reached the migrant until after he had made his own accommodation to the new urban environment. Many social services were located away from migrant neighborhoods. Other agencies with better sites and more understanding found housing and jobs. They also preached hygiene and decorum. The activities of the Chicago Urban League and similar organizations were beneficial in individual cases and spread an awareness of problems among the black elite and white patrons.

Three circumstances prevented the agencies from having more than a marginal impact on the migrant. First, many middle-class blacks, even those concerned with the migrants' fate, were disgusted by their boisterous, slurred speech, repelled by their smells, and fearful of a white reaction against all blacks induced by migrant behavior. Such attitudes prevented full middle-class involvement in social service projects directed at migrants. Second, the resources were unequal to the task, as in Harlem, where the migrant tide inundated the social service agencies during the 1920s. Third, pamphlets and exhibits on public health, housing, and employment assumed a certain degree of literacy and interest. They also assumed that migrants had the wherewithal and sense of community involvement to buy toothbrushes, attend tuberculosis clinics, and repair leaky hall toilets in their run-down apartment houses. The migrants' rural, peasant background ill-prepared them for the public health problems of crowded urban living, but their fatalism helped inure them to the consequences of their ignorance.

Of all the ghetto institutions, storefront churches of the Holiness and Pentecostal variety reached the most migrants. Few migrants attended the established, middle-class churches, which they found to be staid and impersonal. Established churches such as Chicago's Olivet Baptist and Bethel African Methodist Episcopal helped the migrants, but they were unusual. However much the middle-class black preachers, the social workers, and the urban leaguers might deplore them, the emotional "holy roller" services provided migrant men and women with a catharsis. They were a temporary flight from cracked plaster, overflowing sinks, reeking bathrooms, and squalling children. Some of the shouting, chanting preachers were sincere, others were charlatans, but the migrants gave their scarce cash to both.

They also gave up their nickels to the policy, or numbers racket, a black neighborhood institution of sorts. For five cents the bettor chose a number, and if it matched one selected at a central office, he won. The chances against winning large amounts were astronomical, but the policy tickets were tickets to daydreams of wealth for the people who held them. Even blacks who refused to play the numbers often defended the policy racket. It gave work, and mostly "clean" work, to hundreds of blacks who otherwise would have been forced into menial employment or possibly unemployment.

Underworld types and other less-than-respectable sorts pervaded migrant neighborhoods. They were more visible than the social service agencies, and sometimes more helpful. They asked no questions, conducted no interviews, made no exhortations to buy a toothbrush and use it properly. One young black remembered that "Mama always taught me that whenever I was out and down, . . . 'Well, the Christians, honey, you always go up to the Christians and ask them to give you something to eat, and they will.' Well, the Christians would always give me good advice but that was all, so I just got so . . . whenever I wanted anything I used to make it to the gamblers." [7] Other migrants found escape in drugs and in the criminal life required for most of them to support a drug habit.

Some urban blacks struggled for identity, self-respect, and respect from others through pan-Africanism. Marcus Garvey, a talented aggressive Jamaican, founded the Universal Negro Improvement Association in 1914 and moved its base of operations to New York in 1916. Garvey's eloquence, his pride in his blackness, and his refusal to bow to militant white racism appealed to working-class Negroes whose only significant organizations up to that time had been churches and lodges. The UNIA was a kind of secular religion. Its message was the possibility of freedom, economic independence,

[7] *Ibid.*, p. 78.

and abundance on earth under black leadership. Garvey's lavish ceremonial dress, his sermonizing, and his frequent references to God reinforced the parallel between the UNIA and a universal black church. The doctrine was a humane black separatism, similar to the ideas of black separatists half a century later. Garvey's sometimes garish appearance and rabble-rousing speeches masked his content and put off many more who might have been sympathetic.

Unfortunately Garvey was a better promoter and organizer than he was a businessman. Beset by white hostility, the dishonesty of trusted Garvey associates, and Garvey's own mismanagement, the UNIA businesses collapsed. Garvey himself, convicted of mail fraud in connection with a defunct steamship company, went to prison in March, 1925. President Coolige commuted his sentence late in 1927. The federal government deported him as an alien who had been convicted of a felony in December of that year. At its height during the early 1920s, the UNIA may have enrolled as many as 100,000 members, most of them in New York and other cities in the United States. It probably could claim an additional two to four million interested blacks around the world. It declined rapidly in the late 1920s and was scarcely more than a skeleton when its founder died in 1940.

No account of storefront churches, gamblers, and the Garvey movement should imply that any of them necessarily helped black migrants adjust to urban conditions in the North. They did ease the pains of transition for many migrants, either by taking the newcomers' minds away from their worries or by enhancing their sense of belonging and human dignity. They did nothing for migrants' material conditions and, in fact, left them poorer by the amount of cash enticed from immigrant pockets and purses. Neither they nor the social services could alter migrant conditions in any basic way.

The sixth and final proposition about the migration also concerns costs, but costs in dollars and cents, costs more apparent to many government experts and city-watchers than the human toll. As in other areas of urban life, the cities themselves picked up most of the check. Cities paid for black social disorganization in the higher costs of police and fire protection, jails, litigation, and court administration. Most migrants were either school-age children or young adults whose children would be going to school in a few years. They required more buildings and larger teaching staffs. The problem, numerically expressed, seems small to later urbanites accustomed to population figures in the hundreds of thousands or millions. In 1910 the black residents of Detroit numbered 5741 and increased to 40,838 in 1920. The numbers alone say nothing about the origins, age, and general equipment for urban living of the newcomers, or the ability of urban institutions to assimilate them. Percentages are more revealing. Detroit's black population jumped 611.3 percent in the decade while the white percentage increase was 107. The percentage increase in Cleveland's blacks was over 300, and Chicago's almost 150. The white population of New York's Manhattan borough actually declined more than four percent, but its black population advanced 80 percent, from 60,534 to 109,133.

It was true, as Washington Negroes charged, that black children often went to school in hand-me-down buildings in formerly white neighborhoods, while white children enjoyed the new schools. It was true for all cities, not just Washington. It was just as true that without the migration the new white schools and the money to build them would not have been required so soon. Urban taxpayers footed the bill and took little comfort from the debate.

Diseases of all sorts prevailed in black slums, and exacted more than their grisly charges in human suffering. They raised the costs of public relief and hospitalization, which city taxes paid for in the days before state and federal assistance. Most of the support for private charities also came from urban dwellers. No matter how much the social services struggled, black death rates were two, three, or four times as high as the white. Tuberculosis flourished in Harlem because the indifferent white society would neither initiate nor permit a comprehensive attack on the problems of congestion, substandard housing, and poverty, so encouraging to the disease. On the other hand, it is not very helpful to condemn the white community with cries of "racism." The great migration was a complex social phenomenon no more the "fault" of a white urbanite than it was of a farmer, a small-town resident, or of the migrant himself. Yet the white city dweller would have had to pay a disproportionate share of the costs of ameliorating the migrant's condition. Throwing solutions for the migrant problem on the cities meant, in short, that the problem would not be solved.

While it is useful to distinguish white racism from a reluctance to pay the spiraling social costs of the black migration, there was racism aplenty in white America during the teens and twenties. Race hatred and fear of blacks was not the product of the black migration nor was it confined to urban areas. It was an especially ugly manifestation of a nationwide movement to impose a presumably superior Anglo-Saxon culture on all people in the United States. Races not Anglo-Saxon were to be subordinated and carefully held in check by whites. The race riot of 1917 in East St. Louis and the more widespread riots during the summer of 1919 were urban manifestations of the national white attitude. The Chicago riot in which 23 blacks and

15 whites died should not be seen as something so limited as a white response to black encroachment on previously all-white neighborhoods, although black residential expansion exacerbated an already tense situation. In Washington, where the black influx and encroachment were much less, there was a vicious riot. New York with its booming black population escaped any significant disturbance, but the East Texas town of Longview, where race relations approximated the "Old South" model, experienced a riot and several days of tension.

Racial violence expressed a wide range of postwar tensions and emotions. Black service in the war to make the world "safe for democracy" fueled blacks' growing resentment against restrictions imposed by whites. On the whole the "New Negro" movement was positive, a paean to black culture and achievement. Nevertheless it was on a collision course with white racism. The emotionalism and conformism of wartime no longer had an international focus, but turned inward. Xenophobic whites set themselves against all deviants, whether political, cultural, or racial. Spiraling prices, "wartime" prohibition continued past the Armistice by government edict, and the dislocations of reconversion to peacetime production, all helped to heighten race conflict.

The riots led to several salutary investigations of the black situation and race relations in cities, the most comprehensive resulting in the Chicago Commission on Race Relations publication, *The Negro in Chicago* (1922). The indifferent white community greeted this and other findings, released long after the "trouble" had died down, with yawns. Riot investigators confronted the same wall of white serenity facing social workers who spoke of drug addiction, crumbling flats, overcrowding, and juvenile delinquency, all signs of the serious social pathology in black neighborhoods. Whites were hostile to breaking the interlock of residential restrictions, low-paying "Negro jobs," and deteriorating housing that circumscribed urban black opportunities.

The few whites with the power and will to do anything thought in terms of a wholesome community life for blacks, not in terms of altering blacks' relationship to the rest of society. Chicago's self-made utilities magnate, Samuel Insull, dragooned the city's Gold Coast society into founding a community center for blacks in 1922, and a South Side Boy's Club a year later. Insull, scarcely the monster that local reformers pictured him, gave generously of his own money from altruistic as well as practical concern for the social health of the black community. Had Insull been truly original he would have developed a compensatory hiring system for blacks while enlisting bright, proven black executives for significant jobs with his operating companies. That he didn't is not to say that Insull should be condemned. He did more than most. But it does suggest that most reforming whites shared many of the assumptions of hostile whites about the proper relationship between the black and white communities.

The only way for blacks to break their urban bonds was to join the flight to the suburbs. Moving to the suburbs would not have solved all blacks' problems any more than it brought heaven on earth to white suburbanites. Those blacks who were able to escape would have fled the encircling ring of white housing closed to them by deed restrictions limiting sales to whites. They would have fled their deteriorating environment, with its evermore crowded conditions, its aging houses, and its rising crime rate. They could not escape, not even in one of the most suburbanizing areas in the United States during the 1920s, Los Angeles and its surrounding communities.

In Los Angeles and its suburbs racial residence restrictions alone did not satisfy whites. Some playgrounds were segregated before 1920. Blacks failed in attempts to found country clubs in Santa Monica, Huntington Beach, and Corona during the 1920s. Whites were especially hostile to their efforts because blacks intended the clubs to become centers for residential development. When blacks tried to establish a seashore residence and resort area at Manhattan Beach in the late twenties, the city condemned all beach property owned by blacks and segregated the beach to boot. The National Association for the Advancement of Colored People challenged the segregation in court and won, but a campaign of terror drove most blacks out of Manhattan Beach. Whites in the working-class suburb of Watts chose annexation to Los Angeles in 1926 rather than face the prospect of a black mayor. Blacks had settled in Watts even before the great migration and their continuing settlement there made a Negro mayor a virtual certainty if the town remained independent.

Rumor credited the Ku Klux Klan with forcing the annexation election in Watts and with instigating some of the anti-Negro activity in other suburbs. Klansmen probably urged the segregation and restriction of blacks, but the Klan was far from powerful enough to initiate or direct the pressures. The Klan had suffered a serious loss of prestige in 1923, when 37 Klansmen raided a suburban home believed to contain a winery, and one of the raiders died in a subsequent gun battle with a town marshal. When confiscated Klan membership lists revealed Klansmen in local, state, and federal officialdom, the reaction gathered momentum. That a secret society noted for weird regalia and ritualistic mumbo jumbo could conduct a vigilante raid on a residence and could claim the loyalty of the Los Angeles Chief of Police, among others, was too much for many citizens. Widespread denunciation of the Klan stemmed from fears of its hidden influence, not from concern for the rights of blacks. Anyway, Los Angeles Klansmen feared crime, lax sexual morals, neighborhood decline, Catholics, and other presumed demons more than they feared Negroes. In the cities of the North and West the Klan attracted largely lower-middle-class white men who were overwhelmed by urbanization and technological change, and who felt that their childhood certitudes were rapidly slipping away. They sensed, probably unconsciously, that the blacks were hemmed in well enough and needed their special attentions less than other deviants from the Anglo-Saxon ideal.

THE HARLEM RENAISSANCE

Whites interested in flourishing talents, and the people attracted to the bizarre, patronized the "New Negro" movement and the "Negro Renaissance," which occurred nationwide but centered on Harlem. What is often called the "Harlem Renaissance" comprised two related, but distinct trends. One, to be discussed later, centered on revues and nightclubs. The other involved literature and the visual arts. Among its leading lights were Claude McKay, Langston Hughes, Countee Cullen, and Aaron Douglas. Harlem attracted young black literary and artistic talent because it was large, variegated, exciting, and (viewed from the outside at least) free from provincialism. Harlem represented, not degradation, but hope. There the young talents could express the rising black anger against white repression and appeal to sympathetic whites for understanding of the Negro condition.

Growing white realization of the cruelties embedded in racial segregation fed well-to-do white patronage of black authors. White interest in blacks was one truly "new" feature of the "New Negro" movement. Therefore much black writing was didactic, freighted with a message about the black environment, its heroes and heroines merely "types" created to display the impact of blacks' limited opportunity. Not much of this output sold very well, a few novels such as Claude McKay's *Home to Harlem* (1928) excepted.

Not all black writing dealt with exclusively black themes. McKay's poem, "If We Must Die," now rediscovered and widely reprinted, was not specifically black protest. McKay intended to articulate the undiscovered courage of all oppressed people, whatever their race, wherever their location. The mannered, refined, superintelligent

Countee Cullen hoped to be a great poet, not a *black* poet. Cullen explored the black condition in "Shroud of Color," "Harsh World that Lashest Me," and other poems, but he did so without rancor. Bitterness was foreign to the Romantic tradition and established verse forms in which he wrote. He wished to "make it" as a poet within the larger, Western white culture, and he succeeded.

Langston Hughes was one of a handful of black authors who expressed the black experience in the black idiom. His earthy poems of struggle, love, and death captured African oral traditions. They bespoke a poor people's concerns in blueslike rhythms. On the other hand blacks working in the plastic arts borrowed from easily visible African sculpture. The paintings of Aaron Douglas reveal definite art deco influences, but the shapes and stances of his figures are just as definitely African-inspired. Sculptor Sargent Johnson's works are Western, but their grace and apparent simplicity are of African origin.

The answer to the puzzle, why did so few black authors "go African," lies deeper than the lack of an African literary heritage. It lies instead in the relation between black authors and their largely white patrons, publishers, and readers. That relationship was subtle and complex but two aspects of it are clear. First, sympathetic, emancipated urban whites wanted to learn about the condition of urban blacks in the twentieth-century United States. They were not much interested in black folk literature.

Second, black authors who pushed "blackness" too far found themselves face to face with a weird refraction of the white image of blacks. Whites—emancipated whites especially—believed that blacks were "primitive." Whites of the 1920s in revolt against "civilized" traits of duty, industry, and sexual continence embraced an imagined "primitive" black spontaneity, irresponsibility, and sexual license. That was one reason why black literature so enthralled the urban white *avant garde.* It was also the reason why black authors celebrating blacks' greater humanity and artistic talent had to stop short of allowing these traits to become mere primitivism. Primitivism attracted whites, yes, but a black who found himself wallowing in primitivism was in danger of losing whites who wanted information on the hard realities of black life. He also ran the risk of encouraging even the most understanding whites to relegate himself and other blacks to a second-class "primitive" status.

The second, theatrical side of the Harlem Renaissance appealed most directly to white images of what black life was really like— filled with carefree laughter, spontaneous song, and unabashed sensuality. All-black musicals of the twenties both revived and refined slapstick minstrelsy. Jazz, the blacks' gift to music, came of age in

Shuffle Along (1921). *Runnin' Wild* (1924) gave the world the Charleston. *Blackbirds* (1926) was equally sensational and provided a generic term for the black musical revues of the late twenties. Nightlife was important, too. The chorus entertainment at the Cotton Club (for whites only) and a cluster of speakeasies with jazz bands formed the nucleus of Harlem after dark.

The "lighter" side of the Renaissance developed a pool of black talent and catered to white desires for relaxation, entertainment, and escape. Although both races sensed the ambivalences in Renaissance entertainment, the white seeking and black providing was no more pathological than many other racial contacts of the time. The white slumming parties and the white men searching for black prostitutes with whom to realize their sexual fantasies were not unique to the Renaissance. Such morbidities predated the black cultural boom and they survived it. The Great Depression stilled the enthusiasm, and the money flow, that had made the Renaissance possible. The end of Prohibition signaled the demise of the special Harlem cabaret. After 1933 drinks flowed and blacks performed in white New York.

Some serious drama of the twenties and thirties utilized black themes and performers. It was not really part of the Renaissance, because it was written by whites. This new theatrical view of blacks was an improvement on the darky shows, of course. But much of it persisted in seeing blacks as tragicomic, primitive types given to fantasies and earthy emotions. Smash hits such as Marc Connelly's play *The Green Pastures* (1930) and George Gershwin's opera *Porgy and Bess* (1935) catered to white beliefs about blacks even though they were tastefully done.

The political impact of the great migration in urban, state, and national politics was slight until after World War II. Blacks enjoyed their greatest political success in Chicago, where Mayor William Hale "Big Bill" Thompson recognized black claims to patronage, and vice protection, from his first election in 1915. Although blacks had elected an alderman and had traditionally held places in the civil service, Thompson increased black representation in the city government, including prestigious jobs such as those in the prosecutor's office, to a figure approximating the race's proportionate share. In 1928 Chicago's First Congressional District elected Oscar De Priest, a veteran ward politician, the first black Congressman from the North, and the first black to sit in Congress since Reconstruction. De Priest's two terms were not a symbol of the decline of western civilization, as many whites supposed, but neither were they very useful to blacks, except as an indication of their gradually increasing political power in the North.

Harlem blacks elected assemblymen and aldermen but failed to muster the numbers needed to send one of their own to Congress until 1944, when Adam Clayton Powell, Jr., gained a seat. White opposition to black candidates and district lines that split the Negro vote accounted for the failure. The black political situation should not be seen in terms of Congressional success alone, for civil service and even policymaking positions opened to New York blacks. Los Angeles Negroes took government jobs early in the city's premetropolitan age and held them through the twenties and thirties, the years of growing restrictions against blacks there and elsewhere. None of these political advances should be confused with success. Black representation was pathetically small in proportion to numbers and, while blacks were gaining ground in politics and the urban civil service, they were losing it in other areas. The sad truth was that urban blacks were, in general, more poorly housed, less well received in places of public resort, more discriminated against, and more segregated after the great migration than before it. And the white hostility confining blacks to certain jobs and certain sections of the city was mostly to blame.

By 1930 large areas of the black sections in American cities were ghettos in the sense given the word some 30 years after. That is, they were virtually 100 percent black, most whites having moved from their isolated, interstitial dwellings, and they were slums typified by aging, crumbling buildings. They were the visible result of the web of white restrictions, exhibiting the extreme social pathology of a slum: crime, juvenile delinquency, prostitution, and disease. There was something psychic as well as physical and social about them, too, for they spoke volumes on race relations in the United States.

In 1935 Harlem gave the country a foretaste of the ghetto rioting endemic to cities three decades later. The "background causes" were not new to Harlemites or to social workers. Blacks already embittered by chronic underemployment had withstood an added five years of depression. In Harlem, a well-developed ghetto by the mid-twenties, about three percent of the population lived in dank basement flats without partitions or flush toilets. Housing for many was better only because it was above ground. Men had lost jobs and self-respect. Women stood on one of two prominent "slave mart" street corners outside of Harlem, and sold their labor or their bodies for a pittance. Twenty cents an hour was the top wage for a washerwoman hired under those conditions. The unemployed could go to the welfare office, but there was red tape, some discrimination, and inadequate support. Some 50,000 blacks neither worked nor received welfare payments.

With such a background, the immediate cause could be trivial, as indeed it was. On March 19, 1935, a Puerto Rican youngster was charged by employees of a five-and-ten-cent store with stealing a small knife. There was a scuffle while black shoppers looked on. When the blacks saw the white male employees roughing the boy, they attacked the employees. The Puerto Rican lad was soon released without charge. As in many hyperemotional situations, however, rumor shoved fact aside. In rumor the boy first became black, then he became beaten to death. That none of it was true made no difference to the vengeful crowd of 3000 people milling about the store late that afternoon.

The actions of police reserves only fed the blacks' anger. When speakers harangued the crowd about injustices, including the white merchants' employment discrimination against blacks, the police pulled the orators from their stepladders and arrested them. As afternoon turned to evening, wedges of mounted police and plainclothesmen charged into the crowd, trying to break it up. The police drove their cars along the sidewalks, shoving aside resentful blacks with bumpers and fenders. The police tactics could break the huge crowd into smaller crowds but they could not disperse it. Instead of dissolving into its individual human atoms, the crowd grew in size and militance, and became a mob. Resentment against white store owners, against the police, against denials of opportunity and dignity, suddenly burst into riot and destruction. Bricks flew at police and through store windows. Looting blacks sprinted away with armloads of merchandise. Bands of rioters, each several hundred strong, poured through Lenox Avenue and other streets, breaking up and looting some 200 stores. The police and physical exhaustion finally quelled the mobs in the early morning hours of the twentieth.

The riot was not all destruction and terror. In its aftermath Harlemites told the tale of the Chinese laundryman who hastily placed a sign in his window reading "Me colored too." Possibly the story was apocryphal, but the one about the young black appropriating a new coat while muttering over the unavailability of alterations was true. When the humorous is balanced against the grim, the riot becomes more terrible than not. Three blacks died, and some 30 people required hospitalization, while hundreds of others sustained minor injuries. Property damage totaled over two million depression-style dollars. About 100 people, the majority black, were arrested on various charges.

Most whites blamed the riot on agitators and Communists, taking comfort in reports of Communist activity among rioters. Abundant testimony from black leaders, and from ordinary blacks during the investigation that followed, should have refuted white views. But the truth was too uncomfortable. The report of the city's riot commission was, as usual, indifferently received when it was published a year afterwards. The New York riot was not a "race riot," for the mob target was property not persons, and its deep source was systematic discrimination, not more evident race hatred. Its only positive result for blacks—apart from the temporary gains of looting—was its impetus to an ongoing campaign for greater job opportunities waged by prominent Harlemites against the city's public utilities and other large employers.

AMERICANIZATION

Other migrants besides blacks came to cities after 1915. Settled urbanites mildly resented or ignored rural whites but raised no special barriers against them. Newly arrived Europeans generated much more concern among the people who wished to infuse American ideals. The crusade to "Americanize" the immigrants took on a crazed, xenophobic cast after the United States entered World War I, but the later Americanization movement should not be judged by its wartime aberration. Americanizers were not of one breed. They divided into three types, with some overlapping in individual cases. Some of them clustered about social service agencies such as the settlement houses and the YMCA. Their work centered on the agencies themselves, or sometimes, on persuading the public schools to adopt civics, "citizenship" courses. Others, more concerned with industrial development and welfare capitalism, tried to teach English and the fundamentals of American life to immigrant factory hands. The militant Americanizers had been in the wings since the turn of the century although their heyday came with World War I.

A great deal of ink has been spilled to advance the argument that there was no essential difference between the moderate-social-welfarist Americanization and the militant brand. The settlement house and welfare capitalist crowd preached cultural pluralism with the idea of enriching the American heritage and gradually sinking the urban immigrants' distinctiveness in the larger American civilization. The militants wished to strip him brutally of his Europeanisms and clothe him in an ill-fitting Americanism, all without regard for his humanity. Either way the immigrant lost his heritage, so the argument runs.

There was a similarity between the brands of Americanism, but in a different sense than the argument supposed. The social settlement-welfarist wing was more interested in outward conformity than in a thoroughgoing revolution in the lifelong attitudes and habits of first-generation Americans. They changed few attitudes and habits. Militants like Frances Kellor, obsessed by fears of radicals preying upon susceptible foreigners, also accomplished little even during wartime. True, the Ford Motor Company, through the Ford School, insisted upon a knowledge of English and placed heavy emphasis on its workers' external conformity to "American" norms, but this was a prewar practice that it enlarged after the declaration. Most employers refused to go beyond routine exhortations to naturalization and the hanging of patriotic posters. Employers' militance, when it existed, quickly shaded off into welfare capitalism or returned to work safety concerns. Since schooling workers in concepts of "Americanism" had no impact on the workers' efficiency or safety record, it was uninteresting. Besides, the cultural pluralists offered steady resistance to the militants. At best the militants could only ride the cresting wave of war-induced conformity. They could not reach into immigrant homes and alter life-styles. Both types of Americanizers, therefore, could claim no more than marginal results. Acculturation, as a total social process, proceeded much more rapidly with second-generation Americans.

There were cruel ironies imbedded in the Americanization drive. Southern blacks were as much immigrants as the veriest European "greenhorns," yet nothing was done to Americanize them. A wholesale effort to teach them the rudiments of urban living and of standard English, the usual furniture of "soft" Americanization, might have eased the blacks' transition. But blacks were considered to be Americans already, if they were considered at all. Part of the problem was that the Americanizers wanted the immigrants to Americanize, but not too much. If blacks had truly Americanized, the specter of racial amalgamation would have risen. The same difficulty existed with the European immigrants, although to a lesser degree. The Inter-Racial Council established at the end of the war in November, 1918 exemplified the problem.

The Inter-Racial Council was Frances Kellor's private Americanization group formed when the federal government withdrew its support from her efforts. To later generations the idea of an Inter-Racial Council having nothing to do with blacks or other racial minorities seems bizarre. It did not seem so to a generation that equated race with nationality and ethnicity. The equation spoke volumes. If there were a "Polish race" or a "Russian race," then their thoroughgoing Americanization would have involved, in time, "interracial" courtships, marriages, and residence patterns. The militants showed no interest in this sort of assimilation. Had they looked into their own hearts, would the militants have found a desire for more than outward conformity? Probably not.

Jewish immigrants and old-stock Jews were not a separate problem for Americanizers. They were a problem for other twentieth-century citizens who looked on Jews as more than a religious or cultural group. To most non-Jewish Americans, they were the most distinctive "race" in the country, excepting Negroes and Orientals. Their presence in the United States from colonial times bothered only a few old-style anti-Semites, Christians obsessed with Jewish deicide. Jews faced entirely different attitudes by 1915. The new situation resulted partly from the drive for "Anglo-Saxon" or "Nordic" superiority that began in the nineteenth century. Jews, although not so repressed and confined as blacks, just as certainly failed to qualify as Anglo-Saxons or Nordics. Jews remained Jews whatever their residence or country of origin. Barriers were building rapidly against them when the "new" Russian Jewish immigration burst upon the United States. In the nineteenth century the number of Jews, increasingly those fleeing the Russian pogroms, climbed to a high of 76,373 and a 13.2 percentage of total immigrants in 1892. After the depression of 1893 the Jewish influx followed the larger migration, strong from about 1900 to 1914, dropping rapidly during wartime, then regaining momentum until the restrictive legislation of the twenties staunched the flow. Because of their numbers and their culture the Eastern Jews were more visible and more strange than their Sephardic and German predecessors.

By 1915 the days when Jews were considered to be merely a part of the German community in Milwaukee had passed. Cincinnati's Commercial Club had excluded Jews beginning in the late nineteenth century, a practice fairly widespread among the business organizations of midwestern cities. The practice grew in the twentieth century. It became common in the transitional early 1900s for business and social clubs with older Jewish members to deny membership to the sons or other young relatives of the older Jews. Country clubs, the archtypical social expression of twentieth-century suburbia, vigorously excluded Jews, forcing them to establish their own.

Jews were the most urban of Americans, 98 percent in the mid-1950s. In 1940, one-half of American Jews lived in New York and Chicago. In the twentieth century they faced growing resistance to their entrance into universities and professional schools, which operated on formal or informal quota systems. Similarly, the barriers rose in professions such as medicine. The movement for Jewish hospitals developed in part from the refusal of Gentile hospitals to allow affiliation by Jewish doctors. Most Jewish lawyers counseled a largely Jewish clientele or belonged to firms that did so. Yet ambitious and talented Jews crowded the professions, partly because of discrimination in areas such as banking, finance, and insurance. Ten percent of them were professionals in 1940, compared with less than seven percent of the general population. Jews in "trade" were 50 percent compared with slightly more than 20 percent of the general population, but the statistic scarcely strengthens the "rich Jew merchant" image. Most Jews in that category were clerks, salespeople, tradesmen, and small shopkeepers. Jews were underrepresented in several categories including services, transportation and communication, agriculture, and public service.

The distinctive Jewish occupational profile resulted not only from discrimination but also from Jewish preference and traditions. To the extent that they suffered from discrimination, Jews chafed, sought protection in a highly developed network of voluntary organizations, and were guarded in their contacts with the outside world. But few emigrated. The undertow of departures from the United States, large though it sometimes was, was often obscured by Americans' concern over immigration. In 1915, for instance, departures were over 60 percent of admissions. During 1917 and 1918 the figure soared over 80 percent. Jewish departures were much lower. In 1918, a year of low immigration, the percentage of Jewish emigration peaked at 18.9 percent, although the number of departees was only 687. During the depression thirties, people left the United States in growing numbers, and more people left than arrived in the years from 1933 through 1935. Jewish emigration ran from around 300 to 450 persons per year, at most 16 percent of arriving Jews, but usually only about five or six percent of Jewish arrivals. During the prosperous twenties, when about one-quarter as many people left the country as came to it the percentage of Jewish departures to arrivals was one (or less) to four. No matter how much Jews disliked their peculiar situation in urban America, most of them preferred it to life elsewhere.

The Jewish experience belied assumptions about ethnic minorities in cities. Many Americans assume that the city is the place where the "melting pot" operates, if it operates at all. In the Jewish experience the reverse was true. Isolated Jews found it impossible to observe religious holidays and practices, while big-city Jews in large Jewish communities maintained their religion and their distinctiveness. Interfaith marriages were infrequent, touching 10 percent only in a few homogeneous, mobile communities—San Francisco and Washington, D.C.

Some superficial indicators could mislead an observer into believing that the Jews were melting into the larger society, for secularization overtook Jews as it did other urban populations. The decline of Orthodoxy, the rise of Reform Judaism, the withering of the Yiddish press and exclusively Yiddish organizations, all pointed to a growing religious indifference. Through the twenties and thirties the nineteenth-century immigrant ghettos declined. Few fresh immigrants arrived from Europe once the restrictions took effect. As Jews prospered, they moved to "nicer" residential districts. Their once-fascinating neighborhoods, a jumble of "kosher" shops, tenements, and the vigorous street life, decayed and succumbed to the invasions of more recent immigrants, often blacks. Jews did not, however, meld with non-Jewish whites. Instead they clustered in their own settlements within the new housing developments or the suburbs. The absence of traditional Jewish shops and of Orthodox observants in their distinctive garb gave the new districts the appearance of any other residential area. Close observers were not fooled. As early as the 1920s the sociologist Louis Wirth observed that most Jews had merely exchanged one type of ghetto for another. The new one was less provincial but it was also less secure.

After 1915, with the exception of a few years, immigration to the United States dwindled, but immigration to the cities did not. The cities had to meet the problems of the migrants, most of whom were poor and who adopted the middle-class culture slowly if at all. The most conspicuous migrants were Southern blacks, but major cities contained several distinctive minorities who resisted assimilation in part from preference, in part because it was denied to them. It was bitterly ironic that the larger, more "urban" a city became the less urbane it grew, the more it developed fragmented social and ethnic provincialisms. For many years the Jews, whose highly developed social service agencies saved cities a great deal of welfare expense, were no special burden to their communities. Even their determination to "take care of their own" withered during the 1930s. Few city dwellers, of course, were interested in "solving" the racial-ethnic-immigrant problem. Such provincialism, bigotry, and inaction cannot be condoned, for sympathetic awareness of problems must precede their solution. Yet it is reasonable to ask whether greater awareness would have helped the cities much during the interwar period. Employment discrimination, abominable housing, drug addiction, and militant nativism were especially virulent in urban areas, but they were not bounded by the city limits. They were national dilemmas requiring national action. Some people, but not enough of them, understood that.

CHAPTER THREE

The Promised Land

Toward the end of the twentieth century most city-watchers deplored suburbia and the public policies that allowed suburbia to happen. They scorned the automobile manufacturer, the real estate man, the permissive town council, the land speculator, and the suburbanite himself, each of whom, in his own way, helped to make suburbia a headquarters of withdrawal from the urban realities of fear, racism, drug addiction, rising crime, and tasteless sprawl. The critics spoke of a special kind of suburb, the automobile suburb that began developing in the period just before World War I. The critics dealt .heavily in motives and feelings. To introduce the suburbia of yesteryear we might begin with a fantasy of motive, in part to show the dangers of that approach to so complex a problem.

Ours shall be a fantasy of conspiracy. The chief conspirator, the evil monarch of the suburban scene, is wily, hatchet-faced Henry Ford, hiding behind the five-dollar day, the rural myth, and other smokescreens, chuckling hideously while perfecting the cheap, durable Model T car, 577,036 sold in 1916 alone. "Aha," says Ford, cackling and rubbing his hands, "I have made an inexpensive gasoline car, stimulating the demand for cars in all price ranges, a car that will run wherever there is a road (and some places where there isn't), a car that will drive out the relatively pollutionfree electric and steam cars. With this car a man can live anywhere within a 30-mile radius of his work; therefore people will spread out over the landscape in bland, undifferentiated suburbs. Heh, heh!"

Enter next the real estate agent, a red-faced, paunchy character out of Sinclair Lewis. He is a corner-cutting wheeler-dealer, sharp and crafty, who "develops" tracts for as little money as possible while selling the houses on them for too much, whether "too much" is measured in terms of their quality or what their purchasers can afford. "Aha," says this Babbitt type, "I shall reap enormous profits

33

while I blot out prime agricultural land, uproot ancient trees, despoil recreational areas, and desecrate scenic views. I shall create mass suburbs boring in their similarity, and expensive in their utilities servicing. Ford and those other fellows who are building autos are making all this possible. I am in league with them. Ho ho. In the end we shall destroy the public transit system and the urban sense of community."

"Damn the sense of community, anyway," growls our third villain, the suburbanite. "I want to escape foreigners and other people whose habits and attitudes are different from mine. Negroes are coming out of the rural South in ever larger numbers. They are beginning to take over white neighborhoods and everyone knows that they are impossible neighbors. I'll let somebody else pay the taxes to maintain the city's utilities and services, and to coddle the good-for-nothing Negro poor. Because I am culturally a clod I care nothing for operas, symphonies, and museums. Let 'em rot. Thank goodness for enterprising men like Ford and that real estate fellow who are making my escape possible. There'll be nothing left of the city when all of us are through with it."

Our fantasy is what Henry Ford said of schoolboy history, "bunk." If we believed that people understood the full consequences of their actions, and that they were capable of channeling mass social movements, a conspiracy theory might reasonably explain suburban development. Instead most people saw obvious short-run advantages to automobiles and suburbs. For most, the long-run consequences were incomprehensible.

THE AUTO SUBURBS

The auto suburbs of the interwar period developed simply because millions of people wanted to live in them. The satellite areas of all central cities that had reached a 100,00 population by 1910 grew at a rate far greater than the central cities or the population as a whole. They grew from 6,985,696 to 17,376,710 in 1940, a gain of almost two and a half times. The central cities added a few million more people, from over 21 million to over 35 million, but their rate of growth was much slower. Older cities registered even more dramatic differences between the center and the ring. From 1920 to 1930 Baltimore grew 9.7 percent, its ring, 52 percent. Buffalo's ring held 197,306 souls in 1910 while the city contained 423,715. In 40 years the city grew to 580,132 but the ring population had soared to 509,098. Some suburban rates of increase strained credulity. From 1920 to 1930 Beverly Hills, California increased 2485.9 percent;

Shaker Heights, Ohio, 1000.4 percent, and Elmwood Park, Illinois, 716.7 percent. Low population densities characterized suburbia. Scarsdale, New York boasted a density of only 1446 persons per square mile in 1930. Less posh Dobbs Ferry was more compact— 2392 persons per square mile—but much more dispersed than city densities often exceeding 15,000 persons per square mile. While these figures must be refined and extended for an entirely accurate view of residential suburbia, they indicate the strength of the pull to the satellite areas outside of the central cities. When so many people want suburbia, it is hardly necessary for them to conspire in order to get it.

Sheer growth of the suburban ring tells nothing about motive, only that a lot of people moved to suburbs. The answers to "why" have to be inferential and tentative, because relatively few people have been asked the reasons for their move to the suburbs, and they were asked during the second half of the twentieth century. Not all were able to articulate a reason. Within the limits of inference a strong argument may be made for one reason—an escape to a rural ideal. The argument is based on building styles, suburban appearances, the devices for suburban control, the activities of some developers and the federal government, and the selectivity of suburban growth.

From 1915 through the early forties suburban house styles represented an idealized rural environment. The bungalow or cottage style, a story and a half high, was popular from the 1910 decade through the early thirties. Gently pitched roofs supported by brackets, a small front porch, and simplicity throughout were characteristic. There was sometimes a downstairs bedroom in addition to the small living and dining rooms and kitchen. The attic contained one or two bedrooms, or was left unfinished. Lots were narrow, 40 or 50 feet, but wider than the cottage lots of the late Victorian era. These houses were built for homeowners of modest means, usually by small builders who might put up a string of them a block or two long. Others might go up one at a time, built by carpenters to order for individual customers. Beginning in the twenties a vaguely English bungalow style competed for popularity with the earlier design. The English model boasted a steeply pitched roof with side eaves sometimes falling well below the upper line of the front windows. The front door often had an arched top, and the walkway leading to the backyard might pass under a second archway, open but attached to the house. Again the rule was inexpensive simplicity: no shutters, porches shrinking into stoops, frame construction or brick veneer, composition roofs, and small lots. Garages were common by the early thirties.

Even in these cheap examples the suburban house expressed a return to the clear air, neatness, spaciousness, and one-class neighborliness of an imagined rural existence. But not a complete return. In this idyll there was no place for dawn-to-dusk labor, demeaning poverty, primitive medical care, isolation from schooling, and the other burdens of rural living. The suburban neighborhood instead bespoke a carefully selected, refined ruralism. The freestanding house with its rural architecture meant enough isolation from others for the suburbanite to enjoy his immediate family. The lot might be small, but there was room for a garden, a few trees, and a place for the children to play in safety. The homogeneity of the neighborhood insured that everyone enjoyed about the same income and shared the same view of the world, that is, that everyone "belonged." These were the sought-after features of rural living, too difficult or too expensive to secure near downtown. Otherwise, the suburbanite was a city dweller tied to the metropolitan web of services. He was as angry and frightened as any other urbanite when any part of the complex system failed him.

In their prime, as yet near open fields, even the inexpensive suburban tracts appeared to be a blend of the best of city and country. Or so they seemed to an optimist. Harlan Paul Douglass, in *The Suburban Trend* (1925), thought that he was witness to a benign juncture of urban and rural. In brief articles a few years before Edward Yeomans and the brilliant young critic Lewis Mumford had already staked out dissenting opinions. In 1920, anticipating much of later critiques, Yeomans found a suburban type, smug, well-to-do, largely indifferent to suffering. Women were intent on middle-class pleasures. A few men were aware of the gulf between rich and poor, even feared class warfare, but were too caught up in moneymaking to do anything about it. Mumford surveyed suburbia in 1921, finding there the same segmented, culturally starved, empty life already pervading the cities. The cities themselves had no shared institutions; they were merely congested places where life was sliced up into getting, spending, and socializing. The fleeing suburbanite was doomed to dullness because he created nothing to replace the cultural sahara of the city. He was condemned to suffer a perpetual case of the blahs.

Relatively few people read Yeoman's critique in the *Atlantic Monthly* or Mumford's in The New Republic. Not that it mattered. In the twenties the important thing was what people were seeking, not what they were getting. They were seeking an ideal. Feeble criticisms scarcely matter to questers of the grail.

Striving for the ideal was more evident as the suburbs rose on the income scale. (Usually this accompanied a rise on the distance scale from the central city.) Soon the cottages and the duplexes, similarly styled, were left behind. Larger lots, two-story and sometimes three-story houses, and more expensive cars were the visual expressions of higher income. Styles underwent a change, although several larger versions of the English cottage style could be seen. More prevalent was the Southern colonial, or as it came to be called, the "colonial" without a modifier. This style, a perennial favorite since its revival in the late nineteenth century, featured a floor plan with a center hall dividing the living room from the dining room, and an upstairs hall with four bedrooms opening onto it. The basic design was popular because it was highly flexible and accommodated so many internal and external variations. The colonial house suggested a leisured, not a rude, rural atmosphere. So did the large "cottage" houses and the popular Dutch colonial design.

House styles continued to evoke the rural ideal in the upper middle-class suburbs. Lots became spreading lawns. Austere colonials gave way to sprawling brick colonials with colonnades and bays outside, libraries and billiard rooms within. Lavish Tudor and Norman brick houses suggested aged country estates. Tudor houses replete with stucco, half timbering, and leaded glass windows were especially favored. Frequently they hid behind blankets of shrubs and trees, hinting at the rural delights of elaborate flower gardens and scenic views beyond their barely visible chimneys and steep roofs. Other well-to-do homeowners adapted Renaissance styles to recall the splendor of Italian villas. In the Southwest, Spanish Mission styles were popular in all price ranges, suggesting in their way the wide open spaces of a bygone era.

A few daring souls commissioned houses in Frank Lloyd Wright's prairie architecture style with its low silhouette and wide eaves. In the thirties a few, even more daring, built in the international style. Most homeowners and developers were more comfortable with historic styles or with eclecticism. Only in a few cities did frankly urban styles persist. Around Philadelphia and Baltimore builders put up modest row houses on expensive land for the middle and lower middle-class market. In still other Eastern seaboard cities row houses appeared, but only in strings of three or four, and usually in already well-developed suburbs. Once in a while something reminiscent of a federal period townhouse would rest upon a broad suburban lawn in any part of the country. But such urban penetrations of the suburban ambience were rare.

More than just expensive houses marked the well-to-do suburbs. As suburbs became more exclusive, the utility wires went underground to provide unblemished vistas. The grid street pattern broke up. Streets narrowed, bent to the contours of the land, dipped down hollows, and wound up hills. At intersections they occasionally circled around fountains and statuary. All this, a carry-over from well-planned nineteenth-century suburbs, enhanced the countrylike setting. The really important changes were invisible but were calculated to freeze the expensive suburbs in their contrived bucolic molds for decades, or even forever. These changes came in the shape of deed restrictions on each lot. They bound the owner to build a house rather than hold his land for speculation, required a substantial house, imposed setback regulations, forbade commercial uses, and so on. Such restrictions avoided the visual embarrassments of older suburbs; a scraggle of houses built now close to, now far back from the street, or cheap houses thrown up on the leftover lots of an aging, well-to-do neighborhood.

The so-called "restrictive covenants" by which the buyer agreed to sell only to another Caucasian, have caused a furor disproportionate to their effect. Although the clauses were in force until the Supreme Court overturned them in 1948, they were neither the most important idea behind the elaborate deeds, nor were they the first line of defense against neighborhood heterogeneity. Few members of minority groups could afford to buy in most restricted suburbs, and those few would have been barred by the web of informal restrictons, the "gentlemen's agreements" persisting long after the covenants were struck down. The economic segregation of suburbia is obvious. What is less obvious is the sometimes strict ethnic segregation in yesteryear's suburbs. By unwritten agreement between owners and real estate men there were definite Protestant, or Italian, or Catholic, or Jewish areas in the suburbs. Sometimes these "gentlemen's agreements" were less strictly enforced, so that white families of mixed ethnic or religious background lived side by side. Generally speaking, the more expensive the neighborhood, the more rigid its definition of the people who "belonged."

Muncipal zoning confirmed the character of suburbia. By 1929, 56 of 68 cities of over 100,000 population had adopted zoning. Zoning also spread rapidly through the suburbs on their periphery. In some residential suburbs one purpose of zoning was to fix lot sizes and, practically speaking, the cost of the houses to be built on them. Zoning legislation almost always fixed land at the highest residential classification, excluding apartment houses, duplexes, and stores. Stores were carefully herded into shopping districts not always conveniently located to serve their scattered customers.

Unfortunately all but the most carefully planned suburbs soon lost the illusion of an idealized rural landscape. Wide boulevards and thoroughfares were the sites for some of the largest upper-middle-class houses. Rapid building along them quickly diminished the sense of spaciousness. As the automobile traffic load steadily mounted through the twenties, noise and congestion robbed the boulevard districts of their serenity. Deed restrictions reinforced by zoning regulations preserved the neighborhoods, but the boulevards had forfeited their quietude to the side streets and the newer suburbs.

Industrial suburbanization and deconcentration were less spectacular than residential suburbanization. Employers continued their outward movement up to World War II, but neither the moving nor the remaining industries attracted their share of the population after 1930. Highly industrialized cities and their industrializing suburbs generally continued to grow, but at a lower rate than urban areas having a low proportion of their population engaged in manufacturing. Metropolitan areas with a high industrial concentration grew 5.1 percent in the thirties, 17.2 percent in the forties. Growth rates for areas of low concentration were 18.1 and 34.8 percent for the same periods. Taking the suburbs alone, residential suburbs added almost 32 percent to their populations in the forties, while "producing" or "employing" suburbs gained only 17 percent. Clearly the residential suburbs added more than their proportionate share of the population.

The rapid growth of many central cities in the midwest, southwest, and west was another parallel development. These cities—Kansas City, Dallas, Denver, and Los Angeles among others—grew rapidly by annexation, by building up large vacant tracts within their limits, or both. Building up vacant areas and annexation of surrounding unincorporated territory (providing fresh vacant areas) were significant because the incorporation of adjacent, independent towns was practically impossible in most places by 1915. In effect these newer cities suburbanized the outlying areas within their city limits. The development is a contradiction in terms only if one stands upon a definition of suburbanization as necessarily involving the movement to the economically related but politically independent towns surrounding the central city. In several trans-Mississippi cities there are "suburban" developments in the central cities contiguous to and identical to, residential neighborhoods in suburban towns. It is obvious that the same mixture of human ecology, human aspiration, and technology was applied to the intracity developments as to those outside the central city. Of course this suburbia within the central city could not occur on the eastern seaboard, where cities were surrounded by thick suburban rings and most residential land was long since utilized. There suburbanization had to assume the form of a flight from the city. We should be wary of applying eastern necessity to western experience. Had people really been fleeing from crime, rising taxes, noise, and soot, all but the least affluent would have settled outside the central cities, no matter where they were. That simply did not happen. A brief automobile tour of the gracious residential developments well within the limits of Omaha, Seattle, and other western cities demonstrates that many of the more affluent stayed "in town" to build their rural retreats.

Differential growth rates, east and west, provide still more evidence for this conclusion. The explosive growth of western central cities (beyond the western boundary of Kansas) contrasted sharply with rates of growth to the east. During the twenties northeastern and middlewestern central cities grew less than 19 percent while western cities increased 32 percent. In the depression decade eastern cities slowed almost to a halt, growing only 2.5 percent, while western cities spurted ahead by 13.5 percent. In the forties the eastern cities increased more than 7 percent, but western cities surged nearly 30 percent. Individual cities made spectacular growth gains. From 1920 to 1950 Houston grew from 138,276 to 596,163; Oklahoma City from 91,295 to 243,504; San Diego from 74,361 to 334,387; and sprawling Los Angeles from 576,673 to 1,970,358. The percentages and figures are not listed to celebrate mere growth, nor are they presented in ignorance of the qualitative changes in population that were working against cities. Given, however, trends toward deconcentration, continued growth at the margins of central cities, and the visual evidence, it is clear that a portion of some of this rapid population increase involved central-city neighborhood development indistinguishable from suburbanization.

J. C. NICHOLS AND THE SUBURBS

The career of Jesse Clyde Nichols, a real estate man but scarcely the prototype Babbitt, is a study in superior suburban development. Nichols was born in 1880 at Olathe, Kansas, about 20 miles southwest of Kansas City, Missouri, where he would later make his fortune. He possessed incredible energy, drive, brilliance, and character. Although his father was a well-to-do storekeeper, he took his first job at the age of eight, worked during his high school years, and worked his way through the University of Kansas, where he was an extracurricular dynamo and scholastically at the top of his class. From Kansas he went to Harvard intending to study law, but a classroom assignment diverted him to land development. After leaving Harvard in 1903 with a second A.B. he spent a year in old Mexico and the Southwest, in part to study real estate problems. The next year he returned to Kansas, turned a quick profit in some land deals, and in 1905 he began selling real estate in the largely undeveloped southwestern section of Kansas City.

Nichols sold his first lots with "pep," "hustle," and "abundant naïveté" on the part of both buyer and seller. He made money but clearly something was wrong, because the buyer was left to struggle with contracting for a house, with poorly graded streets, with the extension of expensive utilities to his lot, and with the hazards of property unprotected from adjacent jerry-building or commercial encroachment. All this did nothing for Nichols' reputation as a businessman. Through his own experience he came to realize that development was a fleeting phase of residential real estate, whereas the buyer, the seller, and the community had to live with the results forevermore.

Nichols' solution was the nineteenth-century romantic suburb adapted to automobile use. In part, local situations and developments conditioned his thinking. Southwestern Kansas City and the adjacent area over the Kansas border were topographically well adapted to romantic treatment. The terrain featured moderately to steeply rolling ground occasionally slashed by ridges, creeks, and wild ravines. Little bluffs with limestone outcroppings dotted the area. Some of the timber was scrubby but, on the whole, there were plenty of tall, spreading oaks and elms. A few blocks to the north and east William R. Nelson, the corpulent editor of the Kansas City *Star*, had already established a residential area, the Rockhill district. The street plan was mostly rectilinear, but the houses were done in the shingle style and other rustic designs.

The city's most important inspiration was its park system, designed by George E. Kessler, a talented landscape architect and planner in the best City Beautiful tradition. Kessler emphasized the beauty of the natural terrain. Man should enhance it, but not clutter up the landscape with a lot of phony romantic grottos and rills. Nichols wrote Kessler that he had profited "by the example set by such men as yourself" [1] but, in fact, the young real estate man had to leave the local scene to complete his inspiration.

The elder Frederick Law Olmsted and his firm had brought the nineteenth-century romantic suburb to perfection in Roland Park, an upper-middle-class development outside of Baltimore. At Roland

---

[1] William H. Wilson, *The City Beautiful Movement in Kansas City*, University of Missouri Press, Columbia, Missouri, 1964, p. 131

Park, Olmsted conquered the rough natural landscape with winding drives, wrote deed restrictions, and developed a homeowners' association to enforce them. This was the formula Nichols applied to Kansas City in a 1000-acre tract he had assembled under several ownerships by early 1908. Nichols' plan was not original—innovative work would come later—but he did conceive of the huge tract as a unit, built broad boulevards to public specifications, and deeded them to the city to expand its already impressive system. Kessler and other able designers perfected the layout. Although a purchaser could build a house for as little as $3000, much of Nichols' advertising appealed to people wealthy enough to own cars. By 1915 the Country Club district was frankly an automobile suburb. By the late forties the district covered 5000 acres in southwestern Kansas City and the neighboring subdivisions of Mission Hills and Indian Hills in Kansas. It contained 10,000 houses, some apartments near retail areas, and about 50,000 residents. Several thousand acres of independently developed land abutting the Nichols properties substantially conformed to the precepts of the Country Club district.

As Nichols grew in experience, he multiplied lot restrictions and the services the J. C. Nichols Company offered to its customers. A customer could ask the company for financing assistance, usually necessary because the price of improvements was figured into the lot and minimum house prices ran up to $50,000 in pre-World War I dollars! The J. C. Nichols Company insisted on the right to approve the floor plan, facade, external color scheme, and siting of the house. For that reason, some customers asked the company's design department to handle those matters. The company assigned English designs to certain areas, colonial designs to others, and frowned on contemporary styles. Persistent customers were grudgingly permitted contemporary houses, provided that they bought lots in designated locations. Lot minimums increased in some areas to 200 by 300 feet. Residential streets became narrower and steeper to discourage traffic. No billboards were permitted anywhere. Nichols activated homeowners' associations to police violations in each subdivision. The homes associations ruled every established subdivision in matters sanitary and esthetic. Every property owners' deed carried an agreement to pay the assessments levied by the associations for keeping up public parks, trees, and shrubs, as well as all vacant lots within the subdivision. The associations arranged for, and assessed for, refuse collection and, if needed, street cleaning and any other sprucing up. In unincorporated areas the homes associations maintained the streets and organized fire departments. Nichols was proud of the fact that no resident had ever refused to serve on a homes association board.

Nichols devised deeds with restrictions in force for 25 years. They were automatically renewable for another 25 years, unless five years or more before expiration the holders of a majority of the land in the subdivision petitioned to end the restrictions. The difficulty of doing so virtually assured restrictions in perpetuity. The energetic realtor himself often took to his car, noting unkempt laws and garage doors left carelessly raised. Then he telephoned the offenders, coupling his remonstrance with a brisk pep talk on the beauties of the Country Club district. Residents might consider such activity awesome, or quaint, or merely officious meddling, but they could not doubt that Nichols, his company, and the homes associations effectively controlled the area.

Nichols' contributions to the design of retail shopping centers made his Country Club Plaza internationally famous by the end of the twenties. Early in the decade he began developing a retail district in the Brush Creek hollow west of 47th and Main streets, immediately north of the Country Club district and four miles due south of downtown. He rested his case for "Nichols' folly," as scoffers called it, on two related arguments about the automobile and the psychology of its use, one objectively stated, the other intuitively grasped. First, automobile congestion was approaching the saturation point in the downtown retail districts of the early twenties. The congestion was there for anyone to see and draw his own conclusions. Nichols saw it and wrote about it. More important, he understood, though he did not articulate, the car's overwhelming appeal: if people could not drive downtown to shop, they would drive somewhere else rather than take a trolley downtown. Dispersed shopping districts already existed, of course, but they looked like helter-skelter collections of neighborhood shops or the gimcrack offspring of downtown. Although they usually straggled away from all four sides of a favorably located intersection, their jumble of building styles and heights, their confusion of overhanging signs, gave a motorist approaching from any direction the impression of a garish "strip" development. Many of them survived into the late twentieth century. One such hodgepodge assaulted the eyes merely a mile east of Nichols' Country Club Plaza. Few "strips" provided off-street parking even though it was nothing new. The Olmsted firm had pioneered a parking lot in a small Roland Park shopping district back in 1907.

Instead of strip storefronts Nichols planned a rectangle roughly three blocks by four, with wide streets to encourage cars. The wide streets permitted diagonal parking and the storage of two and a half times as many cars on the streets. Nichols included parking lots— "parking stations" he called them—to handle the overflow from the streets. With one exception the streets were curved to add visual interest and discourage speeding. Short blocks and abundant safety islands encouraged pedestrians. He dotted the Plaza with benches and the same type of sculpture he used in the round points and pocket parks in the residential district.

Nichols chose a Mediterranean motif for the buildings. He kept heights to one or two stories and severely limited the signing so that commercial appeals did not overwhelm the facades. The architecture was pleasing even if derivative and incongruous in the Middle West. Because he believed that office workers monopolized parking space better used many times each day by shoppers, Nichols forbade offices other than doctors' and his own. He constructed special alleys for loading and unloading, and decreed that most remodeling and noisy maintenance work would be done at night. Unlike many commercial developers Nichols sold nothing, retaining full control of his property while renting it for a fixed sum plus a percentage of the gross. Retailers paid through the nose and liked it, for the Plaza did a land-office business. Nichols' triumph was an automobile shopping center, built to a human, pedestrian scale.

Some other urban real estate developers were inspired by Nichols or, as in the case of the combine that developed Los Angeles' Palos Verdes Estates, they drank directly from the fount of inspiration. Federick Law Olmsted, Jr., was one member of a team that designed the residential and commercial area that had a dramatic view of the Pacific Ocean in 1923. Robert C. Gillis' Huntington Palisades development followed a few years later, with a similar romantic design, perpetual restrictions, and a homeowners' association to enforce them. It is difficult to criticize these suburbs from any frame of reference allowing for capitalistic land development. The formal racial restrictions were deplorable but not unlawful when they were written. The belief was widespread that they should be a part, although a minor one, of the deed restrictions in high-grade residential areas. Racial covenants themselves were a nineteenth-century device. Near Los Angeles' southside they did not prevent black invasions of white neighborhoods, if the covenanted areas were near expanding black districts and whites could sell their houses at a premium. It is easy to sneer at developments for "only" the wealthy and the middle class; it is just as easy to forget that they housed a lot of people. The Country Club district alone was home to more than one-tenth of the population of Kansas City, Missouri by the late forties.

Although of low density, the interwar developments were compact by later standards. They usually included ample grounds for public recreation (less needed because of the large yards and the financial ability of the residents to "get away"), for schools, and for public services. Many post-World War II developers could have copied their layouts with profit to the later suburban environment. There is no point in discussing a "failure of the suburbs" when the problem was a social failure to harness the expertise of suburban developers for working-class and minority-group homes. In 1914 Nichols called for deed restrictions and the careful planning of utilities for working-men's residential areas. Without the controls afforded the well-to-do districts, workingmen could not protect their families against changes in land use or overcrowding of adjacent lots. Because utilities typically were not provided before blue-collar lots were sold, the worker paid for his sewer, water, curbs, and street grading through special tax assessments. The amounts raised the cost of his lot, on a per-square-foot basis, to some of the most expensive residential property in the city. Nichols maintained that reformers gave too much thought to the worker's structural housing needs, while treating his neighborhood environment too casually.

The celebrated private developments of modest houses in the twenties and thirties did not reach low-income people. Projects such as Chatham Village in Pittsburgh, built from 1931 to 1936, rented to lower-rung professionals and executives, not to manual laborers. Earlier in Pittsburgh the Chamber Housing Corporation, an arm of the Chamber of Commerce, really tried to finance improved workers' housing to better the city's competitive position in the labor market. The Corporation built a grand total of 304 houses from 1921 to 1924. It lost almost $12,000 while making its minuscule contribution. A later private agency, the Pittsburgh Housing Association, believed in rehabilitating existing dwellings and in keeping up working-class housing standards by strict code enforcement. This fatuous notion was one of the depression's early casualties. The eviction rate soared while workers lost their jobs and fell behind on their rent. Landlords found it impossible to cover their mortgages and operating expenses, to say nothing of pouring money into rehabilitation. Had Nichols or someone else of his caliber been invited to deal with the problem in Pittsburgh or elsewhere, there is a chance, although a slender one, that he might have been able to develop an ingenious national housing solution for all but the most destitute. He was never given any incentive to act on his proposals of 1914, nor did he think to do so on his own initiative.

SUBURBS, PLUS AND MINUS

The long-run benefits of suburbanization were substantial for the suburbanite. He gained a larger lot, more light and air, and more dwelling space for his family. If he lived in a perpetually restricted suburb, he may have enjoyed an appreciating real estate investment along with his other amenities. He may have suffered a few twinges of regret over leaving the city's cultural and recreational facilities, if he had moved too far away to enjoy them regularly. If later surveys are any guide, however, he soon found replacements: yard and garden tending, informal visiting, the rapidly developing phonograph and radio, neighborhood movies. Suburban retail centers replaced downtown for all but major shopping forays. These gains were more than enough to sustain him as certain short-run benefits were lost. The sense of living in a rural-like retreat soon vanished. The initial freedom and exhilaration of running a car over improving streets sometimes turned sour when the car became common property. In some areas the increasing automobile load deteriorated the service and decreased the speed of suburban and interurban trolleys. None of this affected everyone equally, especially not the majority of suburbanites who turned their daily auto commuting into a game or a series of challenges, or who had no conscious thoughts about it.

In short, there is no evidence for any discontent or unrest in the suburbs that is traceable to suburbanization, or to conditions in suburbia. Was there any real "loss," did anyone "pay"? The answer is yes. The older central cities already ringed by suburbs paid the highest price. They had no more land left within their boundaries for suburban-type residential development. They reaped none of the benefits but suffered all of the ills of suburbanization. They picked up the check for the suburban motorist who operated over their streets. They lost retail revenues (relatively, not absolutely) to outlying centers, and they gave up the cream of their taxable population to the suburbs. They endured growing slums and expanding "blighted" areas, both residential and commercial. The motorcar was urban America's most phenomenal development, and, in terms of its public requirements, one of the most expensive.

AUTOMOBILES AND CITIES

The torrent of private automobiles let loose upon the United States in the teens and twenties represented nothing less than a revolution. No truly conservative society would have permitted such machines to run rampant if they uprooted and flung out urban populations into low-density suburbs, caused taxing and bonding into the billions of dollars for new boulevards, harder street surfaces, and traffic control, spewed foul-smelling fumes into the air, and altered social behavior.

A more permissive society might have banned all cars and trucks except emergency vehicles from population centers and decreed that anyone who wished to travel great distances would do so in the comparative speed and safety of limited trains. A brutal, coldly realistic, but somewhat shortsighted society might have summarily executed anyone caught manufacturing or possessing a car. If it is asking too much of people to have strangled the car at birth on the grounds that it did not at once assume its monstrous form, the grounds for ignorance had passed by 1915, when there were 2,332,426 autos. But American society devised no way to control its technology, nor did it want to. Had there been a national referendum on the car, even a loaded one such as "Do you want automobiles even though they are fouling the air, wrecking the streets, and tearing apart the cities as we have known them?" the answer probably would have been an overwhelmingly enthusiastic yes. Nobody seriously questioned the right of anyone to produce cars if he could, or to buy one if he had the money, and to drive it where he would.

Why would so many people make a car the centerpiece of their lives? The positive and immediate advantages of the car far outweighed its disadvantages, which only slowly accumulated, like the effects of an insidious narcotic. First and most important was the tremendous sense of liberation and exhilaration a car gave to its owner. No longer was he confined to interurban rails and schedules when he wanted to joyride in the country. No more would he have to take the streetcar to the amusement rides in the "Electric Park" at the end of the line. Never again would he have to ride the rattling, swaying, crammed trolley to and from work. Of course a lot of this presumed freedom was illusory: the motorist was going to work in any case; the rides at "Electric Park" were the same whether he drove or rode to them, and so was the title on the movie marquee.

The second point in favor of the car was that it granted enough margin of speed, comfort, convenience, and zest in driving to give some substance to the illusion. On a frosty morning in the spring of 1920, Sinclair Lewis' fictional character Babbitt condescendingly offered a ride to a waiting, shivering trolley passenger during his drive downtown. Both Babbitt and the "victim" of his generosity were acutely aware of the difference between sitting on the cushions of Babbitt's car and standing in the aisle of a lurching streetcar, stuffy in a winter overcoat, jostled at every stop by other stuffy, encased bodies. With delight Babbitt "devoted himself to the game of beating trolley cars to the corner: a spurt, a tail-chase, nervous speeding between the huge yellow side of the trolley and the jagged row of parked motors, shooting past just as the trolley stopped—a rare game and a valiant." [2]

In more prosaic language a 1930 traffic control study of Kansas City pointed to the time advantage of cars over trolleys in the outbound evening rush. In the downtown area itself trolleys and cars moved bumper to bumper. But as soon as the car was free to move subject only to infrequent traffic signals, it spurted ahead. In two miles from the retail district the car had gained five minutes on the trolley. It could reach the southwestern city limits, 7½ miles from the retail district, in 25 minutes. An especially swift streetcar running on its own right-of-way for some of the distance, arrived at the same point 15 minutes later. Further east, on less favored lines, the 25-minute auto ride required an hour by public transit.

Third, the car was a rolling status symbol impressing people with the owner's affluence wherever he drove it. At first it was enough simply to have a car in the days when a dependable auto such as the massive Locomobile cost $5000. Merely owning a machine was insufficient by 1915, when Ford sold 355,276 Model T's at $440 for the basic touring car. By then auto manufacturers had discovered the principle of marketing different grades of cars for buyers of varied circumstances. Respect for car and owner was due the Cadillac, the Packard, the lordly Pierce-Arrow, and their possessors; the Model T, usually the first car of a low-income family, was an object of ridicule.

The advantages of the car seemed chimerical only retrospectively, when the country's streets and highways strangled on their load of cars and her citizens choked on exhausts. Driving a car was more expensive than taking a trolley, but it was counted a small price for convenience, speed, comfort, and status. Babbitt saw no inconsistency in berating the streetcar company for its seven-cent fare while priming his car with expensive ether on the coldest mornings, paying 31 cents for a gallon of gasoline, and buying an electric cigar lighter while straining to justify its utility. The noise of early auto traffic was inconsequential to people whose heads were full of the sharp clatter of horses' hoofs and the screech of streetcar flanges on the rails. The stench of automobile fumes was scarcely significant to shoppers who dodged the feces left in the streets by giant draft horses, or who smelled the horses' urine running in the gutters.

Not until the midtwenties did urbanites express ambivalence about mass car ownership. Even then their worries were not those of the late twentieth century. There was only mild concern about the future of "downtown." There were denunciations of the mounting

---

[2] Sinclair Lewis, *Babbitt*, Harcourt, New York, 1922, p. 30.

toll of traffic deaths. Frets about death and the urban economy competed for importance with bother over the morals of young people
whisking away from parental supervision in cars. In any case nobody
seriously suggested a reversion to the horse-and-buggy days.

So Americans bought cars. The number of them shot up more than
a million a year, on the average, for the five years after 1915. The
2,332,426 cars of 1915 had become 8,131,522 at the end of 1920.
Auto registrations bounded up through the twenties, peaking at
23,120,897 in 1929. A depression-induced decline amounted to less
than two and a half million cars and lasted but four years. In 1933, 58
percent of all registered motor vehicles were in places of 1000 or
more population, the density of cars corresponding roughly to the
density of people. After 1933 the number of cars increased again for
every year but 1938, reaching a new height of 29,624,269 in 1941.
The depression affected auto ownership so little because many families had altered their budgets to give the car top priority.

To some people the car had become a necessity, and not only
because of a shift in values. Some public transportation had deteriorated under the onslaught of the car, or had not kept pace with suburban growth. By 1940, 13 million people lived in communities
beyond the reach of public transportation. Even in the depths of the
depression auto sales stayed above their 1915 levels, spurred by
rapid advances in power, comfort, and styling. Flowing fender lines
were common on cars by 1933 and within two more years the last
traces of the boxy body styles disappeared. Improvements in engine
mounting and design, and suspension systems kept pace.

World War II's restrictions took more cars off the road than hard
times, a little over four million. Civilian automobile production
ended early in 1942. Gasoline was severely rationed and most people found tires difficult or impossible to get. But the country's residential structure, to say nothing of its commerce or its war effort,
would not permit the federal government to order cars off the streets.
By the end of 1945 the number of cars was rising rapidly and reached
almost 26 million.

The cities' bill for this engorgement by cars has been obscured by
the conventional history of governmental response to the motor vehicle. That chronicle concentrates on the "good roads" campaign to get
state roads "out of the mud," the introduction (in Oregon, in 1919) of
the gasoline tax, the rapid spread of that tax, and its steady increase
in most states. The 1916 Road Aid Act and the Federal Highway Act
of 1921 are trotted out to show how the national government encouraged states to establish highway departments, to designate certain roads as primary highways (the foundation of a federal system),

and to spend money on highways by granting matching funds.

The conventional history largely accepts the notion that the gasoline tax was "fair" because it was a "user" tax, the revenues from the driving public being paid out in road construction. Like most arguments for the equity of taxation, this one was mostly flapdoodle. The gasoline tax involved serious imbalances for cities, which saw few state-assisted roads built within their borders. The roads that were constructed were not eligible for federal matching funds during the interwar period. A lot of driving was intraurban or suburban, over streets paid for entirely from local property taxes. The commuting "users" received few street construction benefits from the taxes on their gasoline. Some states granted gasoline tax rebates or exemptions to certain commercial users who operated motor vehicles entirely within urban areas, such as dry cleaners or local bus lines. Other states returned a portion of the collections to cities for use in street building. The basic purpose of the tax was to finance nonurban mileage, however, which is where the bulk of the revenues went.

The conventional history fosters the comfortable illusion that road building was the only major governmental response to the automobile. It was not. The residents of central cities paid for signing and illuminating city streets. They paid for increasingly sophisticated traffic control equipment. The task of traffic control quickly outran the abilities of a few patrolmen at busy intersections. The police were first supplied with manual signals, usually operated from a platform in the center of the intersection. Hand-operated signal lights were in use in New York by 1922, and lights timed to permit an uninterrupted traffic flow were installed on Cleveland streets in 1924. From the early twenties onward cities chose between the historic functions of the urban street, vehicle storage, and vehicle travel, in favor of the latter. On the advice of their traffic engineers city councils banned curbside parking or limited it to off-peak hours to create more lanes for moving cars. To keep the cars moving, they forbade left turns at all intersections along the major thoroughfares.

Cities spent millions of dollars in rebuilding their existing streets. In many places even the thoroughfares were made of old-style, "water-bound" macadam, a fine-screened chat laid over a gravel base, kept resilient by rolling and sprinkling. The growing numbers, weight, and power of cars and trucks battered macadam surfaces unmercifully. Street departments at first thickened the traditional surfaces, then applied "bituminous" macadam and concrete. Cobblestone and high-grade wooden streets, satisfactory in the days of light traffic, cracked and sagged under the weight of thousands of treads. Brick streets remained popular even after heavy vehicle traffic assaulted them, for they were durable. They also had to be slowly laid by hand, were bothersome to repair and, like stone, slippery and bumpy. Miles of brick streets disappeared under asphalt as they became worn and rough. Cities not only repaved streets, they widened them, as Boss Pendergast's organization did in Kansas City after 1931. Backed by a lavish bond issue, contractors plowed up parkings, slaughtered tall, arching street trees, and cut deeply into boulevard median strips to give the cars more traffic lanes. Even those who did not like Pendergast hailed the resulting "progress."

None of the preceding discussion denies that cities received some benefits. An incredible amount of employment in garages, salesrooms, parking lots, gas stations, trucking, warehousing, and so on battened on the motor vehicle. One estimate has one job in four dependent directly or indirectly on motor vehicles by 1930. Good roads enhanced the central city's "imperialism" toward the surrounding countryside. Cities found ways to make some money from cars, such as from licenses, usually windshield stickers sold for a nominal sum, or from public parking lots (1924), or coin-operated parking meters, first installed by Oklahoma City in 1935. But the conventional history needs some balance to its explications of "good roads" and the benefits of motor vehicles.

The car was one more of those instruments of change that was "nobody's fault." There would have been room for relatively few cars, and few new expenses, had public policy maintained cities and suburbs in their preautomobile form. But public policy is, in the end, the responsibility of the public. And the public wanted cars. Thus the automobile, the automobile suburb, and the growing debility of the central city were fatefully interwoven.

Cities also suffered qualitative changes in their populations. These changes caused concern at the time, but nothing like the alarms of the late twentieth century. There were, however, portents of things to come. The urban-suburban distribution of Detroit's 2500 families in the social register altered dramatically against the central city in the period 1910 to 1930. In 1910 more than 50 percent of them lived within three miles of the business district, preserving the nineteenth century's close relationship between wealth and its work. Fewer than 10 percent lived beyond the city limits; the rest lived on the fringes of the central city. All that changed in 20 years. In 1930 only 7½ percent of Detroit's elite lived near downtown, while one family in two had retreated to the suburbs of Grosse Point, Bloomfield Hills, or Birmingham. The number of Detroiters inclined to delinquency and dependency increased while the upper-class families moved away.

Sprawl, the ravages of the car, blight, and the slipping urban tax base could have been lessened or prevented if only the cities had maintained their efficient, centralizing rail transit systems, or so the conventional wisdom of the late twentieth century had it. The painful efforts of San Francisco to reestablish rail transit in the sixties and seventies seemed to confirm that judgment. Conventional history coincides with conventional wisdom to the extent that the former decries the decline of railroad and electric interurban traffic and mileage. Conventional history sees the decline of the railroads as the major price paid for the motor vehicle.

Unquestionably the railroads declined. Through the teens and twenties railroad trackage increased slowly, reaching 429,883 miles in 1930. Thereafter it dropped each year, although the demands of World War II slowed abandonments, until 398,054 miles remained in 1945. The number of rail passengers plummeted through the prosperous twenties from the all-time peak of 1,269,913 in 1920 to 707,987 in 1930. Continuing automobile and motor bus inroads plus the depression hurt still more. Travel during World War II improved things somewhat, but in 1950 the number of passengers fell below 500,000. Statistics important from an accounting standpoint, such as passenger miles and revenue per passenger mile were not so depressing, but the long-term trend was unmistakable. The 1930s aside, railroad freight tonnage gradually increased, but trucks were carrying 10 percent of the intercity tonnage in 1941. The more convenient trucks devastated the railroad's business in household goods, livestock, and processed meats. A fair inference is that while trucking itself may have generated some increase in the total amount of freight shipped, the railroads actually lost business to the trucks.

The interurbans were harder hit. Interurbans were oversized electric streetcars running between two cities or towns on their own rights of way. Although never an integrated system, they totaled 15,580 miles in the peak year of 1916, with a heavy concentration of connecting mileage from the trans-Appalachian region through the Middle West. The fortunes of the interurbans fell as rapidly as those of the automobiles rose. Although some lines were poorly located and financed, that scarcely explains the disappearance of almost 13,000 miles of interurban track in 30 years. Nor does rail competition explain it, for the railroads began giving up their local trains in the twenties.

The automobile was the real villain. It developed hard on the heels of the interurban and was noticeably cutting into its business by 1916, although one optimistic interurban developer predicted that "The fad feature of automobile riding will gradually wear off, . . .

and the interurbans will carry their old time allotment of passengers." [3] By 1926 the power and comfort of cars and the quality of highways forced the interurbans to abandon 689 miles of track in that year alone. Additionally, bus competition and the depression shoved abandonments above 1000 miles each year from 1930 to 1933. So much for optimistic predictions. Some interurbans tried to shift to short-haul, less-than-carload freight traffic. The railroads' reluctance to establish joint tariffs, regulatory problems, and competition for the same freight business from the more flexible trucks prevented all but a few lines from making the transition. By the late thirties the local steam train and the interurban were doomed and the long-distance passenger train was in decline.

Late twentieth-century critics were much agitated about the resulting crush of cars in the cities. Here, they argued, was the best place to conserve space, freshen the air, reduce overall transportation costs, and check sprawl. The way to do it was to rebuild the vanished rail-born public mass transit of the central city and its suburban ring. Why, when they were blessed with mass transit, didn't people think to save it?

The answer is that a few people did think to save it. But attempts to salvage rail transit foundered because of public indifference and hostility. Many transit companies had poor reputations. The bad old days of thieving traction lines were not ancient history to adults living in the twenties and thirties. Long-term giveaway franchises, high fares in proportion to wages, rumored and actual bribery of city councils, overcrowded cars, poor service, rattletrap equipment, and incompetent or indifferent management still raised public hackles. Not all lines suffered from these defects, and in the early twentieth century improvements in equipment and service were the rule from city to city. Unfortunately the improvements failed to keep pace with public expectations, and the bad odor remained.

Nor would the public pay for operating costs plus a reasonable return on investment. This public attitude was justified insofar as it recognized that many transit systems were overcapitalized. That is, the lines were deliberately overvalued to force fares up to provide larger dividends to stockholders. One way to do this was to distribute more stock than the company's assets warranted. Another was to retire creaking mule cars to a dilapidated car barn when the line electrified, but to keep both cars and building as "capital investment" on which a return had to be made. Many municipalities imposed but

[3] George W. Hilton and John F. Dué, *The Electric Interurban Railways in America*, Stanford University Press, Stanford, California, 1960, p. 235.

nominal real estate taxes on their traction companies, an arrangement that the public correctly recognized as a form of subsidy.

The trouble was that changes in public attitudes lagged far behind the deteriorating situation of the trolley lines. The higher price levels of the World War I and postwar eras raised true plant and equipment investment to about what the lines said they were. Costs of operation rose much more rapidly than fares. Fare increases were difficult to come by. If the lines were private, increases usually required approval from the city council or a local rate commission, even though the franchise might grant the company a specified return on its investment. Approval was costly in terms of public relations and passengers, more of whom deserted to the motor car with each increase. If the lines were municipally owned, the increase was opposed on the grounds that municipal ownership had been sold to the public as cheaper and more efficient than private ownership. Fares should drop, not increase.

The stubborn public attitude was incomprehensible to many people living in the late twentieth century. They were willing to pay undisguised subsidies to rail transit because they were well aware of the alternative, a stagnating jam of cars and insatiable demands for still more land-gobbling highways. In other words, in the late twentieth century rail mass transit was seen to be a social good, for it handled large numbers of people with reasonable speed and economy, and at a density the motor vehicle could not match. Nor, indeed, could the motor vehicle handle the people at all, unless by expanding highways and streets to the point of having all pavement and no destinations. Because rail mass transit was a social benefit, few people argued in the late twentieth century that the rider should pay all the costs of a rail service expected to approximate automobile standards of comfort, convenience, and speed.

Public expectations in the twenties and thirites were far different, and not only because the car was much more exciting and much less menacing then than later. At that time it was widely believed that enterprises such as public transit lines demonstrated their social utility by making money, not by just existing. If a line could not provide steadily improving service at a price the public would pay, then the most socially useful thing it could do was expire. Such "old" modes of travel giving way to "new" was "progress." The trolley's demise was not seriously thought about, however, because most people believed that the streetcars could be made to pay if their managers really wanted them too. Finally, the public then did not appreciate the "hidden" costs of truck and bus travel. That the highway was a form of subsidy was not well understood, although publicists for the railroads, the interurbans, and the street railways strove to conquer ignorance.

Under these unpleasant circumstances the street railway managers shifted as best they could. They kept old cars in service and postponed improvements. With the more flexible busses, they expanded routes, which required no outlay for rails and wires. At first the busses only fed the trolleys, but their advantages soon caused the managers to substitute them for the railcars. The number of local and overland busses rose from 17,808 in 1925 to 162,125 in 1945. Trolley busses (trackless trolleys) answered automobile drivers who complained of bumpy tracks; with the rubber-tired trolleys the tracks could be filled in, the line could be extended at the cost of only the overhead wire, and the trolley bus could pull up to the curb for its passengers just as the motorbus. The bus and the trolley bus ran on the same portion of the street as the car, thus slowing all traffic, a disadvantage not fully grasped at first.

The rise and decline of Los Angeles' great Pacific Electric Railway place those rail transit problems in focus. Wealthy Henry E. Huntington organized the Pacific Electric in 1901 and thrust its tracks beyond the fringe of settlement to the lands owned by his Huntington Land and Improvement Company. Huntington subdivided his land and garnered traffic for the Pacific Electric at opportune times. Within a few years of Pacific Electric's founding, Edward H. Harriman, president of the Southern Pacific, became its principal stockholder. In 1911 Huntington bowed out of the Pacific Electric and took control of the Los Angeles Railway, the city streetcar operation, while the Pacific Electric became a subsidiary of the Southern Pacific. The 1911 reorganization added a number of other interurban lines to the Pacific Electric.

Through all of these corporate evolutions the line improved its roadbed and equipment, extended its mileage, and upgraded its service. During the twenties the P.E. operated about 1000 miles of track, some of it double and even quadruple. Its route mileage (counting overlaps) was 760 and radiated in all directions from downtown Los Angeles. Most of the routes ran in an arc from due west to southeast, plus a cluster of tracks in the northeast, and a long run over 60 miles due east to San Bernardino and beyond. The P.E.'s "big red cars" ran at a headway (time interval between trains) of 7.5 minutes on the busiest routes. The fortunate Angelenos who lived along overlapping routes could expect cars at even shorter intervals.

The Pacific Electric was strong in part because it covered the Los Angeles area so well. It also enjoyed a considerable carload freight interchange with the parent Southern Pacific. Prior to the twenties it was only once seriously hurt by auto competition, in 1914. Nineteen fourteen and 1915 were the years of the "jitney," a nationwide phenomenon coinciding with the recession at the outset of World War I. In Los Angeles numbers of unemployed persons cruised the streetcar routes in secondhand jalopies offering rides to trolley patrons for the price of a fare or less. City councils across the country quickly legislated the jitneys out of existence, but they were a portent of the future. Relative to cars the P. E. lost passengers, but not absolutely until after 1923. It fought back more effectively than most electrics, establishing its own bus company in 1923 and offering door-to-rail truck freight service in 1929. In hard times, as in the period of rapid cost increases during World War I, it could count on the Southern Pacific to pull it through.

For all of these reasons, plus the rapid growth of the Los Angeles area, the Pacific Electric remained in relatively good condition through the thirties, and its passenger traffic boomed during World War II. It dropped a few unproductive routes in the twenties, but extensive abandonments did not begin until after 1935, although crowded streets and aging equipment caused a deterioration of service. A number of important runs survived into the 1950s. The P. E. was originally an interurban, but metropolitan growth made it a suburban streetcar line, except for the San Bernardino route. The runs west to Hollywood, Beverley Hills, and Santa Monica were really local trolleys.

The planning commissions of Los Angeles and Los Angeles County, and the California Railroad Commission all recognized that the P. E. and the Los Angeles Railway were vital to metropolitan passenger transport. In the early twenties they urgently recommended improvement and extension of the line to combat the glut of motor vehicles. By 1923 downtown Los Angeles was strangling on the hodgepodge of cars, trucks, busses, streetcars, and jumbled local and through traffic clogging its streets. No wonder, for auto registrations in Los Angeles County, under 20,000 in 1910, rose to over 100,000 in 1920, passed 500,000 in 1924 (when 262,000 cars entered and left downtown daily), and neared 800,000 in 1930. In the area's mild climate the relatively open and inefficiently heated cars of the teens and early twenties could be operated comfortably. The resulting demand for good streets and roads produced more cars, busses, and trucks, which encouraged greater deconcentration of industry, retail business, and residence tracts. The commissioners' recommendation to stave off further sprawl and paralysis by beefing up rail transit was one that any late twentieth-century critic would applaud.

But it was not to be. There were several reasons. First, the wailing and gnashing of teeth over the disappearance of the "big red cars" has obscured the fact that Huntington built his lines, not to make money from them, but to exploit his real estate holdings. Although well managed, the Pacific Electric never made enough to attract the capital needed for the tremendous improvements that the midtwenties' public demanded. Second, the rail commission could not conscientiously compel the privately owned P. E. to retain its weaker lines, however socially desirable the service. Third, tying the P. E. albatross to the healthier Los Angeles Railway would work only if both lines became municipally owned. The P. E. was capitalized at $100 million, the Los Angeles Railway at $20 million, and the city's buying them out, while often recommended, was never successfully negotiated. Fourth, the suburbs bitterly objected to public ownership, which they saw as a move to shore up the choking urban core at the expense of decentralized retail, office, and industrial districts. Their opposition probably prevented county participation in any public ownership scheme. Fifth, there was no way to compel the railways to extend their lines or improve service in the face of their poor financial showing. Sixth, the belief that private ownership was more "efficient" than public was as strong in Los Angeles as anywhere else. The idea that metropolitan transit might be a social necessity and yet beyond the resources of private enterprise, was an idea born too late to save the Pacific Electric.

Seventh, to a planner gifted with short-range vision only, it seemed that the car might be cheaper to cope with than rail transit. Banning parking here, widening a street there, establishing speed limits, synchronizing traffic signals, building a few grade separations, and abolishing left turns would take care of the car. By the midtwenties it was clear that such makeshifts, important as they were for safety and smooth traffic flow, were not taking care of the car. Next the county proposed a series of auto highways to handle the load, and the people happily authorized bond issues to pay for them. Los Angeles had jumped on its unending treadmill of providing more road surface for more cars, thus encouraging more cars and requiring still more road surface.

If the interwar developments in the suburbs, in motor vehicle use, and in rapid transit demonstrate anything conclusively, it is the public's indifference to the few people with foresight. Most people wanted urban sprawl, they wanted cars, they cared little for the fate of public transit, and less for those who warned of mistakes and inadequacies. The cities and their residents paid for these attitudes, and will continue to pay for them. In the twenties and thirties, most people counted the results as worth the cost.

CHAPTER FOUR

Varieties of Politics

Council-manager government excited more interest and comment among political scientists and students of public administration from 1915 to 1945 than any other single development on the urban scene. At first blush it is difficult to see why. After all, council-manager government came close to being the norm for small and medium-sized cities after World War II. Postwar students largely occupied themselves with the relationships between councils and managers in various situations, rather than with fundamental questions about the success or failure of the scheme itself. Success, if the spread of the plan could be called that, was assured.

COUNCIL MANAGER SYSTEMS

Widespread acceptance of the council-manager form dates from its adoption in 1913 at Dayton, Ohio, in the wake of a disastrous flood. Dayton was a good-sized manufacturing city. Its success in reducing infant mortality, collecting garbage cheaply, and introducing an eight-hour day for municipal employees gave the plan a cachet. By 1916 some 50 cities, mostly small-to-medium-sized by the standards of the day, had accepted the plan. For the next several years urban America went on a council-manager binge. In 1920 almost 160 cities had acquired managers and the other trappings of the plan. During the twenties many states eased their cities' paths to the council-manager system. State legislatures passed laws increasing home rule, that is, granting greater local control of urban departments such as police or sanitation. Before, governors often had appointed the department heads, thereby holding powerful offices for state patronage or for bargaining with urban political leaders. Legislators took that power from the governors and gave it to city councils or to the urban electorate directly. Legislators also passed enabling acts or option

58

bills empowering cities to choose among the generally accepted plans of governance.

By 1930, exactly 388 cities had switched from commission and mayor-council forms to the council-manager form. The rate of adoption, slowing through the twenties, continued to drop through the thirties and forties. By 1945, nonetheless, 637 cities had converted to council-manager government. There were 28 backsliders by then, especially among larger cities. The voters of Akron in 1923 and Cleveland in 1931 turned out the council-manager form after trials of three and seven years, respectively. Citizens in Rochester reverted to partisan elections in 1931 after three years of nonpartisanship. Exceptions aside, the council-manager plan had advanced very well, especially in small and medium-sized cities.

This advance encouraged students of local politics and public administration, almost all of whom endorsed the council-manager idea. They were eager to examine, and to propagandize, a municipal development that seemed to prove that decent government would triumph. Time, at last, was on their side. These professional analysts were excited, too, because the council-manager plan stood at the center of a congeries of reforms, most of them considered essential to the plan itself. But each had its own virtue, and reform-minded students of municipal government were concerned for them, individually and collectively.

Reformers had worked out the programs during the late nineteenth and early twentieth centuries. It remained for the National Municipal League to unite their ideas, so far as urban government went, in its Model City Charter, completed in 1916 and periodically revised since then. The reforms included a home rule provision, already discussed; a unicameral council elected by the voters as a whole, abolishing ward-based representation under the old aldermanic system; a mayor chosen by the councilmen from among themselves and confined mostly to ceremonial duties; a city manager, the "chief executive officer" of the city, responsible to the council as a whole and empowered to appoint most of the heads of administrative departments; departments of law, health, works and utilities, safety and welfare, education, and finance, with emphasis on departmental grouping by function and provisions for adding or deleting departments; an urban civil service; a utilities policy developed for public benefit; and advanced systems of finance and accounting. Because so many jobs were to be filled by appointment, the ballot would be short (confined to the most important offices) and preferably nonpartisan. Later revisions concerned mostly changes in finance, taxation, and civil service; extensions of the planning and zoning function, and clarifications of contratural relationships with outside agencies.

The rationale for the council-manager plan had been thought through by 1915 but its greatest employment, coincident with the spread of council-manager governments, occurred after that date. The basic argument—the council-manager plan is similar to a business organization—was repeated endlessly through the years. Unfortunately it degenerated into a catchphrase, "business government by businessmen, not politicians," or some such remark, as though that were a sufficient justification in itself. Scholars rightly deplored such mindless equations, pointing out that government was a complex operation of aids and services not reducible to nice profit-and-loss calculations. Businessmen as a group, they argued, possessed no special qualifications for running a city.

Recent historical research has gone farther, coupling the "business-in-government" argument to a reappraisal of urban reform. According to this reinterpretation, the urban progressive reformers who introduced the council-manager form were not middle-class do-gooders or professionals such as doctors, lawyers, teachers, or ministers. They were not driven to reform by perceptions of evil, or by fears of powerful labor unions, or great corporations, or a loss of status relative to the new men of business. Instead they were business and industrial leaders themselves, hard-eyed, cynical men who knew what they wanted and how to get it. What they wanted was a centralized urban administration that would efficiently organize the city's services—transportation, sanitation, welfare, and the rest—according to the business view of what was good for the city. Public transportation to improve blue-collar journeys to work was one such businessmen's concern. Another was a citywide department of education that would speed the assimilation of future workers by teaching standard English and United States history in immigrant-district schools.

The centralized manager administration, professionally staffed, was not only more efficient than the mayor-council form, it reduced or eliminated the lower- and lower middle-class influence in government that interfered with businessmen's citywide concerns. No longer could persons of no economic importance importune their ward aldermen for street paving or playground equipment. New-style councilmen left such matters to the professionals who regarded the needs of the city as a whole. Businessmen worked this revolution in urban government by using the manager plan-business analogy to win over colleagues, by adopting the rhetoric of democracy when on public display, and by adroitly turning the media (owned by large businessmen) to their advantage.

This interpretation of the businessman as reformer is compelling as far as it goes, and its proofs carry it a long way. Prominent businessmen initiated the council-manager plan in city after city, large and small. George Eastman, head of the giant Eastman Kodak firm, was the driving force behind Rochester's adoption of council-manager government in 1925. In Dallas, the Chamber of Commerce, George B. Dealey, the influential publisher of the *Morning News,* and a gilt-edged association for civic improvements urged the council-manager plan as a replacement for the commission system then in use. The rapidly growing Texas city adopted the council-manager form in 1930. In Janesville, Wisconsin, a small industrial and trading city, the charter reform movement began with businessmen. The movement succeeded in 1923. Two manufacturers organized the drive for a council-manager system in Charlotte, North Carolina, after discussing the idea at their country club. In 1929, when Charlotte's population was 83,000, it joined the growing list of middle-sized cities with council-manager governments.

Voting returns lend further support to the view that the council-manager movement was a reform of the upper class. In a typical city the council-manager elections went heavily in favor of the new form in wealthy and well-to-do wards. The plan carried middle-class wards handily, but it did less well as the wards dropped on the economic scale, suffering overwhelming defeats in working-class wards. In Janesville, heavy majorities in the wealthiest wards overcame two-to-one opposition in the blue-collar side of town. Rochester's council-manager charter went over well in the higher-priced residential areas but fared badly where workers lived. Union labor led the fight against the council-manager scheme in Charlotte. In Berkeley, California, opposition to the 1923 charter changes came mostly from West Berkeley, where Mexican-Americans, blacks, and recent European immigrants lived, and from South Berkeley, an area of modest to cheap houses.

The evidence for council-manager government as an upper-class reform is persuasive but it is not conclusive. For one thing, the reformer's equation of the council-manager form with business organization was more thoughtful and realistic than is usually admitted. In the beginning the reformers had to counter the argument that the old mayor-council government was sound because it followed the forms of the federal government. Ninety-five percent of the business of local government was not legislative, they argued, it was administrative. The cry that "there is no Republican or Democratic way to lay a sewer pipe" would not have been raised unless there had been, in fact, partisan interference in matters within the realm of administration and expertise. The reformers believed that the mayor and council, once having established a policy—where sewers were to be laid and how they were to be paid for—should have withdrawn. Instead mayors and councils, unlike the President and Congress, frequently interfered with the award of contracts, with inspections, and with payments for completed work. Reformers often watched in dismay while well-intentioned councils occupied whole evenings in the uncongressional activity of passing upon routine city expenditures. To them it was obvious that mayors and councils were not following the national models of legislation and policymaking but were fooling around with administration and petty details.

If most of the activity of urban government·was administrative, what organizational and procedural model should it follow? Reformers had the answer: the corporate form, which separated policymaking and administration. Before the reformers could equate the council-manager plan with business methods, they had to reject a similar agrument in favor of the commission plan. Galveston, Texas first used the commission form in 1900 in the wake of a hurricane and tidal wave that destroyed the city. The old aldermanic government, bumbling in the best of times, was utterly unable to cope with the disaster. In the emergency the governor of Texas appointed a commission of five businessmen. His appointees rebuilt the city, cut the tax rate, and retired some of the old municipal debts. The commission was ratified by law in 1903, when the commissioners were made elective.

The commission scheme spread rapidly until about 1915, when roughly 500 cities and towns had adopted it. Along the way it picked up other reforms, including the nonpartisan ballot and the assignment of each commissioner to specific departments, such as police and fire. By the late teens commission government was declining rapidly. Municipalities reverted to the mayor-council form or, more often, adopted the city manager plan. The basic problem with the commission plan was this: what was good for a municipal emergency was not good for policy or administration over the long pull. The commissioners tended to approve one another's budget requests, to protect one another's reputations, and generally to run a government-by-logrolling. Even though they were administrators, voters elected them to their part-time offices for other reasons, including personal popularity. Nevertheless the apology for the commission plan was that the commissioners resembled a business board of directors.

Richard S. Childs, the tireless young business executive and reformer, did not agree. In 1910 he read the commission–board of directors analogy and shook his head. No, the commissioners were not a board of directors, and they would not be until they got out of administration and appointed the equivalent of a general manager to oversee the departments. Childs, already the leading advocate of the short ballot and the secretary of his brainchild, the New York State Short Ballot Organization, thereupon fathered another reform idea. He imagined a municipal executive endowed with complete administrative control, the commissioners retiring to strictly policymaking roles. The commissioners became, in effect, councilmen with limited powers, but the new scheme was known for a time as the commission-manager plan to give it the appearance of a variation on the theme of commission government. Childs named the urban chief executive the "city manager," a title which stuck so firmly that the council-manager system is often called the "city manager plan."

Now the way was clear for developing the similarities between the council-manager form and the forms of business organization. The council, like a corporate board of directors, would concern itself with policymaking. Periodically it would review the administrative work of the chief executive officer and his department. Corporate board members did not fiddle with administrative matters, nor did they devote a lot of time to the business. The council would behave in the same way. Just as corporate directors were chosen for their breadth of view and keen perception, traits well-suited to policy formation, so would councilmen be selected. Men of ability would agree to campaign and serve, moreover, because they would need to devote so little time to municipal business.

The arguments favoring other reforms were similarly well thought through. At-large elections gave the citizen a chance to determine who all of his local governors would be. The short ballot limited to important offices would replace lists so long that not even conscientious citizens were able to evaluate all of the candidates. These arguments were open to attack, of course, but they were not shallow or silly. In all, the council-manager reformers had developed a careful rationale for their system. That it was on occasion reduced to superficiality is no argument against it.

Other problems with the upper-class reform interpretation have to do with the wide acceptance of council-manager reform, or some of its components, in all types of cities except the very largest. Middle-class people generally upheld the council-manager emphasis on honesty and efficiency. The idea of efficiency mesmerized engineers, professors, and others who were by no means industrialists or business leaders. For instance, business leaders often contributed to municipal research bureaus but others were interested, too. The bureaus were organized to investigate the city administration and publish their findings with suggestions for greater efficiency. The ideal municipal research bureau was to be absolutely nonpartisan and to stay out of policy questions, relying instead on its revelations to generate citizen response. The first bureau, founded in 1906, was financed in part by Andrew Carnegie and John D. Rockefeller. It was not financed entirely by them, however, and well-known professionals served on its first board of directors. The spread of the bureaus after 1915 was not always at the behest of industrialists, or chambers of commerce. Some, like Toledo's, were government agencies.

Middle-class interest in at-large elections and other features of the council-manager plan equaled or outran that of the rich. Proportional representation (or "PR" as it was known), was almost entirely a middle-class enthusiasm. Under the popular Hare system (named for its English originator) there were no primaries; candidates circulated petitions for their places on the ballot. Then a number was chosen, usually the number of qualified ballots cast in the previous local election. Next, one more than the number of elective positions was taken as the divisor of the first number. This procedure guarded against a decline in voter turnout and facilitated the counting. The quotient became the quota each successful candidate had to reach. If the number of qualified votes was 50,000 and the number of positions to fill was 10, then each candidate's quota became 50,000 divided by 11, or 4546 (the quotient, rounded up). The voter marked his first choice on the ballot, then his second, his third, and so on, as far as he wished to designate choices. Usually the names were rotated by voting district to give all candidates choice locations near the top of the ballot. During the counting, as the first candidate reached his quota, his surplus votes were distributed to the other candidates according to each voters' second choice. At each count, the candidate with the least votes was declared out, and his ballots transferred to the surviving candidates on the same basis as the surplus votes of the leading candidate.

If this recitation of the procedure makes PR seem like pretty dull stuff, be assured that it was really an electoral bombshell. It was so revolutionary, its implications for representative democracy so startling, that it was little tried, and where it was tried, abandoned after trials of greater or lesser length. Consider the implications for a political machine. The machine could not field candidates through a more or less controlled primary election but had to gather names on a petition. Gathering names on a petition was no problem for a disciplined organization, but the petition system destroyed the real purpose of the primary: to limit the candidates in the primary to one "real" candidate and possibly a stalking horse or two, or to limit the general election by a deal across party lines involving the other party's deliberate nomination of a weak candidate. Now anybody with a cause, and a petition with names equal to two percent of the voters in the previous election, could get on the ballot.

What was worse, the dominant party could not control the election by rolling up huge majorities for its candidates. Under the old ward system the majority party could win in a ward by a slight majority or even a plurality, but the votes given to losing candidates counted for nothing at all. This was all the more true if wards were carefully gerrymandered to follow the principle "when you win, win a little, when you lose, lose big." Under that arrangement the dominant Democrats, say, fixed boundaries to include a safe majority of Democrats but also a significant minority of Republicans, whose votes would be wasted. On the other hand, Republican districts would be drawn to include as many Republicans as possible, and to waste few Democratic votes on hopeless candidates.

A shift to "nonpartisan," at-large elections might make the situation potentially more lopsided. In the absence of significant independent voting or ticket splitting the dominant Democrats (in our hypothetical situation) could, through disciplined effort, capture the entire slate, leaving the Republicans with no representation at all. Actually the threat was less serious because, among other reasons, it was difficult to gerrymander wards in a rapidly growing city with shifting ethnic populations and because at-large elections encouraged independent voting. Nevertheless it was true that dominant parties secured representation disproportionate to their vote. In New York City, in the final, non-PR, aldermanic election, the Democrats got out 66 percent of the vote but captured 95 percent of the places, while the Republicans took only five percent of the seats even though they gained 26 percent of the vote. The remaining eight percent of the voters received no representation for their pains.

With PR, control by machine was virtually impossible in an honest election. Granted, the machine could distribute sample ballots properly marked, just as it did in "nonpartisan" elections, or it could inform its members to vote for the party designation after the names. But control by those means, while theoretically possible, was practically difficult. Even machine voters were likely to rank machine candidates in different orders. New York City's first PR election in 1937 was a dramatic shift in the direction of true representation: the Democrats received 50 percent of the places with 47 percent of the vote; the American Labor Party's 21 percent of the vote garnered it 19 percent of the seats, and the Republicans' 8.5 percent of the vote earned them 11.5 percent of the seats. In no instance did the vote and the representation diverge by more than three percent.

The revolution did not stop with ousting the machine, however. That partly explains why reform ardor toward one of the most truly representative of systems cooled so rapidly. Under PR it was just as difficult for a powerful reform organization to seize control as it was for a machine to do so. Also, by giving proportional weight to minorities, PR opened city councils to Communists, blacks, and "foreigners" in greater numbers than the older system could have allowed. But partial explanations are not total explanations; thus it would be wrong to dismiss anti-PR reformers as cynical fascists. Some were dubious of the long, drawn-out vote count necessary with PR. Others doubted its constitutionality. Others feared that so radical a departure, however good in itself, was too vulnerable to be relied on.

As it was, four or five cities and towns (not always the same ones) used PR in their elections through the late teens, the twenties, and the thirties. It began to catch on during the early forties despite the distractions of war. By 1946, ten places, including Cincinnati, Toledo, and Boulder, Colorado, had gone over to PR. The spreading repeals of PR did not come until the late forties and early fifties. The timing suggests a reaction against minority dissent springing from the current internal security phobia rather than from local dissatisfactions with PR. The fact remains that the 1915–1945 period witnessed experiments with one of the most far-reaching democratic electoral reforms ever proposed.

There were frequent deviations from the model city charter in matters more important than proportional representation. Several cities elected their mayors, a fact that gave the mayors more moral authority than the councilmen, whether or not their powers were greater. In some cases mayors were given a veto or more appointive power than the model-charter purists wished. Some cities violated the canon of at-large elections, either by retaining the ward system or reverting to it, or by electing a part of the council from districts, and a part at large.

Council-manager governments were not always, in practice, the tools of the rich. Often they expanded urban services and spent more money, though usually more efficiently, than the governments they replaced. Rising expenditures for health, welfare, and recreation usually aided poor people and, in some cases, taught them the value of playgrounds and health ordinances. In Janesville, prolabor councilmen carried the third election under the council-manager charter. The city manager worked successfully to reopen a woolen mill, a

Chevrolet assembly plant, and a Fisher Body Corporation plant, and to persuade a furniture factory to locate in Janesville, actions that greatly assisted labor. In Dallas the first city manager offended important businessmen when he refused to consider public works projects that would have enhanced the value of their riverfront properties, and when he insisted on vigorous law enforcement. Lower-middle-class and working-class people were offended even more by his cold aloofness and his economical, impersonal administration. In 1935 middle-class and lower-class voters united against the upper class to vote in a permissive council with the understanding that it would more closely control a new manager. Even though the reformers returned to power after a few years, the reform council kept a close watch on the manager and made no attempt to restore the old efficiency regime. The manager system in Kansas City well served the interests of the Pendergast machine.

In several other cities the council-manager scheme fell flat, or stumbled badly, but these failings were not always the fault of the plan. The Jackson, Michigan charter was the brainchild of groups concerned with prohibition and industrial progress. In their zeal for strict saloon licensing and for ending public works benefits to low-income wards, they allowed several contradictory, ambiguous clauses to creep into the charter. Under that document the city manager was simply another administrator who shared important budgetary and appointive powers with the council, the mayor, and the city clerk. Alliances and personalities played large roles in administratively gray areas. From 1915 to 1921 professional city managers centralized much of the administrative authority in their office. Misuse of bond revenues under such "expert" administration plus the disgust of low-income citizens with "professional" evenhandedness produced a council of ruthless cost-cutters in 1922. The managership fell first to a parsimonious former assessor and then, after an interim period, to a capable but gregarious man who worked hardest at being a "good fellow." The administrative fabric of the first years rotted away.

San Diego, California had never been noted for the quality of its government and the council-manager system did not raise it much. In 1913, when the city was under the commission plan, the city fathers had hired a rainmaker to solve a water shortage. The deluge that followed may or may not have resulted from the rainmaker's work, but it did burst a dam. The angry commissioners not only refused to pay the rainmaker, they even muttered threats of legal action against him. By 1926 the city had returned to a mayor-council system but its water supply problem remained. Against expert advice the council directed the building of two dams, only to abandon them both at a loss of most of the bond funds earmarked for their construction. The city had done well in some administrative areas, notably planning and police recordkeeping. But unsolved civic problems, including the dumping of raw sewage into the harbor, induced a change to the council-manager form in 1932.

The first manager had made a good record as an engineer in another city, but in San Diego he devoted his time to speechmaking, visiting public works, and quarreling with the council and the department heads. The council ended his six-week career after his car struck a pedestrian. Next the council divided over whether to permit reasonable vice activities in the port city or require strict law enforcement. Disagreements on most other policy matters followed. The council was almost unanimous, however, in badgering the manager for special favors to constituents. When the permissive element became a majority on the council, it dismissed the second manager, appointed a successor who was a combination clerk and yes-man, and dealt directly with department heads. Criticism from local newspapers and a recall campaign by middle-class devotees of good government stung the mayor, who resigned. The council equipped his successor with an expensive official car, which the new mayor promptly wrecked. While the mayor was serving out his office in jail for a traffic conviction, the city attorney was indicted by a grand jury for misusing public funds and later convicted. After his conviction he gave the proceedings a slapstick climax by turning in a false fire alarm. In 1935 a group of well-to-do citizens with a strong sense of civic responsibility organized to rescue council-manager government in San Diego. Their organization swept the election and gained a majority on the council. The new city fathers infused their government with the spirit of the council-manager charter, but they could not end factionalism. After 1935 various interest groups—organized labor, some neighborhood leaders, even the Chamber of Commerce—were at odds with the council at one time or another.

In Charlotte, North Carolina, the lack of effective home rule hampered the council-manager system. State-imposed limits on the city's power sometimes were trivial, if irritating, such as the legislature's *pro forma* authorization of local tax assessments. Legislative interventions could be serious, especially when the county delegation was at odds with individual councilmen or members of the administration. In the early thirties the legislature's vindictiveness limited the park and recreation budget, excepted the garbage department from council and manager control, and increased the size of the council despite opposition from the council and from proponents of the council-manager system. Charlotte's lack of home rule, like Jackson's poorly drawn charter and San Diego's sometimes madcap government, stood in the way of one-class control of the city's affairs.

Council-manager systems could well serve the interests of more than one class. In several instances labor or lower-class interests seized control of the civic machinery, but they retained the forms of council-manager government. Referenda against the plan itself were fairly uncommon. A referendum was not easily organized in tranquil times, but significant changes in urban government were certainly possible when the citizenry or any significant part of it became aroused. Referenda, after all, had voted in most of the council-manager plans. Through 1945 there had been 120 referenda on abandonment, and 28, or less than one-fourth, had carried. The 28 reversions were minor by comparison with the defections from the mayor-council and commission plans. They were not large compared to the 619 cities that either lived under or had voted in the council-manager plan by the end of 1945.

The managers themselves were partly responsible for the permanence of the plan. Most of them early abandoned the idea that government equaled administration, and that efficiency was their grail. They came around to a view of city hall as the place where interest groups resolved their conflicts and each received its share of the loaf. Solutions to group conflicts varied with situations but, generally, the managers agreed that no powerful group could be eliminated without jeopardizing the council-manager plan and its principles. Many managers helped to make policy and to "sell" the policy to the public. Many also acquiesced in "suggestions" about appointments and other administrative matters emanating from their councils. A few managers never altered their myopic "efficiency" view of urban government. Their stubbornness is understandable, for most of the first managers were engineers, the chief worshippers at the shrine of efficiency. Those who hewed to their "politics-is-engineering" approach were sometimes successful in small cities where little was at stake or where one element or a coalition was firmly in control.

City managership quickly became an institutionalized profession, in keeping with the fashion of the day. Eight of the 17 city managers met to found the City Manager's Association in 1914. In short order the association was equipped with a canon of professional ethics, a full-time staff, and a magazine. Within the breast of many a manager loyalty to his own profession and to his ethical code soon competed against devotion to any local faction or group. Besides, an able manager might not have to stay in one particular city. As the city manager movement gained momentum, cities questing after experienced managers found them in short supply. Frequently they got them from smaller cities that could not afford the pay and perquisites of the new position. Large universities, quick to see a "subject field" in the latest profession, began training in public administration. Bright young men found a new ladder of upward mobility. Success as a manager was judged as much by whether one moved from city to city (the moves had to be to evermore important jobs, usually in larger cities) as by competent service to one community rendered for a generation or more.

Middle-class supporters of the council-manager plan abetted professional ambitions when they urged cities to appoint managers from out of town who were unsullied by ties to local factions. They hailed the rise of C. A. Harrell, who began in 1928 as Cincinnati's assistant manager. Three jobs later, in 1945, he was managing Schenectady, New York. He would return to manage Cincinnati after two more positions in nine years. L. Perry Cookingham reached the apex of his career in Kansas City, where he was called in 1940 from Saginaw, Michigan. For many years Cookingham gave exemplary service to the reform government that replaced the notorious Pendergast machine. An aspiring city manager had more than the Harrell and Cookingham models to emulate, for the profession might lead to greater, or at least different, careers in other fields. Although Clarence A. Dykstra had been a university professor before he became a public administrator, he won his spurs as the manager of Cincinnati. From that job he became, in 1937, the president of the University of Wisconsin. In 1945 he was named provost of the University of California.

The growth of city manager government and the professionalization of city management helped to entrench the council-manager form. Persons and institutions developed an interest in its perpetuation. Universities with public administration curricula naturally favored the system. The manager form encouraged professionalism in urban administrative departments, with everyone from personnel administrators to recreation directors equipped with organizations and codes of ethics.

The council-manager system could not be saved where it had not been tried, and it was rarely tried, and if tried not usually retained, in the largest cities. In 1940, none of the 15 largest cities (the list extended below the 500,000 population mark) was under the plan. One of them, Cleveland, had abandoned it. The great cities stayed with the mayor-council form. Usually they developed some variant of the "strong mayor" arrangement, whereby the mayor held the appointive power and dominated the council through patronage and the veto. In the big cities the loaves and fishes of politics were too tasty and too abundant for their recipients to surrender them readily. Proportionately larger numbers of poor people and ethnic minorities, groups traditionally hostile to the council-manager reform, lived in the largest cities.

Finally, politicians in big cities had come to recognize a basic truth in the council-manager ideology: cities were going to have to become more efficient in order to survive. Faced with demands for improvements in sidewalk extension, welfare, traffic control, schooling, and the whole range of urban services, cities of all sizes had to abandon old shoe methods. From the eve of World War I to the advent of the New Deal the cities bore an increasing financial load without developing basic new sources of revenue. The heads of departments in major cities had to produce, or their subordinates had to produce, for them to keep their jobs under the new regimes.

NEW YORK: REFORM'S SUCCESS

Big cities, then, did not need managers in order to reform. Reform could come to them without the fundamental structural changes so dear to the heart of the good government crowd. Reform came, and stayed for years in the greatest city, New York. Reform in New York is traceable partly to the flatulence of bossism and to the vitality of the reform spirit in the early 1930s.

New York's reform began with the increasing inability of the regular Democratic organization to cope with the city's growth and complexity. The Manhattan, or Tammany Hall, group dominated the Democratic political scene, and New York City, until Fiorello La Guardia's election in 1933. Tammany suffered from a reputation for monumental graft, corruption, and incompetence, a richly deserved reputation as we shall see. Things were not always so bad, were in fact run competently enough under Charles F. Murphy, the leader of Tammany Hall from 1902 to 1924. Murphy was a tough, intelligent Irish kid in the gashouse district of Manhattan's lower east side. Genteel occupations were closed to his sort, so he went into the saloon business and politics. A superb administrator, he sacked corruptionists. He insisted on close communication between himself and his district leaders, and between them and their constituents. Murphy, "Mr. Murphy" to all but a few close friends, led an exemplary personal life, was true to his word, and expected the same behavior from his subordinates. He shunned the limelight, worked hard, and never spoke two words when one would do.

Murphy sometimes promoted reform. Under him Tammany favored direct primaries, home rule for New York City, woman suffrage, and factory legislation. The leader himself advanced the political careers of urban liberals. Al Smith was one of the greatest, if not the greatest, reform governor of New York. Robert F. Wagner achieved permanent national fame in the Senate with his sponsorship of important, successful bills concerning labor relations, social insurance, and housing. Murphy could have destroyed both men when they were young and unimportant but he did not. Lest the Tammany leader be thought of as a paragon of virtue, it should be said that in important ways Murphy reinforced the image of the old-line machine boss. Although he supported occasional reformers, he was not himself a reformer. The differences are important in the light of recent historical scholarship. That scholarship has penetrated the antimachine rhetoric of reform groups to show that urban bosses often advocated fundamental reforms and that reformers frequently built machines. Granted, the operational similarities of boss and reform governments were sometimes striking. It was nevertheless true that machine politicians and reformers held fundamentally different views of politics and society.

First, when a politician like Murphy sponsored a reform, it was to perpetuate the organization and not for the sake of reform. Indeed, Murphy opposed reforms until he learned that the voters who benefited from them would vote for the reform party out of gratitude. Murphy's pleasant surprise at this discovery says something about his limited view of things. Reformers, on the other hand, placed reform first. They built machines, or tried to, not primarily for getting out the vote and rewarding the faithful, but for preserving and extending reform. Of course bosses could be altruistic and reformers, especially after a term of office or two, could grow cynical and organization-minded. The distinction, however, must stand. It may seem trite, but it was not lost on either Murphy or his opponents. For Murphy, politics was a serious, full-time business, his life's work. If reform fit his framework, but only if, he accepted it.

Second, Murphy practiced so-called "honest graft," anathema to reformers. The New York Contracting and Trucking Company, a Murphy family enterprise, did a great deal of business with private companies in New York. When New York Contracting and Trucking bid on a job, it was considered wise to award the contract to Murphy's company, whether or not its bid was the lowest. Firms failing to do so might find needed ordinances or permits blocked until they came around. Ocean shipping concerns often found it convenient to lease docks from companies controlled by the boss and his friends. All this allowed Murphy to live comfortably in a substantial townhouse and a sprawling Long Island retreat, to take up golf, to indulge quietly in charitable giving, and to leave a large estate at his death.

Moreover, though he was intolerant of dishonest graft—taking protection money from vice operators and the like—Murphy condoned honest graft in his subordinates. Most typically honest graft operated in connection with city condemnation proceedings, but it was really limited only by the human imagination. With respect to honest graft, at least, Murphy's men were gifted with extraordinary imaginations.

Third, for a group of closely related reasons Murphy departed from the ideal, or even tolerable, reform image. He was uninterested in structural reforms that would eliminate a large number of jobs useful chiefly as political rewards. During his years in power he developed a corps of men who were industrious, capable enough in their secondary jobs, and who generally did what he expected of them. He did not groom any talented young men to assume command after his demise. Despite his administrative ability he had bad luck with his mayoral selections. He never cared much for upgrading New York's municipal services to keep pace with its growing population or the special needs of areas such as Harlem.

Murphy's chickens began coming home to roost in the late teens. In 1917 his candidate for mayor was John F. Hylan, "Honest John," who was honest, ambitious, and hardworking, but not much else. A hulking man who refused to be bossed by Murphy, Hylan was a poor judge of character, was indecisive, and lacked the intellect to get things done. Murphy still ran the machine, and he forbore Hylan through one re-election and most of two terms. In 1925, the year after Murphy's death, most thoughtful machine Democrats wanted Hylan out. In his stead they chose James J. Walker, son of a Tammany politician, a state senator, and another protégé of Murphy, who had liked him. It was hard not to like Jimmy Walker. A man of extraordinary verve and charm, Walker was highly intelligent, dapper, and a master of the *bon mot*. When he appointed the plodding ex-mayor Hylan to be judge of a children's court he quipped, "the children can now be tried by their peer." [1] New Yorkers loved Walker for his funny cracks, his appearances at the great prize fights and the Broadway openings, his partying, his extramarital affair with an actress, his trips abroad. They might have loved him longer had he found the time to be mayor in fact. Walker was Hylan's antithesis in every way including his attitude toward disciplined hard work. After Walker resigned under pressure in 1932, the Democrats chose (and New Yorkers ratified in a special election) another man in the Hylan mold: a sincere, unimaginative malaprop named John P. O'Brien.

[1] Arthur Mann, *La Guardia Comes to Power, 1933*, University of Chicago Press, Chicago, 1969, p. 60.

Back at Tammany Hall things were no better. The men who followed Murphy in power were mostly characters of the party wheel-horse type, but they were not leaders. They limited their intelligence and activity to perpetuating the machine in power. In one sense they were not able to do that, for Murphy had assumed a first-among-equals position with the other borough leaders, and his successors failed to hold his gains. The result was that the citywide Democratic organization was not only incompetent to deal with New York's mounting problems, it was also unable to silence the bickering within its own ranks. From 1929 to 1934 the Tammany leader was John F. Curry, a man of no qualifications for the job, save tenacity. Curry and his associates continued their own kind in lesser party, elective, and appointive offices.

The state of things under such caretakers went from bad to worse. A series of scandals led to calls for investigation that Governor Franklin D. Roosevelt and the legislature could not ignore. There were in fact three investigations, but all were conducted simultaneously under Samuel Seabury, so it is unnecessary to distinguish one from another. Seabury, a wealthy patrician, tall and white-maned, a reform crusader since the nineteenth century, was backed by a staff of young, hustling, ambitious, and idealistic investigators. Despite his elaborate courtesy, Seabury showed his disgust with the Tammany system and its works in his witty but relentless questioning.

The Seabury investigations revealed so much and suggested so much else that it is impossible to do more than indicate by three examples the depth of corruption, political favoritism, and incompetence. John Theofel, the Democratic leader of Queens borough, was also chief clerk of the Queens County Surrogate Court, put in office by the man he had installed as the court's presiding judge. Seabury's questions revealed that Theofel had little idea of his duties, took long vacations, and made a lot of money in honest graft. Theofel was the part owner of an automobile agency where Queens politicians bought both official and personal cars. Thomas M. Farley, the sheriff of New York County, denied that his tidy fortune came from the protection of gambling. The source of it, he said, was saved money kept in a "wonderful" tin box at home. The magistrate's courts were staffed with political appointees, as one of them, Magistrate Maurice Gottlieb, freely admitted. When asked why he was a judge, Gottlieb replied that his position was a reward for his services to Tammany Hall.

All this was grist for the mill of the middle-class and upper-class civic groups that were the organized indignation of New York. But it

took more than the outrage of the wealthy and comfortable to overturn the Democratic Party, still entrenched, still the favorite, as the
1932 special election showed. There was more fuel for reform fires in
the shape of the Great Depression, crime, the determination of the
indignant to organize effectively, and the mayoral candidate himself.
Except in the very poorest wards, which remained loyal to Tammany, these influences conditioned New York's voters for change.

That the economic crisis of 1932 profoundly influenced popular attitudes is a truism so painfully trite that the shift in the public's
thinking may be seriously undervalued. In prosperous 1929 Jimmy
Walker could have done no wrong. In 1932, in the midst of a catastrophic depression, the revelations of Walker's financial careless-
ness, if not corruption, did not sit well with thoughtful citizens. The
Seabury revelations had little effect on lower-class fatalism, but
crime did. Prohibition, by driving the satisfactions of liquor underground, placed an enormously lucrative business in underworld
hands. From liquor dealing criminals spread into other activities, notably protection rackets at the docks, in produce marketing, in unions,
and in various businesses. Poor and laboring people were often
the direct victims of the rackets. Also, they were the most frequent
targets of petty criminals and of the general social disorganization of
the slums. Public prosecutors and the police were too undermanned,
too demoralized, and too often bribed to be effective. In their com-
placency the Democratic leaders had forgotten that permitting some
vice and crime was one thing, but protecting rampant major and
minor crime was something else.

To put reform over, the reformers had to capitalize on the discontents born of corruption, incompetence, depression, and crime. And
to seize on the discontents, they had to compromise their ideals to
some extent, organize with all the anti-Tammany elements, write an
attractive platform, and find an appealing mayoral candidate. It is to
the reformer's credit that they were able to submerge personal differences, unite with the regular Republicans in the City Fusion
Party, and write a reform program that firmly but undogmatically
committed them to nonpartisan government. The Fusion platform
called for various structural reforms, especially the reduction of
purely patronage jobs; strengthening the civil service; proportional
representation; and perhaps a city manager. The Cincinnati experience in overturning a corrupt machine and replacing it with a model
government under a city manager inspired the New York reformers.
On the other hand they recognized that not all members of the Fusion coalition shared their enthusiasm for such trends as proportional
representation and the council-manager form. They stressed dif-

ferent parts of the platform to different groups of voters.

As its candidate for mayor the reform coalition chose Fiorello H. La Guardia, a most improbable selection. Short and chunky, with a voice that somehow combined the qualities of a high-pitched scream and a rasping croak, La Guardia was definitely not the sort whom many upper-crust reformers admired. A man of jumbled ethnic and religious background, La Guardia emphasized his Italian heritage and generally kept his mother's Jewishness quiet. La Guardia entered law and politics on the side of the disinherited. He served a term in Congress, next as president of New York's board of aldermen, then again in Congress. In 1929 he was the mayoral candidate of the Republican party (to which he gave nominal allegiance) mostly because nobody else wanted to run against the fabulous Jimmy Walker. Walker and Tammany crushed him. In 1932 he lost his Congressional seat to a Tammany nonentity. In 1933 he had the reputation of being a fighting but hopelessly vulgar politician, a disheveled little "wop," and (worst of all) a loser.

Yet on New Year's Day, 1934, La Guardia became mayor of New York. He won the Fusion nomination partly because he so passionately wanted it. Several potential candidates, including Seabury, refused it. Others, including the brilliant but colossally egotistical Robert Moses, builder of the state park system, had too many powerful enemies. La Guardia was sincerely interested in honest and humane government, and could make extremely clever but dignified speeches to that effect before blueblooded reform audiences. He cultivated important friends among the New York elite, men who admired his demonic energy, his quick and penetrating mind, and his determination. Adolph A. Berle and Newbold Morris, later Seabury himself, were in this group. They remembered what the stocky little man had said about Tammany corruption in his 1929 race for mayor.

La Guardia won the election for all the reasons mentioned (corruption, crime, the depression, reform vitality, his own personality) plus some others. He and his advisers presented an ethnically, religiously, and politically balanced field of running mates. La Guardia campaigned hard, promising to end partisan government in New York. To the poor he promised improved, apolitical health services, welfare, and housing. The Italians considered Fiorello one of their own and voted overwhelmingly for him, despite their Catholicism and his Episcopalianism. By late summer the New Deal had given New Yorkers a federal example of the sort of governmental activism that La Guardia was talking about. O'Brien, the Tammany candidate, was patently unequal to the task. Joseph McKee, a capable reform Democrat, was a much more formidable opponent. McKee had been the acting mayor between Walker's resignation and O'Brien's election. Tammany passed him over, but President Roosevelt probably induced him to run to defeat Roosevelt's old enemy, Tammany, and the Republicans allied with La Guardia. But McKee entered the race late and could not field the lesser candidates or the organization to match La Guardia's. Shortly before the election La Guardia charged McKee with anti-Semitism to counter a similar accusation by McKee. Both charges were equally baseless but, unfortunately for McKee, an article on public education that he had written many years before gave a slight color to La Guardia's claims. La Guardia did no better, or worse, with Jewish voters, who decided for him or against him largely along economic lines. The accusation did cut McKee's ties with the White House, robbing him of important administration support.

La Guardia gave New York 12 years of good administration and about half as many years of dynamic innovation. Although most recent political scholarship looks to other than personal reasons for the explanation of events, in this instance La Guardia's extraordinary intelligence and energy transcended the usual politics. His triumphs are all the more compelling when set against the backdrop of New York's problems and his own limitations.

Some of the limitations were personal. The little mayor was sensitive about his height. He was intensely competitive and combative. He dished out merciless tonguelashings to subordinates, from secretaries to prominent commissioners. Although he usually kept his temper, La Guardia was liable to screaming tantrums. He gave an impression of boundless energy and wide-ranging attention to detail, an impression largely correct. All the same, he tended to flit from problem to problem, interested only in the matter of the moment, never focusing intently on one subject for any extended period. He made good his promise of nonpartisan government, but his administration was necessarily political. By awarding patronage to minority elements within parties and interest groups, he built up personal loyalties but not an organization capable of carrying on reform. These characteristics cost him some excellent administrators, and some administrative continuity over the years.

Other problems inhered in New York's ramshackle government. County government was already what it would become in many urbanized areas, an anachronism. Each of the five boroughs was also a county, replete with sheriffs, recorders, and many other people who had virtually nothing to do, because city officers duplicated most of their functions. County jobs were useful chiefly to reward adherents to the Democratic machine and insure a loyal cadre of voters. The entire weight of the county apparatus was against reform.

On the city level the mayor had to struggle against divided authority and a top-heavy administrative system. Several important elected officials enjoyed considerable autonomy within their own spheres. The mayor shared executive and administrative powers with the Board of Estimate, composed of himself, the elected presidents of each borough, and other officials. The Board of Aldermen, the chief legislative authority, was limited in power and unwieldy in size. Several quasi-independent commissions controlled large administrative areas. The later Charter of 1936 and accompanying acts (most of which became effective in 1938) changed these situations relatively little.

La Guardia was elected three times, but his personal popularity should not obscure the fact that New York remained a Democratic city. In 1933 there were many grievances against the hardheaded, dim-witted machine that Tammany had become, and he masterfully capitalized on them. Yet most New Yorkers preferred either the Democratic party as it was or the Democratic party reformed. La Guardia won 868,522 votes, a plurality, but O'Brien, the Tammany candidate, polled 586,672, and McKee, the Recovery (reform) Democrat, 609,053. The Democrats' total vote was 1,195,725, or more than 327,000 ahead of La Guardia's. Although La Guardia carried a bare majority on the Board of Estimate, the Democrats controlled the Board of Aldermen, the borough presidencies of Manhattan and the Bronx, and all the county offices. Late in 1935 a Fusion member of the Board of Estimate died, and La Guardia lost his majority there.

La Guardia ran on his record in the next two elections. In 1937 La Guardia triumphed, receiving about 60 percent of the vote, thanks to heavy support from organized labor. Fusion captured all but one of the seats on the Board of Estimate, and carried other important offices. Even in Fusion's glory year, the Democrats clung to a majority in the Council (formerly the Board of Aldermen). By 1941 La Guardia had become an independent political force and largely ran his own campaign. It was a slick campaign, the slickest of all, but with the former evangelism notably absent. For that reason and others La Guardia's majority dropped to 53 percent. The little mayor's running mates, most of them not personalities in their own right, suffered by such tactics. Democrats reduced the Fusion majority on the Board of Estimate, increased their majority in the Council, and swept most of the other offices.

During 1940 and 1941 La Guardia took on other jobs, giving much of his time for a while to the Office of Civilian Defense, of which he was chief. He was badly overworked and more given to public and often petty disputing with subordinates. He wasted lots of energy in a futile quest for a brigadier generalship. The Second World War's manpower shortage decimated his civil service. His final four years were largely caretaking, a welcome relief for ordinary men but a pall over the reputation of a dynamic reformer. In 1945, with his old reform coalition vanished, his public stature diminished, and his health deteriorating, La Guardia decided not to seek reelection. Two years later he died of cancer.

Despite the limitations, La Guardia's triumphs were great ones. First of all, he *was* the mayor. He played on his gifts for showmanship to dramatize the city's activities and his own crusades. He read a proclamation against the artichoke racket to the accompaniment of blaring trumpets. He bashed in confiscated slot machines with a sledge hammer during his administration's crusade against the slots. After the city had negotiated the purchase of the privately owned transit lines, La Guardia donned a motorman's cap and overalls, and drove the first city-managed subway train out of Times Square station. His fire chief's hat and slicker were always at hand when the sirens wailed.

The showmanship was interesting and important because it stood for something. La Guardia was uninterested in piling up a fortune, and he was almost phobic about grafting and dishonesty in others. New York's finances were in a perilous state when he took office. He imposed ruthless economic discipline on the departments, cut wages in the early thirties, and hiked taxes, but left the city much stronger financially than he found it.

La Guardia waged a vigorous and exceptionally successful war against organized crime. It would be wrong to think that he eliminated crime, for some crime—gambling, for instance—catered to human desires and fantasies so powerful that eliminating it would have entailed unacceptable enforcement and social controls. Despite minor victories most forms of gambling, along with prostitution, continued to flourish in New York. The doughty mayor earnestly tried to improve the police department and to raise morale through an honest merit system. He succeeded to a commendable degree, but the take from gambling and prostitution was so great that large bribes were offered and sometimes accepted. La Guardia did force some gamblers and madams out of the city; others had to stay on the move or take extraordinary precautions.

He was more successful in breaking up racketeering in the produce markets, where criminals controlled the sale of garden truck by elaborate systems of theft and receiving of stolen goods, communities of interest, bribery, and intimidation. Federal authorities helped by prosecutions for income tax evasion and violations of the Sherman Anti-Trust Act. In 1935 La Guardia instructed the police to cooperate fully with Thomas E. Dewey, a youthful, ambitious, intense, and extremely capable special prosecutor for the State of New York. Dewey's investigations exposed industrial racketeering, begun in the twenties when some businesses hired hoodlums to break strikes. The hoodlums soon turned the tables. They found that businessmen were highly vulnerable to work stoppages. The threat of one usually produced a payoff, and if it did not, then a "strike," a stink bomb, or damaged equipment served as an object lesson to others. Dewey broke such racketeering, first as special prosecutor, then as the District Attorney for New York County (Manhattan) from 1938 to 1942. Dewey's brilliant work was so effective that other prosecutors, grand juries, and committees followed up his leads for years.

Neither La Guardia nor the men he aided stamped out racketeering, of course. It survived in the unions, and was unchecked along the waterfront. Important criminals with home bases in Brooklyn were protected by their ties with the county government. Yet La Guardia had helped to control a rapidly deteriorating situation in which growing numbers of citizens were held in thrall to criminals.

La Guardia's greatest single contribution to his city was its social and physical reconstruction. Except for education, in which he interfered inordinately, he kept his nose out of the day-to-day departmental operations. His special enthusiasms were likely to surface at any moment, but they were as brief as they were intense. Beside his negative policy of noninterference he helped the programs in several positive ways.

First, La Guardia appointed as administrators men and women who were talented and who were impatient with interference in their administrative domains, whether the interference came from the mayor or anyone else. The best example of such an appointment, and among the best of the lot, was Robert Moses'. La Guardia named Moses, an arrogant and opinionated but also energetic and brilliant man, to head the Department of Parks. Moses laid down conditions: he had to remain at the head of the state park system and he would lead only a unified city system, not the five uncoordinated borough systems. State law prohibited Moses' accepting an additional job, so La Guardia asked the legislature to rush through an act permitting him to hold unpaid city positions in parks and recreation, public works, and planning. Under Moses the Park Department hired a professional staff; cleaned, modernized, and expanded the parks and playgrounds, and reconstructed the rundown zoos. Moses' phenomenal achievements included the reclamation of Flushing Meadow, a marshy dumpground in the Queens, to be the site of the 1939 World's Fair. After the fair closed the site became a magnificent park. In parks and recreational activities, La Guardia's administration showed a bright contrast to its Tammany predecessors, who had allowed the city's recreational plant to go to wrack and ruin.

Second, La Guardia took new initiatives that moved his administration beyond the traditions and precedents of previous reform mayors. His work in housing and urban renewal was his most significant pathbreaking venture. On the promise of the New Deal that Public Works Administration money would be forthcoming, La Guardia wrung an enabling act from the state legislature. Early in 1934 the city established the first Housing Authority, with broad powers to condemn and convey land, destroy blighted areas, rebuild, and rent housing. Then cautious Harold Ickes, WPA administrator, refused to release the funds immediately.

The Authority was forced to improvise a quick solution to the dilemma of rehousing the occupants of some dilapidated tenements on the lower east side. It prevailed on the wealthy owner of most of a tenement block to accept Authority bonds for less than half the appraised value of his property. Next the Authority borrowed from a philanthropist to purchase the remaining buildings. Finally, it arranged with relief agencies to remodel two abutting tenements and tear down every third, to allow for play spaces as well as for light and air. By reconstructing the tenements rather than demolishing them all, the Authority was able to open the first public housing project in the country on December 3, 1935. The Authority would have razed all the tenements if it could. Therefore it would be false to credit it with a neighborhood redevelopment concept involving the remodeling of salvageable buildings rather than their mindless destruction. But the project did save some houses; thus it was more sophisticated in its execution than its hard-pressed administrators imagined.

Beginning in 1936 large amounts of federal money were available. WPA funds built projects in all the boroughs; the federal government then lent them to the Authority for operation. Federal money was essential but La Guardia did not rely upon it alone. Under the state's housing law of 1939 the city enacted a special tax and guaranteed the bonds of the Authority, thus becoming the first municipality to entirely finance its own housing projects. Projects such as the ones New York undertook should not be criticized from the standpoint of later years, when the limitations of public housing had been complicated by the middle-class flight to the suburbs and waves of poverty-stricken migrants. Public housing was a forthright, if limited attack on a problem of the depression decade. In attacking the problem La

Guardia did more than merely redeem a campaign promise: he gave substance to the hope that the great cities could cope with their social ills.

Third, La Guardia was adept at wringing money from the New Deal agencies. His financial reforms made the city eligible for federal funds. He unfailingly kept files of worthwhile projects at hand, ready for submission to the appropriate agency. La Guardia and Roosevelt got along well together, the stocky immigrant son frequently confronting the Hudson River aristocrat with appeals for federal aid to the cities. His hand was strengthened in 1936 with his election as chairman of the United States Conference of Mayors. Growing evidence of an urban voter surge to the New Deal was another strong suit. La Guardia made friends with Harold Ickes and Harry Hopkins, the two "great dispensers" of federal money. Some of his activities helped other cities, but he helped New York the most. PWA grants and loans for New York through June, 1940 totaled over $250,000,000; WPA funds were nearly $300,000,000.

Fourth, La Guardia really cared about the disadvantaged people of New York. Under Tammany, relief was financed by borrowing, frequently lacked continuity (many families received relief every other week), and often was dispensed with politics in mind. The La Guardia administration imposed special relief taxes, gave regular and increasing amounts to all who needed relief, and, as soon as the legislature authorized it, began to make relief payments in cash rather than in the humiliating allotments that tradesmen usually discounted. Welfare departments are almost always controversial, and La Guardia's was especially so because of the presence of Communists. The Communists were active but had little influence except in matters such as enrolling eligibles for relief. On the whole, La Guardia's Welfare Department was capably run and was a glowing contrast to what had preceded it. In the allied field of health La Guardia developed a plan of comprehensive insurance for all workers of modest means and began operating it in January, 1945. It was the culmination of a far-reaching concern for health that had earlier manifestations in an expanded tuberculosis program and additions to city hospitals.

La Guardia made real efforts to help New York's blacks. He was not the first big-city mayor to do so—"Big Bill" Thompson of Chicago had granted important jobs to them years before—but there was idealism as well as political realism in La Guardia's fight for black rights and opportunities. New York's black population, some 350,000 in the thirties, was too large for a politician to ignore, of course. But the mayor could have confined himself to tossing a few bones to the blacks while pandering to the prejudices of the larger white community. He did not. As a "wop" who smarted under demeaning references to Italians, La Guardia broadened his sense of injustice to sympathize with others more discriminated against than he. La Guardia placed his departments on notice that discrimination against blacks would no longer be tolerated, a move as fundamental as it was unspectacular. The police were told to stop their discriminatory treatment of blacks. Harlemites' irritation with the police did not cease, but La Guardia's action did improve relations. The mayor broke the Irish grip on the civil service, with the result that more non-Irish, blacks included, gained city jobs. La Guardia enforced nondiscrimination in welfare, a boon to blacks, the "first to be fired," in depression times. By 1936, 21 percent of welfare recipients were black. Negroes moved to top administrative positions in education and hospitals. Harlem received more parks, recreation, and housing projects. There was the glitter of big appointments, too, a tax commissioner, a magistrate, a judge in the court of domestic relations, a reappointed civil service commissioner.

All this was not without its faults. Wretched conditions remained endemic to Harlem, as the riots of 1935 and 1943 testified. Covert discrimination, as elusive as it was pervasive, remained. Blacks got a break in New Deal work relief, but almost all were assigned to menial jobs. La Guardia himself played politics with blacks. For instance, he reappointed Ferdinand Q. Morton, boss of the black Democrats, a civil service commissioner in return for Morton's promise to abandon the Democrats for the La Guardia-affiliated American Labor Party.

Despite his limitations, La Guardia was extraordinarily successful in getting things done. And because he got things done, he gave American mayors a new vision of what they could do with the governmental machinery and the human material at hand. Soon after he took office, the New York mayorship was said to be the second biggest political job in the United States. It was so recognized because La Guardia made it the second biggest political job.

CHICAGO: REFORM'S FAILURE

Unhappily, big cities did not always reform, as the Chicago experience demonstrated. Chicago's politics had many failings, but its most notorious weakness was its permissive attitude toward organized crime. That situation made the Chicago of the interwar period a laboratory for an investigation of the link between crime and politics. Organized crime was the country's most completely urbanized activity, to the public dismay but secret delight of dozens of chambers of commerce. Organized crime required large concentrations of people because the money was there; it could be made from people who were poor (as in the numbers racket) if only there were enough of them. Organized crime also required large amounts of discretionary income to finance extortion, gambling, prostitution, narcotics, and the gamut of illegal activities and merchandise. Cities provided both the people and the money.

Obviously organized crime could not exist unless powerful interests in the cities either encouraged it or were indifferent to it. Men who in their public roles deplored the machine-gun violence of prohibition were privately proud of their liquor closets kept well stocked by a favorite bootlegger. Men who demanded that cheap, vulgar numbers games be closed would calmly accept thousand dollar losses at a swank casino in the suburbs. Men who were shocked by lapses from middle-class morality on the part of Negroes and foreigners went arm in arm with out-of-town customers to a fancy brothel, there to cap an evening's revelry snuggled between lavender sheets with the most desirable inmates of the house. Men who did none of these things, and who deplored the hypocrisy of those who did, might discover that a city's reputation for its "night life" was "good for business."

In Chicago, as elsewhere, a few ingenious men and women soon organized each special illegal activity to ensure protection from the law, to enforce standards, to restrict entry into the business, and to form alliances with others so engaged. Thus, "organized crime." There has been a great deal written to demonstrate that organized crime, or a vast syndicate, does not really exist. The assertions are true insofar as there is no malevolent directing genius, attired in snap-brim hat and pin-stripe suit, with a pencil-thin mustache and a cigar clenched between yellowed teeth, who sits behind a mahogany desk in a plush penthouse office and growls "do this, do that" to subordinates over the length and breadth of the land. Yet it would be false to assert that crime does not respond to the same technology, social and cultural forces, and human will shaping legitimate activities. If commerce, education, and health care are organized, then crime is also organized.

Organized crime was imbedded in the life of Chicago well before 1915. In the early twentieth century prostitution, gambling, and never-close saloons ran wide open in the notorious Levee district of the First Ward under the benevolent but expensive protection of the ward's marvelous aldermen "Bathhouse" John Coughlin and Michael "Hinky Dink" Kenna. Criminal youth gangs flourished, as did

Mafia-type extortion threats and killings. Bombings often marked internecine struggles within the gambling fraternity. In 1907, when able, affable Mont Tennes was consolidating his hold on Chicago gambling, his rivals answered his moves with some 10 bombs in the summer and autumn of that year. Tennes was undeterred by blasts in his garage, his front yard, and his gambling joints. He continued to force the independent hand book operators to pay a percentage to his racing wire service.

Why organized crime was more rampant and blatant in Chicago than elsewhere was probably because of Chicago's unique development. The city on Lake Michigan's southwest shore enjoyed, or suffered, mushroom growth fed by polyglot immigrations from Europe and the rural South. Chicago was almost from the first a series of competing racial, ethnic, and neighborhood interests without any group that could presume, however speciously, to speak for the city. At the same time the need for urban services, intense in all large cities, was overwhelming in Chicago. The city's village legislative system—a two-house council and a veto-wielding mayor—made it virtually essential for ambitious men who wanted to make a lot of money to bribe the council for the ordinances needed to construct the necessary utilities. Charles T. Yerkes, a man of stupefying ruthlessness and arrogance, bribed on behalf of his "legal" traction companies, the stockholders of which included some of the most renowned Chicago businessmen. If "legitimate" businessmen bribed systematically to influence aldermen, assessors, and license departments, surely there were few bars against underworld figures using the same means to get what they wanted.

Official corruption pervaded Chicago when Republican William Hale Thompson became mayor in 1915 after a free-swinging campaign. During the campaign he lent his gravelly voice to calls for a "clean" city, but "Big Bill" intended no such thing. Thompson was, until the debut of New York's Jimmy Walker, the leading *bon vivant* of American urban politics. A rich man's son, a natural athlete, and a handsome six-footer inclined to corpulence by his late forties, he possessed a good mind and superb oratorical skills. He could have moved in select social circles while building upon the family fortune. Instead he indulged a boyhood fantasy by running a ranch in Nebraska, then returned to Chicago to become a Levee habitué and a brilliant all-around amateur athlete. When athletics palled, he turned to politics. Soon his talents came to the attention of shrewd, energetic Fred "Poor Swede" Lundin, the well-known businessman and politician who directed his mayoral campaign.

After a few well-publicized raids and a temporary enforcement of the Sunday saloon closing law, Thompson settled back to preside over the usual corruption and grafting of both the honest and dishonest variety. He turned patronage over to Lundin, who promptly vitiated the civil service by temporary appointments. Some civil servants resigned in disgust. Those who did not faced demands for salary kickbacks and campaign work, or suspension on trumped-up charges. Police corruption was common during Thompson's administration, but in the beefy mayor's first two years it reached from the chief downward. Appraisers of real estate condemned for street widening and other improvements received enormous fees. Lundin himself stood trial for his role as the leader of a ring of honest and not-so-honest grafters who milked the city's school funds for more than a million dollars. Witnesses detailed inflated contracts for everything from boilers to potato peelers. Lundin and his codefendents were found not guilty, but the publicity destroyed Thompson's hopes for a third term even though "Big Bill" was personally untouched by the scandal.

Thompson was to be mayor once again, ironically because the interim reform organization had lived up to its billing, and because of a profound increase in the income from organized crime. Taking the last situation first, the advent of prohibition in January, 1920 was an enormous boon to organized crime. Organized crime's syndicates had paralleled legitimate business development, becoming evermore centralized, integrated, and specialized, as students of crime noted even before prohibition. Prohibition itself acted upon organized crime in somewhat the same way as the realization of a practical automobile acted upon industry—it opened new vistas of production, demand, profit, and new lucrative relationships with well-established activities.

This was especially true of Chicago, where there was little but fringe sentiment in favor of prohibition. Making and selling illegal beer and liquor would become a highway to riches for young men of Italian, Irish, Jewish, or Negro descent who faced too many barriers to wealth in the legitimate world. The possibilities were the more dazzling because gangsters were wealthy in a society that placed a premium on money, not on how it was made. The lives of gangsters, involved as they were with sumptuous homes, fast cars, parties, and women were glamorous beyond belief. Even if he failed to reach the top, a young man could make more money driving a bootleg truck or working in a bootleg warehouse than he could in most available legitimate occupations, or in such criminal activities as robbery, burglary, and extortion of the Mafia type. Indeed, bootlegging was so profitable that it drew virtually all of the old extortionist "black hand" crowd into the new occupation.

Even so, there was an inside track in Chicago's underworld, just as in its upperworld. James "Diamond Jim" Colosimo, gross and coarse, had built a string of brothels into Chicago's greatest vice syndicate when he was shot just a few months after prohibition began. His chief lieutenant and successor, John Torrio, built a sound bootlegging organization on business principles, integrating it with his other illegal activities. Torrio was a man of great intellect, quiet, and conservative, with a distaste for personal violence. He was convinced that cooperation through federations of large criminal organizations was superior to incessant warfare, price cutting, and bloodshed. When persuasion failed the Torrio organization neatly dispatched its rivals in the approved gangland fashion.

Torrio had grown up recognizing the need for protection through close relationships with politicians. He paid out lavish bribes and joined the William Hale Thompson Republican Club. In return for his consideration, Torrio's syndicate grossed up to 13 million each year from its activities in and around Chicago. So things stood in 1923 when reformer and Democrat William E. Dever was elected to replace the discredited Republican organization of Thompson and Lundin.

Dever found an incorruptible, uncompromising chief of police and told him to go after the underworld. The chief did. The underworld reacted in two ways. First, and in the long run most important, Torrio ordered his lieutenant Alphonse Capone to move the base of operations into Cicero, a west side suburb with a large, thirsty German and Slavic population. Capone simply bought the Democratic political machine and became the controlling influence in Cicero. At first neither Torrio nor Capone himself probably fully understood the significance of the Cicero operation, for it was merely on a grander scale what Torrio had done years before, when he suburbanized some of Colosimo's brothels. But it was the scale that mattered, for Capone had not merely bought protection. He had bought out the government of 50,000 people, the fifth largest city in Illinois. Organized crime was so rich and powerful that its money and election-time strong-arm tactics were essential to the politicians. Now the syndicate no longer needed individual politicians, factions, or parties— these could be shuffled at will. Now the criminals protected the politicians, not the other way around. And if it could happen in Illinois' fifth largest city, why not its first?

That development would have to wait for the underworld to run through its second reaction to reform. After Torrio was arrested in the spring of 1924 during a raid on a "closed" brewery, then indicted, it was plain that he could no longer buy protection for anyone in the syndicate. His carefully built empire crumbled rapidly, with its viceroys buying some protection on a ward or suburb basis where they could, raiding each other's territory and machine-gunning each other. Torrio himself crumpled under a machine-gun attack, suffered through a hospital stay, endured a brief prison sentence arising from the brewery raid, and left for Italy in 1925. "Scarface Al" Capone succeeded him and brought a temporary truce in the autumn of 1926. From late 1923 to 1926 some 400 gangsters were killed (either by their own kind or by the police). Chicago acquired an international reputation for violence, and the Dever administration was discredited.

It was hard on Dever. He had been elected on a promise to crack down on prohibition violators and he had done so. He had built more schools and paved more streets in four years than Thompson had in eight, despite the latter's bluster about "Big Bill the Builder." None of it helped. Bickering between schoolteachers and the superintendent hurt Dever, as did overzealous police who broke into houses to confiscate a bottle or two of bootleg. Prohibition enforcement was decisive, however, for it turned the Germans, Swedes, Italians and some Slavs against Dever. It also convinced Capone that he needed to ally himself with someone who could capture the mayorship and let him operate in Chicago once again.

Thompson was Capone's man. In his comeback acceptance speech for the 1927 primaries he obliquely but firmly promised a wide-open town. Capone and his associates made heavy contributions to Thompson's campaign. Once Thompson was elected, Capone—burly, intelligent, utterly ruthless and fearless—returned to Chicago. A new eruption of gang warfare ended in early 1929 with the famous St. Valentine's Day Massacre of Capone's leading rivals. He was then the undisputed head of a grand syndicate at the age of 32. (Much has been made of Capone's youthful achievements, but it was not unusual for Chicago gangsters to have arrived at the top, or to have been slain, or both, by their late twenties or early thirties.)

As for Thompson, his last term was a disaster almost from the beginning. Grafting in his administration was exposed earlier than usual. He suffered a nervous breakdown from which he never completely recovered. The depression followed the gang war, and Chicago slid toward bankruptcy. Thompson refused to economize and fell into lassitude when local bankers threatened to dry up loans to the city. It made little difference to Capone, who was now invincible in Chicago. Practically all politicians held office at his will, including even "Hinky Dink" Kenna. Capone liked Kenna and often went to his cigar store for Kenna's stories about the old days and for his current advice. Displacing Kenna was unnecessary, for the old alderman no longer ran the first ward. Capone did, with a system of handouts and voter marshaling (nominally on behalf of Kenna) that gave him the appearance of a Robin Hood. And so it went in other pliable wards.

Capone's reign was the high-water mark of blatant organized-crime control of politics. The depression took some of the starch out of Chicago's nightlife and the syndicate's activities. Capone went to federal prison on a conviction of income tax evasion in 1931; the syndicate roared on but not in the charge of men of his caliber. In 1931 Anton J. Cermak, a Czech immigrant and consummate ethnic politician, whipped a hapless Thompson in the mayoral contest. Cermak, a tough wheeler-dealer, was no bluenose when it came to the syndicate. Long an advocate of a man's right to drink what and when he wanted, he was tolerant of bootlegging and related activities while chairman of the Cook County Board of Commissioners.

But Cermak was intolerant of disloyalty or rivalry. He insisted on complete obedience after he captured the leadership of the Cook County Democratic party in 1928. While he was mayor he ran Chicago's politics and administration, opening letters, tapping telephones, cowing subordinates, and brooking no interference from anybody. The syndicate switched its loyalty to Cermak before the campaign, and Cermak protected it, but protection was as far as he went. After Cermak's death in 1932, his inheritors, Edward J. Kelley and Pat Nash, treated organized crime as simply another, even if powerful, special interest group. The disciplined Democratic machine with its independent organization took election-time assistance from the syndicate largely on its own terms.

The relative strengths of personalities and organizations do not account for all of it. Organized crime had undergone a significant internal evolution. The end of prohibition in 1933 was the most obvious development. The syndicate's largest source of revenue became legitimate again and suffered immediate losses with the return of legitimate businessmen. The losses were not all that serious, however, because such syndicate businesses as beer distributing and night clubs, formerly illegitimate, were now legitimate. Furthermore, organized crime had insinuated itself so well into legitimate enterprises that it no longer needed the degree of domination it once required. As in other large cities, legitimate businesses wishing to maintain minimum prices or restrict the number of competitors called in criminals to enforce their wishes. Organized crime had developed specialists who could handle such matters subtly or not so subtly, as the occasion demanded. Employers hired criminals to fend off unions; unions retained them to make employers see the light.

Once established, criminals were difficult to dislodge. Usually they seized positions of power in intra-industry protective associations, demanded high salaries, and won the right to invest in legitimate retail outlets. Laundries and cleaners in Chicago were particularly affected, but shoe repair shops, groceries, and other businesses also were involved. The legitimate associates of such criminals were reluctant to expose them, not only because of the potential for violence, but also because the criminals performed a service in restricting competition. Syndicate men in legitimate business had their own protection, and so had less need of it from politicians and the police.

While the Kelley-Nash machine consolidated its hold on Chicago's politics, La Guardia loudly and vigorously reformed New York. Of course there were similarities between New York and Chicago. La Guardia and Cermak both were consummate ethnic politicians. Both developed organizations that danced to their tunes. Both battled a difficult depression situation with courage and resourcefulness. If the Kelley-Nash machine was less dynamic and innovative than Cermak, why so was the La Guardia of the last years less skilled than the early La Guardia. To end the analysis there, however, would be to lose the essence of reform in operational similarities. La Guardia offered to every New Yorker the hope that the city's basic housing problem could be solved, that the schools would educate effectively, that shopkeepers and truck farmers would be free from extortion, and that an efficient civil service would respond to citizen needs. Big cities saddled with the burdens of official indifference and organized crime needed that kind of hope.

There were lessons in the Chicago experience, too, for urban politics and reform. First, Chicago showed that reform (the Dever administration) was too fragile to be mixed up with social experiments like prohibition, which perhaps 80 percent of Chicago's adult population heartily disliked. Second, Chicago demonstrated that administrative incompetence, municipal bankruptcy, and civic degradation (the third Thompson administration) may be sufficient reasons for the people to abandon the men responsible, but may not be enough to drive them into the arms of reformers. Third, Chicago (and New York, too) revealed that reform alone could not succeed in the ethnic welter of most cities: reform required a politician-reformer with a consciously cultivated ethnic appeal.

In the end what mattered was the distinction between reform and mere politics. Formerly, politics sought power for its own sake; good works were the by-products of the search for power. Reform reversed the order: good works were what counted, but to get them one had to be a politician, and to love politics almost as much as good works.

CHAPTER FIVE

Cities Analyzed

American scholars and writers with awakened imaginations, fresh insights, and a lively sense of self-discipline studied the city in new ways during the 30 years after 1915. Whether academicians or novelists, they broke with "problem writing" and its homiletics, typified by Upton Sinclair's *The Jungle* (1906) and the social surveys of the settlement-house workers. Instead they examined urban situations, using new methods, and hoping for improvements in the urban environment through the education of the literate public.

Their approach was born of a postprogressive view of the city as a conditioner of group behavior. The view was at once sober and pessimistic, excited and hopeful. It was sober because some of this behavior, for instance, the impersonality of urban crowds, was mildly psychotic if one took small-town gregariousness to be the norm. Pessimistic, because it was unlikely that cities would cease to overstimulate most humans and that "unnatural" behavior could be eliminated. Excited, because the city was the seat of dynamic social processes that could be understood, or even predicted, if the correct techniques of "data gathering" and analysis were applied to them. Hopeful, because understanding of the city's social processes would lead to controlling them in the interests of all, but especially of the disadvantaged poor.

SOCIOLOGISTS AND CITIES

A small group of hyperactive scholars at the University of Chicago led the way into the new field of urban sociology. Behind the gray Gothic facades on the Midway Plaisance they pored over spot maps depicting the clusters of Chicago's pathology, including the residences of criminals, dance hall patrons, and prostitutes; they sent graduate students out to gather still more data on the city and its human types, and they drove themselves harder than their graduate students. They fed data into computers, but this was in the 1920s, so they called their machines "electronic card-sorters." They avoided the snobbery that academicians in one discipline all too often display toward those in related fields, working closely on several projects with political scientists, economists, historians, archeologists, anthropologists, and social workers.

Some disclaimers must be entered before going further. Chicago was not the only university where things were happening in twentieth-century sociology, but Chicago's prestige outshone that of its nearest rival, Columbia. The theories, investigations, and writings of the men who composed the "Chicago school" covered the entire range of sociology, not just urban sociology. The men to be discussed here as urban sociologists often made contributions in other branches of the discipline. Several men whose major studies were in other fields contributed insights and ideas to the urban sociologists. All the fields of sociology infected and reinforced one another during those heady days. Nor did urban sociology spring forth fully grown in 1915, although Robert E. Parks' article of that year, "The City: Suggestions for the Investigation of Human Behavior in the Urban Environment," marked off a separate field of urban studies. Sociology, urban or otherwise, did not begin with Chicago. Courses in the study of contemporary society and institutions were common in the colleges and universities of the late nineteenth century.

Disclaimers granted, Chicago was at the center of things sociological. Its department of sociology, the first in the country, was established on a par with the other academic departments when the university opened in 1892. The distinguished president of Colby College, Albion W. Small, came to head the department and, soon after, to serve as the graduate dean. Small made little impact on sociological thought. In fact, academic sociologists of the twenties and thirties treated Small's writings with mingled pity and scorn. Yet Small is correctly regarded as one of the giant figures of early sociology because of his key contributions to institutional development. He established the *American Journal of Sociology* in 1895, an elite scholarly publication owned by the university and edited by a member of the department until 1936. He was twice president of the American Sociological Society (founded 1905) during its formative years. The academic luminaries whom Small and his co-workers attracted to his department so added to Chicago's luster that there was a rebellion against "Chicago domination" in the thirties, resulting in the founding of the *American Sociological Review* and a rival society. Small's specific contributions to urban sociology consisted of two precepts that he preached but did not practice: "objectivity" (of that, more later) and the use of Chicago as a laboratory of research. Students followed through on Small's advice. Doctoral candidates completed dissertations with such titles as "A Study of the Stock Yards Community at Chicago," "A Study of the Higher Life of Chicago," and "Some Phases of the Production and Consumption of Literature in Chicago."

Besides Small the Chicago notables in urban sociology were Robert E. Park, William I. Thomas, Ernest W. Burgess, and later, William F. Ogburn and Louis Wirth. Some brief introductions will precede reviews of their shared ideas and individual contributions. Thomas, a pioneer, transitional figure, arrived at Chicago during its first year. He came from teaching English at a freshwater college to take a doctorate, and he remained until 1918. Iconclastic and indefatigable, he early developed a healthy disrespect for the speculation, theorizing, and deductive reasoning then current in sociology. Most of Thomas' work stood outside urban sociology. However, he bequeathed a zest for fact-gathering, a disdain for sweeping, unsupported generalizations, and a concern for the accommodation and acculturation of racial and ethnic types in cities. Thomas coauthored the massive *The Polish Peasant in Europe and America* (1918–1920), introducing sociologists to the use of manuscript materials, to the compilation of careful life histories for analysis, and to the concept of "social disorganization," the declining force of old social rules on individuals transplanted to a new social setting, as were Chicago's Poles. Thomas was also concerned with mobility, although it is fair to say that Park's interest in the problems of urban social relationships (including mobility) and the problems of race would have developed without Thomas.

Park felt three influences most deeply: his early experiences as a newspaper reporter; the thinking of Georg Simmel, whose lectures he heard at Berlin before taking a Ph. D. at Heidelberg, and his experiences while serving as secretary and traveling investigator for Booker T. Washington. His widely read "The City" reflected these influences when it urged sociologists to study intraurban communication, the process of socialization, and the impact of race on the individual's urban role. The impact of the textbook that he and Burgess first issued in 1921 was enormous, if unquantifiable. Two generations of students knew their *Introduction to the Science of Sociology* as "the green bible."

Park came to Chicago in 1914 and retired in 1933, but Burgess, Ogburn, and Wirth stayed on to witness a new burst of academic activity in the late forties and early fifties. Chicago-trained Burgess, although Park's junior by more than 20 years, joined the department the same year as Park. He was primarily concerned with the social evolution of the family, crime, and social pathology, but he also propounded a much-maligned concentric theory of urban expansion. Ogburn arrived from Columbia University in 1927, bringing with him Columbia's greater concern for statistical methods. Urban sociology quickly absorbed statistical methodology, especially in population study, another of Ogburn's interests. Ogburn's investigations of the relationships between technology and society have yet to be fully integrated with other urban studies. Ironically, the concept of "cultural lag," his most fruitful and controversial idea, did not rest on quantification. Wirth, German-born of a Jewish background, was, like Burgess, a Chicago Ph. D. He returned to Chicago in 1933. Wirth shared a concern for minority group and racial issues with other members of the sociology department. Among his many contributions was his fine study of *The Ghetto* (1928) and his article "Urbanism as a Way of Life" (1938), in which he combined a summary and restatement of the views of the "Chicago school" with a call for a theory of urbanism. Thus the "Chicago school" had come full circle, from denying theory to embracing it, in less than half a century.

All three men worked with and through their students, goading them to refine, extend, and overturn past knowledge. They all wrote a great deal but their students felt the impact of their vitality, force, and intellectual capacity directly. These students were almost always graduate students. None of the men, except Wirth, who could be scintillating, was an effective undergraduate teacher. This is not to say that a capacity for scholarly writing and training graduate students, and an ability to reach undergraduates are mutually exclusive qualities. It does mean that these men were "characters" who lacked the temperament to do well with younger students. Small, who was an exception to the statement about vitality and force, used himself up in the university's internecine struggles. Years before he retired in 1923 his lectures had become painfully dull. Thomas took research notes on slips of paper and stuffed them into his coat pockets. While lecturing he would jerk the slips out and comment on them as he went along. Students who took his courses for their content were rewarded, those who required some self-evident organization were frustrated.

Park, the archetypical absentminded professor, would appear before class with his long white hair disheveled, his clothing in disarray. Once a student walked to the front of the room while Park was lecturing, and began tying Park's necktie that was dangling down the professor's shirtfront. Park matched expertise for expertise, continuing to lecture while the student made him sartorially presentable. But students generally found the classroom Park mirthless, gruff, and frowning. When he thought a student's idea was not worth a damn, he said so. Even graduate students who admired his intellect quailed before his verbal shafts. Those who stuck it through found that Park outside of class was a kindly if distracted man who was inordinately generous with his time. Burgess, a small, frail-looking bachelor, lectured in a high voice with frequent hesitations, although his course content was excellent. Ogburn was thorough, patient, and stressed scientific method, but he was no spellbinder.

Personal quirks counted for little in writing, and it was in their writings that the "Chicago school" urban sociologists laid a common intellectual foundation for their work. Their foundation stones included human ecology, objectivity and a dread of theory, the use of history, and the use of statistics and quantitative methods.

Human ecology was simply the "approach" or the organizing principle through which urban sociologists studied the community structure, institutions, and individuals in all of their relationships. Neither a science nor a methodology, it was the "what" of urban sociology, not the "how." Although every urban sociologist studied the environmental influences on people, institutions, and communities, the foundation for a definition of human ecology waited on the work of Roderick D. McKenzie, a Chicago student, first published in 1925. McKenzie defined human ecology "as a study of the spatial and temporal relations of human beings as affected by the selective, distributive, and accommodative forces of the environment. Human ecology is fundamentally interested in the effect of *position,* in both time and space, upon human institutions and human behavior. . . . These spatial relationships of human beings are the products of competition and selection, and are continuously in process of change as new factors enter to disturb the competitive relations or to facilitate mobility." [1]

The early urban sociologists shared certain assumptions that shaped the ecological point of view, and were shaped by it in turn. First, they believed that urban growth was not to be confused with the development of technology, the growth of industry, or the rise of capitalism. Urban growth was the growth of the urban population in a special setting of institutions and community. Of course the technological and industrial situation helped to shape cities, and the sociologist had to be aware of it. Second, the Chicago school believed that

[1] Robert E. Park, Ernest W. Burgess, and Roderick D. McKenzie, *The City,* University of Chicago Press, Chicago, 1925, pp. 63–64.

institutions and communities molded individuals, and not the other way around. Individuals impressed institutions very little unless they acted collectively. Urban dwellers were inveterate organizers because they were so impotent to alter situations by themselves. On the other hand the individual had some choices within the framework of organizational, institutional, and social compulsions. For instance, geographical mobility, an important component of urban development, involved individual decisions about when and where to move.

Third, the urban sociologists refused to confine their studies to the area within the city limits. They argued that urban economic, social, and cultural influences extended far beyond the boundaries of the political city. The metropolitan region (roughly, the area of contiguous urban settlement) was not so much a dominant "core" and a dependent "ring" as it was an area of interdependent activities, always in flux. The metropolitan area, on the other hand, did dominate the lesser cities and the countryside surrounding it. In 1933 McKenzie analyzed the interdependence, the dominance, and the dynamics in *The Metropolitan Community*. Urban sociologists' concerns extended still farther, into rural areas beyond direct metropolitan influences. The great rural-to-urban migrations and the abandonment of distant farms were the most obvious urban-induced changes in remote rural areas.

Fourth and finally, the ecological approach viewed the city with professional dispassion. The urban sociologists took no position "versus" the city. They did believe that the city, contrasted with the rural environment, cradled severe social pathologies leading to a greater frequency of mental derangement. Park made much of the decline, in cities, of the primary group relationships responsible for the individual's socialization. The "artificial" city discouraged those "natural" relationships in favor of impersonal secondary contacts. When people understood one another only in their roles of banker, client, clerk, or repairman, they cared nothing for one another's moral development. Enforcement of the restraints of the primary group relationship shifted to institutions—the police and the schools—and city people became less inhibited.

None of this means that the Chicago school yearned for an arcadian past, or that its members were Jeffersonians, or that they believed the city to be the abode of evil. First, the Chicagoans found the city much more receptive to inventive, talented, and eccentric people than rural areas were. Second, their attitude toward the city was united to their view of social development as a whole. That view, conditioned by the cyclical theories of nineteenth-century philosophers, was mildly cynical. To the Chicago school mere social change was not progress; indeed, it might be retrogressive unless consciously directed toward human betterment. This view sharply diverged from the usual middle-class measurements of progress: the increasing stock of material goods, technological achievements, and profound developments in transportation and communication. To the Chicago school there was no "progress" involved in the spread of automobiles or the rise of radio. Such products might enhance the sophistication, brittle manners, and coldness of the urbanite, characteristics he already possessed in overabundance. By themselves cars and radios did nothing to promote the security, peace, or sensitive awareness of urban dwellers. Everything depended on their use. Usually they simply altered human situations and behavior, without improvement. Life in twentieth-century cities, then, was not "better" or "worse" because it included novel features. Urban life was the product of a larger culture that was morally neutral.

Besides the ecological approach, Chicago's sociologists shared a commitment to objectivity and an aversion to universal systems of thought. Their commitment no more marked a cowardly retreat from reform than it embraced the naive approach to quantification sometimes embodied in the word "objective." They were acutely aware of the social scientists' inability to escape subjective judgments. They believed just as firmly that the time had come for social scientists to turn away from theorizing and clarion calls to reform.

The Chicago school found the cosmic arguments and deductions of nineteenth-century sociologists rather inconvenient and embarrassing. William Graham Sumner was an acknowledged genius, but his failure to gather research data under controlled conditions, his doctrinaire belief in untrammeled individualism, and his powerful arguments on behalf of the status quo alienated men who sensed society's organic and dynamic qualities. Another giant of early sociology, Lester Frank Ward, believed that natural processes such as evolutionary development were wasteful and confused. To permit human society to drift along undirected by man's conscious efforts was to condemn it to the same harum-scarum destructiveness prevailing in nature. Ward's view was more congenial because he called for human intervention. His theorizing and deductions from his own principles, combined with nearly unintelligible prose, made him as unsatisfactory a model as Sumner. The work of the younger men, Edward A. Ross and Franklin H. Giddings, suffered from similar limitations. Clearly it was time to leave system building and do some original research in the real society.

Other nineteenth-century scholars (like scholars in all centuries) had suffered a few serious theoretical pratfalls. Some of their theories, such as instinct theory and the theory of acquired character- istics, were well known to sociologists. Both had been shorn up for a time by self-serving research. Both were on the scholarly scrap heap by the twenties. The unglamorous fate of these theories reinforced twentieth-century sociologists' commitment to careful investigation unclouded by elaborate postulates. Objectivity, then, meant conduct- ing research, not to validate a theory, but to discover what really was going on in the world. New theories, when they came, would be securely inductive, grounded on thousands of carefully mortised bits of information.

Public exasperation with settlement-house workers' careful inves- tigations of urban conditions was a special warning to Chicago's ur- banists to be objective. The settlement houses were privately fi- nanced efforts to improve the lot of immigrant slum dwellers. Young reformers from middle-class backgrounds, possessed by gnawing shame at social inequities, founded and staffed the settlements. Soon they discovered that research in and exposure of conditions would have to precede their understanding of the immigrant neighborhood, to say nothing of intelligent reform. Beginning in the late nineteenth century the settlement-house workers conducted neighborhood sur- veys of situations "deviant" or "abnormal" from their point of view. Housing conditions, employment patterns, sanitation, recreational fa- cilities, and a host of social pathologies including delinquency and alcoholism were subjects for investigation. The Russell Sage Foun- dation (established 1907) and the proliferating schools of social work supported even more extensive surveys.

Ostensibly the surveys exemplified painstaking empirical research, but Chicago's urban sociologists were not especially enthusiastic about them. To the urban sociologists, the findings of the surveys were just as theoretically straitjacketed as the musings of Sumner and Ward. The surveys were products of the conviction that urban life, or a large part of it, was rotten and required overhauling. The settlement-house residents and the social workers marshaled their facts with a zeal and a radical immediatism that became more and more irritating to the comfortable middle class. The Pittsburgh Sur- vey is a case in point. This massive survey began in 1907, ended in 1910, and was published in six volumes from 1909 to 1914. Outsiders did most of the field work, although the survey was partly locally inspired. Their findings vividly contrasted the disorganization and squalor of workingmen's residential neighborhoods with the finely honed precision of the factories and mills. Apply even a bit of the in- dustrial sector's organizational will and skill to the social sector, their message ran, and living conditions would improve dramatically. Writing about social problems was not enough, they believed; they must take action. In their role as agitators the investigators held meetings, wangled speaking engagements, wrote pamphlets and magazine articles, and tried to develop strategies with local reformers. The only noticeable effect was to anger and humiliate residents who resented being thought of as narrow, money-grubbing, unkind dwellers in an ugly, dirty city.

Settlement houses and surveys continued after World War I, but the bloom was off the rose. Social workers themselves sought a professional status reinforced by organizations, journals, and university curricula. They could not live down the reputation, carried over from the settlement-house days, of being professional bleeding hearts, do-gooders, and effete radicals. The Chicago sociologists understood this and strove to overcome the popular confusion between "sociologist" and "socialist." They tried to disassociate their own labors from social work or "applied sociology."

The trace of snobbery in the sociologists' attitude was mitigated by two considerations. First, they were earnest men who were deeply committed to social action and who found the time to practice it. They hoped that their studies, professional and free of evident bias, would lead to betterment of the human condition. Ellsworth Faris, a member of the Chicago department of sociology, summed it up for all of them. "An objective science," he wrote, "does not concern itself immediately with welfare. . . . But science, or knowledge, is always in the service of ends, and the ultimate justification of science, certainly the science of human nature, will be the service it can render to human welfare." [2]

Second, Chicago's sociologists did cooperate with members of many academic disciplines, including social work, on the Local Community Research Committee. Sociologists at other universities and colleges were not so fastidious about keeping formal barriers raised between themselves and social work. Sometimes this was by choice, as at Columbia University. More often academic sociologists were grateful for the "practical" departments of social work in the smaller colleges and normal schools. These departments of social work usually hired a few sociologists to teach their students "theory." Independent sociology departments were more difficult to establish. After all, what was the practical use of a degree in sociology?

[2] Robert E. L. Faris, *Chicago Sociology, 1920–1932*, University of Chicago Press, Chicago, 1970, p. 131.

Urban sociologists armed with the ecological approach and objectivity added a sense of history to their arsenal. Convinced of the organic nature of urban society, they used historical materials with skill and sense to gain perspective on contemporary problems. Wirth's study of the urban ghetto in the United States, for instance, devoted considerable space to the historical development of Jewish segregation. Had Wirth not treated his subject historically, his discussion of the radical modification of Jewish culture in American urban settings would have been pointless. Ogburn was intensely interested in the historical development of society and culture. He speculated on the role of technology, invention, and great men in history. He applied vigorous statistical analysis to business cycles, political trends, and wartime prosperity. His "cultural lag" theory could have been advanced only by someone deeply immersed in historical problems.

The historical sections in the works on urban society were summary in character, not the results of original research. Their authors were sociologists, not historians. They cannot be held responsible for failing to use history more than they did. Probably they found a lot of historical writing conceptually defective and indifferent to their questions. Nor are they to blame for later shifts in historical interpretations that modified some of their assumptions about the past. Historians sometimes change their minds because of fresh insights from other disciplines, including sociology. The Chicago school's recognition of the need to study society through time was unfortunately lost on some later urban sociologists and cultural anthropologists. Those worthies too often placed their faith in their personal preconceptions of the past or in random bits of local historical myth collected during interviews.

Finally, Chicago's sociologists appreciated the need to make quantitative studies and statements about society. Careful measurement of social phenomena was required to support their claim to be studying scientifically what others were merely theorizing about. The various studies of Chicago included tables, graphs, charts, and spot maps, all relatively simple forms of qualitative presentation. But sociologists also developed, refined, and applied correlations, time series, and scaling to social problems. Many of the studies had nothing directly to do with cities, but most of their techniques, if modified, could be applied to problems in urban sociology. Some students discovered deficiencies in social casework categorizations and in urban population projections. Burgess worked out indicies, or "gradients" by which to measure the ecological nature of urban expansion. Still other studies measured the attitudes of Chicago residents toward prohibition, nationality, and race.

Perhaps because they were not the pioneers in quantitative methods, the Chicago sociologists made no sweeping claims for statistical techniques. They were uninfected by that peculiar arrogance that strikes various groups of social scientists from time to time. The most obvious symptom is a declaration that most, or all, social problems are susceptible of quantification and that solutions may be manufactured once the problem situations are fully quantified. The Chicago school held that society was enormously complex and that quantification was hampered by all sorts of difficulties, including the perceptions of the investigator. The investigator could labor long and mightily with little result. Or he might significantly extend knowledge, as Burgess did when he correlated convicts' success on parole with selected personality traits and background characteristics, and predicted recidivism much more accurately than before. They were no more dogmatic about method or technique than they were slaves of theory. A method appropriate to one study might be appropriate to another, or it might not. It was important, they agreed, to try quantification. They hoped to move from analysis to prediction, but the move would obviously have to take place in the future.

Armed with their approach and their convictions, Chicago's urban sociologists plunged themselves and their students into scholarly investigations of the city. The dozens of monographic community studies were the most widely known. They followed Park's injunction to pry into every nook and cranny of urban life. Although they shared viewpoints and methods, they divided their work into five categories: studies of urban areas (slums, ethnic neighborhoods), urban deviant types (hoboes, professional thieves), urban social groups and organizations (gangs, the Chicago Real Estate Board), urban pathology (crime and vice) and black studies (the Negro family).

The community studies betrayed the weaknesses of the Chicago approach. The Chicago sociologists never succeeded in neatly compartmentalizing their reform urges and their professional objectivity. Judgments against the unhealthy social influences of dance halls or movie houses occasionally crept into their books. The Chicago school overemphasized the urban dweller's ennui, his anomie, his tenuous secondary relationships. In bemoaning the loss of the individual's community ties, Park and the others failed to realize that individuals might maintain primary relationships over long urban distances and that a thick cluster of primary relationships might not be necessary to the survival of society.

The Chicago school saw the city as a collection of neighborhoods, or ethnic groups, or organizations with little or no interaction or interpenetration. (In part this was an extension of their view of the isolated, superficial lives of urban individuals.) The tendency to see fragments rather than the whole was partly a condition, partly a result, of the kinds of studies in which the Chicago school excelled. A study of homeless men or taxidancers concentrated on the people and their peculiar society, not on their links with others in the community who might have homes or who did not frequent dance halls. Nor did the Chicago school, for all its concern with geographical mobility, much bother itself with movement in and out of the groups it studied. Certainly the Chicago scholars fretted too much over the lack of urban social cohesion, both because they missed a lot that was there, and because they set too much store by it in the first place. They did not judge the city against a village ideal, but they did measure it by their unexamined assumption that a closely knit community was a good thing.

Three positive contributions of the urban studies more than balanced their weaknesses. First, Chicago's sociologists significantly widened the scope of investigation beyond the social workers' surveys. The sociologists investigated vice and slums, but they also examined hotel life, the police, upper-class neighborhoods, and business organizations. They exposed the city's diversity and social complexity as no one had before. Second, they stripped "abnormal," "odd," or "criminal" subjects of at least some of their taint. The social work surveys had assumed that any situation deviating from "normal," that is, from middle-class values and standards, was pathological. Pathological situations undermined the urban community and had to be reformed. The sociologists, instead, interpreted divergent life styles "from the inside," or in terms of the deviant community's values. The sociologists explained to middle-class minds that hoboes regulated one another's conduct, that black people had a class structure, and that criminal youths strove to emulate the men who had been successful in the underworld. They presented diverse individuals and situations within each deviant group, demonstrating how misleading stereotypes could be.

Because they interpreted "abnormal" people to the middle class, the Chicagoans made a third contribution. They encouraged a more realistic, hardheaded approach to the complexities of urban life. They urged their readers to see "abnormal" groups as communities having rules, expectations about the behavior of their members, and internal mobility. However bizarre these communities seemed to the outsider, they possessed cohesion, structure, and organic logic. Bootleggers, gang youths, prostitutes, and tramps were each of them individuals moving in a society of regulations, punishments, and rewards. Most "abnormal" people found "normal" middle-class communities vicious and hostile, or hypocritical, or simply incomprehensible. All of this encouraged concerned middle-class people to alter some of their preconceptions and to drop the notion that everyone else viewed things much in the same way as they did. Implicit in the sociologists' presentation was the conviction that no successful reform could be grounded in a simpleminded view of the urban world.

Three Chicago urban sociologists made contributions that went beyond those already attributed to them or to the Chicago school generally. Robert E. Park was the first among the leaders of the Chicago school, and it would be a hard matter indeed to single out one of his contributions from the bright array. His relaxed attitude toward race and race issues such as segregation and assimilation has received somewhat less attention, so it will be examined here.

Park was well in advance of most whites—including educated whites—in rejecting racial differences as a basis for segregation or discrimination against nonwhites. Park believed in racial differences, but he was uncertain whether most of them were innately racial or the product of culture. Besides, the differences were only that, not tokens of superiority or inferiority. He argued, for instance, that the racial "temperament" of blacks inclined them toward the arts rather than to intellectual pursuits, and entertained the idea that black people might be more attracted to bright colors and have happier dispositions than whites. But all this was speculative, and even if proven would not be grounds for claims of superiority or inferiority. He did firmly believe, at least for a time, that each race possessed a distinctive body odor that was offensive in heavy concentrations to members of other races. He wisely refrained from drawing any conclusions based on his belief.

Park's comparatively unclouded view of race and race relations opened his eyes to the revolutionary changes in black attitudes during the twenties. The rural black, whom Park knew well from his service with Booker T. Washington, soon dropped his mask of accommodation after he arrived in Chicago. Reinforced by the presence of so many fellow blacks, he became more proud, individual, and race conscious. As president of the Chicago Urban League during the great migration, Park enjoyed a strategic observation post from which to mark the rise of the "New Negro." Park believed that the "New Negro" was a phenomenon of urban segregation in the North. He applauded the "New Negro's" efforts to preserve and extend black culture. He saw, much earlier than most whites, that blacks formed a cultural nation within a nation. Yet he believed that cultural nationalism, no matter by whom practiced, was passé. The long-range trend favored cultural assimilation and, although Park was carefully vague on the matter, intermarriage at some remote time. Park's sensitivity to black culture made him aware of young blacks' difficulties with a school system organized to transmit white culture. Most racial problems were, he believed, cultural at bottom.

For all his racial concern Park was peculiarly myopic about some contemporary trends in the black community and in race relations. He staked far too much on the rise of a minuscule black urban middle class, concluding without justification that most blacks shared the gains. Although he was aware of some differences between the receptions given to European and to black immigrants in the city, he thought they were fundamentally alike. Racial prejudice was little different from earlier ethnic prejudice and would be similarly overcome. Attitudes such as these made Park too optimistic about the future of black-white relations, but they should not obscure his remarkable sympathy for blacks, both urban and rural. How influential all of this was, it is impossible to say, but Park's views probably swayed many educated minds. His writings were widely read among sociologists, and occasionally, among the literate public. His "green bible" text disseminated his views, even though, for scholarly balance, it incorporated the writings of race supremacists. Park helped other whites understand that the urbanization of the Negro was a great cultural phenomenon of their time. That alone makes his writings on race among the most significant of his contributions.

Ernest W. Burgess' hypothesis of urban expansion, published in 1925, survived many debunkings. On one level Burgess' idealization demonstrated the Chicago school's willingness to invent working hypotheses while remaining skeptical of cosmic theories. On the practical, immediate level Burgess constructed a model for studying urban growth. He observed that expansion involved three related processes: extension, or the city's geographical spread; succession, the encroachment of new types of populations or land uses upon established areas; and concentration. Concentration could indicate the collection of highly mobile populations in small urban spaces, such as the central retail district or areas of high-rise residential hotels. Or it could refer to residential segregation by income or occupation.

Burgess accounted for the phenomena of radial urban expansion by representing the city as a series of concentric rings. The inner circle or central business district was the first zone. The second, transitional zone contained factories, warehouses, and various businesses, but was also home to the sort of people who live in disintegrating residential neighborhoods; hoboes, prostitutes, lower-echelon criminals of various sorts, causal laborers, and the poorest of the regularly employed. The third ring comprised an area of modest workingmen's houses, while the fourth was residential but of higher quality, including restricted developments. The fifth ring extended beyond the city limits into the suburbs and satellite cities. Here the long-distance commuters established their homes.

Most of the attacks on Burgess' hypothesis would not have occurred had the attackers read his presentation carefully. Burgess himself wrote that his concentric representation was ideal, and that no city on earth corresponded exactly to it. Geographical features, transportation lines, long-established industrial areas, and community resistance to invasion by business or immigrants, all warped his ideal arrangement. He was aware that Lake Michigan interrupted Chicago's concentric zones, as the Chicago River did to a lesser degree. The mention of satellite cities in the commuters' zone indicated his recognition of industrial clusters in the area beyond the city limits. Burgess knew about other local departures from the ideal: the wealthy Gold Coast section located just north of the Loop; the industrialization of the Lake Calumet area several miles south of downtown; and the ruthless determination of whites to keep blacks out of Hyde Park, a residential section on the doorstep of the University of Chicago.

Other criticisms arose from a failure to understand that Burgess was seeking what was typical of each zone, not what was unique or exceptional. Burgess admitted exceptions. He plotted "bright light" areas and residential hotel sections in the fourth, or better residential zone when he applied his conception to Chicago. The "black belt" appeared as a long, narrow strip running south from the middle of the transitional zone, cutting through the zone of workingmen's homes, and penetrating the residential zone. A "bungalow section," evidently lower middle-class housing located near suburban industry, was found in the fifth, or commuter zone. But these were clearly atypical situations that did not invalidate the zonal concept.

Burgess paid little attention to the impact of transportation lines, although he did mention it. Had he been more explicit he might have been spared criticism on the grounds that urban expansion follows transportation lines and is axial, and not radial as Burgess would have it. That is, both residential and commercial development follow (or followed) trolley and bus lines or major thoroughfares, leaving large gaps between the axes of advance. The axial theory did not conflict with Burgess' position as much as it complemented it. It would be possible to argue that the thrust of settlement, at least in the prefreeway city, was along axes, but that the spaces between them eventually filled with dwellings similar to those at comparable points of the axes.

The sector theory, another anti-Burgess idea, argued that land uses tended to expand from near the central business district outward to the city's edge. For example, the zone of workingmen's homes was not a third concentric zone but, instead, an area shaped like a wedge of pie, with the point toward the central city, the outer edge extending to, or almost to, the urban margins. The theory owed much to the labors of Homer Hoyt, a land economist who was well acquainted with Burgess' concentric scheme. Hoyt objected to radial bands of growth because, he argued, high-class residential areas bunched in the sort of wedge-shaped sectors he described. They were not distributed in a surrounding ring, but in most cities occupied no more than a quarter of the urban margin. Sometimes low-rent areas covered more of the city's ring than high-rent districts.

Hoyt's circular diagrams with their little wedge shapes showed low-rent districts on the urban fringe, but they also revealed that higher rental sectors usually clustered at or near the city's edge. In fact, Hoyt's diagrams were as good a demonstration of Burgess' theory, properly qualified, as they were of his own. Hoyt believed that the concentric theory was of no help in locating, say, high-rent districts, but his sector theory did not offer any better guide to the precise location of high-rent areas in any particular city. Hoyt's observation that certain land uses followed certain land forms (better residential neighborhoods on high, picturesque ground) was only what Burgess had said in other language. It was scarcely the profound insight that Hoyt seemed to believe it was. It was not exclusive to his hypothesis; indeed in application it could modify the sector theory as much as the concentric theory.

A third explanation of urban development, "multiple nuclei," also complemented Burgess' hypothesis. According to the "multiple nuclei" doctrine, the city's functions cluster about separate centers according to specialization (the retail district), the tendency of certain businesses to group together (the wholesale district), the mutual antagonism of some activities (factories distant from expensive residences), and land rentals (storage and low-income housing on cheap sites). Burgess himself wrote about the tendency toward clustering or concentrations, but he conceived of concentration and dispersion as dynamic processes always shaping and expanding the concentric city. He noted the rapidly growing retail districts in outlying sections, "satellite loops" he called them, a form of concentration in dispersion. Walter Firey's 1946 study of land use in Boston argued that cultural factors—the historic associations of Boston Common, for instance—prevent the development of special urban areas according to the doctrine of the land economists. Firey's work has been hailed because it supposedly collapsed Burgess' theory once and for all. It could better be seen as a careful demonstration of Burgess' argument that particular urban locales sometimes successfully resist changes in population or use.

Burgess' hypothesis alone incorporated the dynamics of invasion and succession, of the displacement of old land uses and populations by new. Neighborhood growth, decay, and renewal under the same or different uses was a fact of urban life. Yet the "sector" and "multiple nuclei" theories took no notice of them. Chicago studies of delinquency and the black family could be criticized (but not dismissed) for ordering their data zonally after the Burgess theory. They did reveal that antisocial behavior and pathological conditions declined as the distance from the central business district increased. They did impart a feeling for Chicago's vigor and pulsating life, the tension and movement of its ethnic and racial populations.

Louis Wirth inherited the Chicago school's skepticism of all-embracing theories of society. But the chaotic state of urban sociology, as he surveyed it in 1938, led him to advance a theory of urbanism. In one way, Wirth's theory was simply a talented restatement of the long-standing assumption that cities influenced human behavior. It was more than that, for he wrote from the perspective of the major studies done in the twenties and thirties while proposing a framework and direction for future research.

Wirth defined a city, "for sociological purposes," as "a relatively large, dense, and permanent settlement of socially heterogeneous individuals." [3] That definition, he believed, transcended mere local or cultural influences while including all the types of contemporary cities, whether they were industrial, university, commercial, resort, or suburban residential. A definition, of course, was not a theory. Wirth extracted three variables from his definition—numbers, density, and heterogeneity—to explain the population characteristics, the social organization, and the behavior of urban dwellers. These special phenomena produced the condition of urbanism. The interaction of numbers, density, and heterogeneity would demonstrate not only why a city developed a technology, dominated its hinterland, or attracted certain types of people. It would show why some cities developed so differently or more successfully than others. For instance,

[3] Louis Wirth, *On Cities and Social Life*, University of Chicago Press, Chicago, 1964, p. 66.

sheer numbers forced a city to establish highly specialized communal services based on the average human need, not on individual desires. Density led to spatial differentiations and to functional zoning in cities, as in the separation of residential and industrial areas. Heterogeneity forced urban dwellers to join groups that catered to the narrow, specific common interests of their members. An individual with several strong interests would have to join several groups having little or no relation to each other, and containing a wide assortment of people.

Wirth's theory allowed for all sorts of approaches and for the inclusion of a variety of data. He asked only that urban sociologists consider their problems and proofs in terms of his variables. The practice would have, he believed, two salutary results. First, it would end the proliferation of *ad hoc* community studies. These investigations of everything under the urban sun were begun without reference to an explicit theory. Nor were they producing any theory in the aggregate. Any one study could be nothing more than a pseudoscholarly validation of the author's prejudices. Second, Wirth hoped to build a body of evidence susceptible to refinement and comparison. A large "coherent body of knowledge" [4] that was internally consistent and transferable to similar situations in different cities was, he believed, the true starting point for urban reform.

Urban sociologists neither abandoned limited studies nor embarked on many comparative investigations. Wirth's article did reflect a growing dissatisfaction with narrow community studies and a trend, already well begun, toward qualitative studies of population characteristics, mobility, and class stratification. The class stratification studies were the most influential. More anthropological than they were sociological, they used cities as the sites of their investigations. They were more exciting than the descriptive ecological studies of mobility, migration, and urban growth so important to the scholars of the thirties and forties. The ecological studies were earnest, abstract, sometimes trivial in their categorizations and comparisons, overburdened with statistics, and oppressively dull. The anthropological studies, by happy contrast, were treasures of wit, irony, insight into the human condition, and plain good writing. Nor did they neglect quantification, for they came larded with sophisticated graphical presentations of reams of data.

The most renowned anthropological studies were the Yankee City series (about Newburyport, Massachusetts) by W. Lloyd Warner and his associates, and two books on "Middletown" (Muncie, Indiana) by

[4] *Ibid.*, p. 83.

Robert S. and Helen Lynd. To take the Yankee City series first, Warner and his crew made important contributions to social investigation. In contrast to the Chicago school, Warner was intensely concerned with social class, interclass relationships, and class behavior. The Chicago school dealt with class, of course, but classes, class stratification, and class-induced behavior were not its primary concerns. Warner's approach frankly recognized classes, not just occupational groups. Warner openly discussed the drawing of class lines and other forms of class antagonism.

The Yankee City series was a prodigy of labor. Warner and his associates carried on four years' intensive field work, beginning in 1930, and kept it up much less intensively through the mid-1950s. The investigators, usually graduate students at Harvard University, compiled interviews, studied health records, observed various classes at work and play, toured homes, clipped newspapers. They even stationed one of their number beside Newburyport's major newsstand to observe who bought what reading matter. They compiled extraordinary amounts of personal information on nearly 17,000 "social personality cards," one for almost every man, woman, and child in Newburyport and its immediate surroundings. They reported their subject's conversations with earthy realism. Their methods were elaborate, refined, and systematic. Usually about 10 but sometimes as many as 15 investigators were at work at any one time. As a study of all of the complex interrelationships that human beings have with one another in work situations, organizations, institutions, or wherever, the four-volume Yankee City series is unsurpassed (a fifth volume, published in 1959, is not considered here).

Warner pointed out the direction for the sociological studies of class and behavior so popular during the forties and fifties. There are vast differences between the Yankee City volumes and such later strident, iconoclastic books as C. Wright Mills' *The Power Elite* (1956). Yet they asked some of the same questions about class, power, control, and social cohesion. Mills and other younger sociologists criticized Warner for selecting an atypical city, for confusing class with social status, and for other sins both conceptual and procedural. Warner was open to criticism. Younger scholars were duty bound to criticize. This does not change the fact that they learned a lot about their trade from him.

When the apologies for the Yankee City series are made, however, there remains a vital flaw in those four careful books. For all their subtlety, their understanding, their verisimilitude, they are relics. Unlike some work of the Chicago school, they are period pieces no longer consulted to find out what is going on or even what was going on. The question is, why? The answer is: W. Lloyd Warner was an egregious snob. Snobbery may seem like a trivial or unmannerly charge to hurl at a scholar. But there is no other name for Warner's bias. His snobbery, his belief that the upper classes did (and should) determine basic social values and beliefs, blinded him to many things and led him into many conceptual traps.

Warner's snobbery conditioned everything about his study, beginning with the selection of Newburyport as the site of his investigations. Warner had recently returned from studying Australian aborigines and was teaching in Harvard University's department of anthropology. It was suggested that he extend a study of workers in one of Chicago's industrial suburbs to include the workers' "total personalities." (The argument for the "total personality" approach was that workers' lives are not really segmented, thus if we are to understand the man behind the machine we must understand his social relationships in all their complexity.) To adequately study the workers' "total personalities" it was necessary to study, in great detail, the surrounding community. Clearly it was impossible to do this with Chicago itself. The Chicago school had been at it for years without more than beginning the job. Why not, then, study one or more of Chicago's industrial suburbs, including the one in which the original factory study had been made?

Warner's answer was as revealing as it was incredible. Chicago's industrial suburbs "seemed to be disorganized; they had a social organization which was highly disfunctional, if not in partial disintegration." [5] Now that, with all respect, was malarky. If Warner had really understood the Chicago school studies that he praised so much, he would have realized that "highly disfunctional" social organizations were organic and internally consistent, they only seemed disorganized to a biased outside observer. But if Chicago's industrial suburbs were disorganized, what was organized? Warner answered: ". . . a community with a social organization which had developed over a long period of time under the domination of a single group with a coherent tradition." [6] Where were such communities found? Why, in the deep South and in New England! Warner never tested his belief in the continuity of southern and New England towns dominated by the upper classes; he simply assumed it.

If we allow for the kernel of truth in his assumption, wars, immigration, internal migrations, and profound technological changes

[5] W. Lloyd Warner and Paul S. Lunt, *The Social Life of a Modern Community*, Yale University Press, New Haven, Connecticut, 1941, pp. 4–5.

[6] *Ibid.*, p. 5.

had made mincemeat of most local elites, leaving them too small and divided to "dominate" their communities. Purely local elites might have the power to establish exclusive clubs, to control access to their class, to set certain hometown styles or trends, but not to "dominate" culturally, politically, or in any other way. Indeed, Warner presented a lot of piecemeal evidence that Newburyport's upper classes were culturally impotent, but he failed to see it as such. The apparent meaning of Warner's language was that if one is to do community research, one should do it among the magnolias and porticos of the deep South, or in Massachusetts, somewhere near Harvard. How much more pleasant there than among those uncouth people on the plains of Illinois who had no upper classes to influence their behavior (or to give lawn parties to which social researchers were invited). At last New England won out over the deep South probably because it contained more of those workers whom Warner was supposed to study.

To be fair, Warner was unafraid of primitive conditions, for he was fresh from his Australian researches, and he did intensively study factory workers and the lower social classes. But his choice this time was not between Australian aborigines and a lounge chair in the Harvard faculty club. It was between types of industrial communities, and Warner revealed what he really wanted to study when he chose Newburyport with its supposedly "dominant" upper class.

Warner and his crew gained their introduction to Newburyport through its upper class, and in a sense they never left it. They drew their interviews and surveys disproportionately from the top three classes (as Warner construed them) even though the upper classes accounted for less than 14 percent of the population. Their examples of conduct and class attitudes came as often from the upper classes as from the lower. They reported what upper-class informants told them about Newburyport's history with a tinge of condescension, but they did not contradict the information. The parties and entertainments they attended were usually upper class. Of course some of these situations were unavoidable. Upper-class people probably were more cooperative, more given to the sort of interviewing and recordkeeping required by the investigation, and less suspicious. Upper-class people had a deeper sense of family and community history. It may be the destiny of prominent outside community investigators to become the intellectual lap dogs of the local elite, and to be rather flattered by upper-class social invitations. And it would be a badly proportioned book that spent more time in descriptions of lower-class people only because there were more of them. These circumstances, then, were not necessarily prejudicial. A sensitive scholar could have compensated for them. Warner's failure lay in his inability to see that there was any problem in his implicit acceptance of the upper class.

Warner's snobbery also cut him off from an intelligent use of the past, for he could not admit to a dynamic urban history disrupting his myth of long-term, upper-class domination. He and his investigators sensed the partiality of upper-class historical recollection that stressed the continuity of old families. Yet they could not challenge upper-class history without challenging their reasons for being in Newburyport. They admitted to only one social upheaval in the city's past. After the war of 1812 a cluster of economic and technological changes doomed Newburyport's commerce and its merchant class, but that catastrophe was safely remote and made no difference in the 1930s. Warner knew that textile mills had succeeded the farming-mercantile economy, and that shoe factories later took the place of the mills. But he argued that none of this really mattered, for technological changes did not disturb social class arrangements! Neither could he confess the social importance of the shift in shoe factory ownership from local to absentee control, even though he reported the complaints of upper-class people about "Jews" and "newcomers" settling in town as a result of the change.

Newburyport contained a significant ethnic and second-generation immigrant group. That was one reason Warner chose Newburyport above other New England cities. But he refused to believe that a large influx of Eastern Europeans and Catholics had dented the community's commitment to Puritan values. There were plenty of examples to demonstrate just how far the rejection of old-family values had gone, and it had gone far. Warner devoted several pages to an account of "Biggy" Muldoon, a tough Irish kid whose mother had begun as a domestic but had grown wealthy in commodities speculation. In later years Biggy and his mother purchased a historic house where she formerly worked. After his mother's death Biggy, to the horror of the upper class, asked permission to move the house and build a filling station. The authorities promptly refused his request. Biggy tried again and was again refused. He then tore up the garden, installed a mock graveyard with stones bearing the names of the mayor and council, plastered circus posters on the outside walls of the house, and hung chamber pots from the windows.

After other adventures Biggy was elected mayor. Still the council would not grant his request. Accustomed to direct action in frustrating situations, Biggy cut down the great elms around the house and installed a gasoline pump. For that he was arrested, fined, and jailed. During the next two months he ran the city from his jail cell. He earned a lot of national publicity. Forty thousand people crowded around the jail on the day of his release. As soon as he emerged, a parade formed, and the crowd bore Biggy home in triumph.

For Warner the point of the Mayor Biggy drama, which occurred shortly before he arrived, was the clash of values involved. He told more about the symbolism of Biggy's acts, ripping out the garden, cutting down the trees, and so on, than most readers would want to know. But the implications for his thesis of Yankee domination were lost on him. Warner seemed to be arguing that Biggy was elected mayor, received nationwide publicity, and was met by 40 thousand people on his release from jail, all because he symbolized a revolt against upper-class old-family values. But so far as Warner was concerned, Biggy did nothing to loosen the grip of upper-class, old-family values in Newburyport. To the reader's reasonable doubts, Warner responded with a staggering non sequitur: politicians who defy American values never reach high national office!

What is at issue here is not Warner's failure to understand history. The Warner team gathered reams of historical statistics. Warner himself constructed status indices for eight ethnic groups. They traced status developments beginning in 1850 with an index for the newly arrived Irish. Warner's method was crude, but it is doubtful whether any professional historians of the thirties could have constructed better indices. What confronts us is not ahistorical thinking, but a bias so profound that it had to deny history in order to justify the expenditure of so much time and talent on Newburyport. Whether intensive historical training would have helped the Yankee City researchers is an open question. Their writing suggests that they were among the persons to whom Louis Armstrong referred when he remarked that there are some people who, if they do not know, cannot be told.

The Lynds' two studies of Muncie, Indiana influenced sociologists less than Warner's books because they exhibited much less theoretical concern than the Yankee City series. Conversely, they enjoyed more popular acclaim. Because they were less encumbered with scholarly apparatus, less choked with methodology, they invited their readers to a cogent but relatively undemanding perusal of one midwestern small-city society.

Taken in their entirety, *Middletown* (1929) and *Middletown in Transition* (1937) give the reader an acute sense of *deja vu*. The generation gap was visible and widening in 1924 when the Lynds arrived in Muncie. High school students battled their parents for possession of the family car, drank liquor, violated the prevailing Victorian sex code, and left home evenings for extracurricular activities. In the depression 1930s young people questioned the capitalistic system, or bitterly denounced a society that allowed them no future. Their elders overwhelmingly accepted the system, and many praised it despite the economic buffeting they had suffered. Teenagers drank, possibly more than their counterparts in the "roaring twenties," and some fornicated, perhaps more frequently than before. In any event they talked more frankly, more openly, about liquor and sex.

The Lynds found Muncie's school system only a little less than horrible, for reasons familiar to later generations of critics. The "administration" had grown enormously in 35 years. Administrators busied themselves with devising paperwork and meetings for overburdened teachers. They sent each other, not the teachers, on expenses-paid trips to the annual meeting of the National Education Association. The curriculum on the first-grade level responded to the curiosity, spontaneity, and physical hyperactivity of children, but the later grades increasingly smothered young inquisitveness under layers of pedantry and irrelevance. Middle-class high schoolers were caught up in such an extracurricular whirl that they scarcely had time and energy for the slight demands of their course work. The Lynds' cooly ironic prose captured the Muncie school system like a biological specimen. Their discussion of that system is a classic indictment of the American public school.

The Lynds recorded other situations and problems having an almost eerie timelessness. The poor received inadequate medical care at the hands of sometimes profiteering doctors. Latent class antagonisms occasionally boiled over on specific issues, but political and social apathy was the norm. Local politics and municipal administration were tinged with corruption. The small river winding through the topographically dull prairie city—a single opportunity for distinctive natural beauty—was heavily polluted. Philistinism reigned in culture and organized religion. Spending leisure time creatively was a growing problem. The unemployment and underemployment lurking beneath the surface of Muncie's 1920s "prosperity" gave the lie to its booster claims of a good life within the reach of all. Women fared poorly in the economic sphere. More women worked, but opportunities for self-employed professional women markedly declined from the 1920s to the 1930s. The class position of some women kept them out of the labor market (that is, the wife of a small businessman was considered declassé if she became a file clerk for anyone but her husband). Hiring policies blatantly discriminated in favor of men. Many if not most Muncie citizens were friendly and kind in their personal relationships but were also rather narrow, bigoted people who viewed the world outside with mixed hostility and contempt.

The Lynds virtually ignored the six percent of Muncie's citizens who were black, and this alone gives their book the musty air of the faded, racially secure white world. Introducing blacks would have involved a study of their culture and of race relations, a subject too large for people having more than enough to study. The Lynds' few comments on the black community were astute, but there was no real effort to gather information on black lives. They almost certainly would have produced a keen view of the race problem, but its absence is compensated for by excellent studies of race during the same period, including John Dollard's *Caste and Class in a Southern Town* (1937) and *Deep South* (1941) by Allison Davis, Burleigh B. Gardner, and Mary R. Gardner.

The remarkable immediacy of the Lynds' writing often obscured their investigative structure and their values. As they stated in the first volume, they sought to assay cultural change in a community from the twilight of Victorianism to the mid-1920s. To do the job properly they believed that they should study a community sufficiently compact to be easily analyzed, yet dynamic enough to experience profound change. Change should not, however, be induced by proximity to a metropolitan area, nor should it be dominated economically by one industry or culturally by a large university. To lend typicality, the ideal community should be predominantly native-born, have absorbed both "Yankee" and Southern culture, and be located in the Middle West. The nonwhite population should be small, to insure homogeneity and to avoid problems of racial accommodation in addition to those involving cultural change.

Muncie served the Lynds' purposes about as well as could be expected. It was not typical of manufacturing cities nor of many small Midwestern cities. The Lynds admitted that. On the other hand they avoided a freakish or atypical community. Their research effort was more modest than Warner's: a staff of five, of whom only the Lynds and their secretary remained for the project's duration from January, 1924 to June, 1925. Their assumptions were modest, too. Simply and concisely they confessed that the interviewer, or participant-observer, came to his task loaded with prejudices that were forever getting in the way of accurate reporting. They acknowledged the impossibility of comprehensiveness given the available staff and time. They hypothesized only two classes, business and working (that is, white collar and blue collar). The categories, the Lynds admitted, were both inexact and overlapping, but the broad cultural division in a city of 35,000 allowed them to get on with their work. Similarly their compartmentalizing life's activities in six units was methodological rather than conceptual. Earning a living, making a home, training the young, using leisure, engaging in religious practices, and engaging in community activities were chosen simply to organize the warp and woof of Muncie's culture into a meaningful pattern.

The Lynd's subtle irony, their unobtrusive methods, their modesty and their narrative power lifted *Middletown* above the relic status of the Yankee City series. Their use of history was greatly superior to Warner's and is, indeed, a model of intelligent sociological-anthropological understanding of the past. They established 1890 as a "baseline" for projecting changes in the midtwenties' society. They industriously gathered all sorts of local information about the Muncie of 1890, when it boomed on the strength of natural gas discoveries. Because Muncie was so new, they escaped falling into the "old family" trap that Newburyport's aristocrats laid for Warner. But the aristocrats had Warner's eager cooperation in springing the trap, while the Lynds understood the dangers lurking for the too-sympathetic participant-observer.

Occasionally the Lynds may have overdramatized the swiftness of social changes between 1890 and 1924, for 34 years is a fairly long time in an industrial society. For example, at one point they seemed to believe in the rapid decline of skilled glassblowers with the introduction of mechanization in Muncie's glass industry. Yet later comments indicated an awareness of a more gradual replacement of artisans by machines. They firmly believed in the growing routinization and impersonalization of factory work, the falling job status of factory workers, the increasing rigidity of classlines, and the declining opportunity for upward mobility among the working class. Their beliefs were assumed rather than proven. They may have reflected Middletown's realities, but they were of doubtful validity for the country at large. But these are minor flaws in an outstanding book.

The later *Middletown in Transition* proposed to discover the effects of the depression on Muncie. The second volume resulted from a much briefer field study in 1935 by Robert Lynd and five assistants. The researchers found that while some things had changed, more things had remained the same. There was, for instance, more fatalism in the working class and less optimism in the business class, but these changes were matters of degree. The outside world was closing in on Muncie, but Muncie seemed to be successfully resisting any real comprehension of it. There was, of course, more space given to relief work. Nevertheless, the book was as much about fixity as it was about change.

In fact the Lynds (Helen Lynd helped with *Transition*) were equally concerned with correcting and extending earlier impressions they later believed to have been superficial or inexact. Thus they devoted a great deal of space to the "X" family, a wealthy and philanthropic but controlling force in the life of Muncie. From 1924 to 1935 class stratification had been the object of studies (including Warner's), and these influenced the Lynds. They were led to construct a six-layered class profile of their own, but happily they made little use of it. They noted prostitution and corruption, slighted in the first book, much more carefully in the second. On the whole, however, *Middletown in Transition* simply supplemented and extended *Middletown*. Together they are one of the most graceful, penetrating community studies ever written.

OTHER SCHOLARS AND CITIES

Sociologists and anthropologists led in the scholarly study of urban situations, but other scholars trailed by only a little. Political scientists at the University of Chicago were especially active. Charles E. Merriam and his associates produced *The Government of the Metropolitan Region of Chicago* (1933), a descriptive study. Harold F. Gosnell wrote two penetrating analyses, *Negro Politicians: the Rise of Negro Politics in Chicago* (1935) and *Machine Politics: Chicago Model* (1937). Economists examined urban economic development and economic imperialism sometimes contemporaneously, sometimes historically, as Henrietta M. Larson did in her *The Wheat Market and the Farmer in Minnesota* (1926).

Arthur M. Schlesinger argued that cities were the locus of humane and progressive developments in *The Rise of the City, 1878-1898* (1933). Seven years later in his influential article, he claimed for the city the same formative role in American history that Frederick Jackson Turner earlier accorded the frontier. Most historical studies were much narrower, but it may be asked whether they were narrow enough. Sociologists studied slums or bums, but historians attempted to compress "the history" of a city into one or sometimes more than one volume. "Urban biography" was the name given to these efforts to encompass a significant part of the economic, political, social, and cultural past of a single city. Some were extraordinarily well done, including Constance Green's *Holyoke, Massachusetts* (1939). Taking the development of one industrial town as her theme, Mrs. Green studied entrepreneurship, capital formation, labor relations, and external but contingent developments such as the rise of the paper trust. The city's physical development, its religious, ethnic, and class conflicts, the rise of the Irish in its politics, and kindred matters were handled deftly and sympathetically. Both the limited size of Holyoke (a peak population of 62,210 in 1917) and the book's limited time span (1840s to 1920s) made Mrs. Green's subject comprehensible.

They were not the only explanations for a successful study. Mrs. Green's portrayal of risk-takers *versus* sure-thing men among the business class, and her delineation of small-business sympathy with the mill laborers, revealed a keen intelligence at work.

Bessie Pierce's history of Chicago, by contrast, was the product of a grandiose but directionless project. To attempt to discuss all significant developments in sprawling Chicago from 1673 onward was too great a task, no matter how many eager research assistants scurried after facts. There had to be some thematic treatment, some focus in a history of the city that grew from hamlet status to 300,000 souls in the 30 years before the great fire of 1871. The two volumes that appeared in 1937 and 1940 aggregated almost 900 pages (a third volume published many years later carried the story from 1871 to 1893). These pages were stuffed with information, but they were conceptually naive, not to say ignorant. No themes—the role of the Erie Canal in Chicago's growth, the impact of her dynamic businessmen, the competition with other cities, the growing awareness of the need for civic amenities—appeared to leaven the recitation of events. The Erie Canal, the businessmen, competition, and recreational concerns were mentioned, of course, but only as part of the chronicle and not as the catalysts of a synthesis. In general, Miss Pierce treated human activity in Chicago not as the actions of those caught up in breakneck urbanization, but merely as the doings of people who happened to live in Chicago. She approached historical Chicago so unimaginatively that the chapters on politics discussed mostly the local reflections of national elections and debates. It was as though the relationships between local politics, Chicago's ethnic groups, and the city's rapid growth were worth only the occasional mentions she gave them.

The inadequacies of urban biography were not entirely the fault of historians. To most scholars of the twenties and thirties urban history was simply local history, useful as background in sociological studies, and as a frivolous diversion for antiquarians. Few cared about the historical development of urban institutions. The contemporary police department, on the other hand, was a worthy subject for sociological investigation. There was obvious utility, at least a hope for reform, in a thorough study of the present police operation. Problems in the evolution of a modern police force were considered dated and irrelevant. Many more years would pass before urban historians launched the sort of specific, monographic studies that their counterparts in sociology had done with masterful thoroughness in the heyday of the Chicago school.

NOVELISTS AND CITIES

Twentieth-century novelists wrote about cities with a sociological zest for the details of urban living. They laid bare the lineaments of urban occupations, class structures, racial and ethnic conflicts, the incredible jumble of creeds and convictions, of urban distractions and pleasures. No hero of a city novel escapes feelings of desperate loneliness in the midst of the urban throng. Each man is titillated and isolated by the city, with its stimulating but curiously unsatisfying attractions. The novelists burned for reform, just as the academicians did, and, like the academicians, they suppressed reformist declarations. Their art was the servant of political action just as social science supplied the grist for change.

There were equally important differences. The academicians sought order, structure, and social cohesiveness, while the novelists saw cities through their protagonists' eyes, compelling, distracting, sometimes incoherent. The academicians grounded their conclusions on empiricism and induction, the novelists deduced classes and neighborhoods, occupations and human conflicts from a handful of characters. Their intensity evoked a more sympathetic view of the human condition in cities than the academic studies, with their scholarly limitations and constructions, permitted themselves.

Five of the most striking city novels of the interwar period seem to argue, on one level at least, that the city is too overwhelming for all but the most advantaged or resourceful people. Jimmy Herf, the modestly talented dilettante in John Dos Passos' *Manhattan Transfer* (1925) runs with the theater and café society crowd. Jimmy cannot capitalize on the advantages provided by well-to-do relatives. He becomes frustrated with his chosen field, newspaper journalism. He contracts a disastrous marriage with an actress, a woman pursued (and often caught) by other men, a woman whose only true love had burned himself to death in a drunken stupor. In despair over his personal failure, Jimmy leaves his wife and his job. Other characters have more or less material success than he does, but all fail to find the happiness that the city seems to promise. Only Congo Jake, a vagabond sailor and barkeep turned bootlegger, garners both money and a measure of contentment. Even Congo's success is born of prohibition's inverted morality, and he remains a gauche *nouveau riche*. Jimmy realizes that he cannot shape his destiny in the city. He leaves it with self-possession but little else.

In *An American Tragedy* (1925) by Theodore Dreiser, Clyde Griffiths is defeated by his inadequacy in the face of urban blandishments. The son of street preachers, he has little education and family background, but possesses looks, charm, and ambition. As a bellhop, first in Kansas City, then in Chicago, he yields to urban attractions: expensive clothes, fancy restaurants, entertainment, and girls. Still he is not really getting ahead. By a stroke of good fortune he is employed at his wealthy uncle's clothing factory in New York state. This time Clyde's weak willed impatience is fatal. While waiting and hoping to crack the local small-city society, he falls in love with one of the factory girls under his supervision. Soon after, a society girl becomes enamored of him. While he is maneuvering to end his affair with the factory girl, she informs Clyde that she is pregnant. The factory girl dies in ambiguous circumstances, but Clyde's monumental timidity and ineptitude trap him in guilt. His dreams of social success end with the electric chair.

The central figure of James T. Farrell's *Studs Lonigan* trilogy (1932–1935) is the victim of similar personal limitations. Studs is fundamentally decent, if too emotionally and intellectually narrow, and too willing to adopt the values of his street gang on Chicago's South Side. The high point of Studs' life comes during the summer following his grade school graduation. He falls in love, he whips the neighborhood bully, and he gains recognition from his companions. But he is incapable of purposeful, mature actions thereafter. High school is irrelevant, and Studs is expelled for nonattendance. He goes to work for his father, a second-generation Irish painting contractor, but the job is tedious and it fails to confer on him the adult status for which he yearns. Studs' attempts at sobriety, physical conditioning, and religious involvement do not reap the immediate social rewards that he anticipates. A bout of pneumonia leaves him with a heart condition and diminished chances. He retreats more and more into nostalgia, day-dreaming, and self-pity. A few opportunities yet remain, but Studs muffs them all. He dies as ineffectually as he lived, leaving behind a pregnant fiancée.

Bigger Thomas, the hero of Richard Wright's *Native Son* (1940), is a black slumdweller in Chicago, with all that implies in the way of poverty, deprivation, and blighted hopes. Bigger and his friends, a crowd of socially myopic poolroom loungers, understand in a general way that whites control things and deny them opportunities. Bigger has a chance of sorts when the wealthy Dalton family hires him as its chauffeur, but he accidentally kills young Mary Dalton and burns her body in the furnace to escape detection. For a while he deflects suspicion to others, even composes a creditable ransom note. But he cannot bring himself to clean the furnace of its incriminating bits of jewelry and unburned bone. The dirty furnace smokes in the presence of others; they empty the ashes and discover Bigger's ruse. A city wide manhunt snares him. He is falsely accused of raping and willfully murdering Mary, tried, and convicted in an atmosphere of hysteria.

Most of Bigger's education in the ways of the white world comes after Mary's death, and he skillfully uses his new knowledge to confound his white enemies for a time. In the end the whites savor an ironic confirmation of black inferiority: Bigger, even though black, was clever enough to build an alibi, clever enough to write a ransom note. He was clever enough to know that he could kill his girlfriend because the death of a black girl was unimportant beside the death of Mary, but he was not clever enough to get rid of those bones!

Only George F. Babbitt, of Sinclair Lewis' *Babbitt* (1922), escapes from failure and death. The reasons he does so, however, are not particularly reassuring. Babbitt is a middle-aged real estate agent, a partner with his father-in-law in Zenith, a mythical Midwestern city. He is thoroughly conventional and more than a little bit gross. Through life he has done what was expected of him, suppressing his urges to independence. In his forty-seventh year he rebels. He embraces both radical ideas and other women, and is openly skeptical of middle-class routine. But not for long. His business associates temper economic reprisals against him with expressions of regard and a willingness to receive him again into the fold. Babbitt never surrenders his affection for his family, nor his family for him. His family and the business world may be trivial at times but they represent security, and Babbitt returns to them after his fling. When Babbitt returns, conformity and things-as-they-are claim him as their prisoner.

On one level, then, these five novelists might be considered anticity, and their novels to be tracts "versus" the city. Such a judgment would be extremely narrow. It is true that the heroes of these city novels are used up at frighteningly early ages: Bigger Thomas executed at twenty; Clyde Griffiths at twenty-two; Studs Lonigan dead at thirty, and Jimmy Herf defeated at the same age. But why? Is it really the fault of "the city" or of "society" that such things occur?

Bigger's inability to clean out the furnace and escape detection cannot be traced to his ghetto upbringing, to white oppression, or to foolishness. His failure is a failure of nerve, a very human and personal failing. Clyde's ineptitude and indecision prove to be his undoing. Studs cannot persevere. Studs' father, though bankrupted and shattered in the end, has lived a life of direction and purpose. A portion of even the father's problems, like the son's, are laid to gambling in the stock market. Jimmy is one of those young men over whom older people cluck their tongues, hoping he will "find himself."

Jimmy does not conform or rebel, he escapes.

Nor is the city the home of unrelenting material standards, the place where all things human are subordinated to money values. Dos Passos comes the closest to defending this position in *Manhattan Transfer*, but Jimmy and some of his friends reject mere wealth. Bigger, writing his ransom note, lusts for money and freedom it will bring, but Wright shows on every page how the hero of *Native Son* is hemmed in by much more than poverty. Some of the most powerful passages in Studs Lonigan concern the black invasion of the Lonigan's South Chicago neighborhood, and Irish hatred of Jews, Italians, and their ever-encroaching black neighbors. The black invasion and the ethnic and racial hatreds have economic causes and consequences, but the human consequences are also noneconomic and nonrational. Studs himself embraces some non-economic values, including the pleasures of lolling in the park or swimming at the beach.

Clyde Griffiths wants money, yes, but the hero of *An American Tragedy* is refreshingly hedonistic. Money means summer houses, boating, riding, swimming, tennis, parties, and lavish dinners. It means power. Clyde also understands that getting and keeping money requires unremitting labor, or at least working hard when one is not playing. For all that, money captures Clyde. Yet it does not concern his family very much. Nor does money and its concommitant social position overawe Roberta, Clyde's girlfriend from the factory, until she loses him because of it. In any case, money values pervade society, not just cities. Lewis states this last position especially strongly. When Babbitt "escapes" to the Maine woods, he find the guides just as physically lazy, just as absorbed in dreams of money, as anyone in Zenith. Babbitt recognizes nonmonetary values, just as he realizes his inability to abandon himself to them. Instead he takes vicarious pleasure in his son's decision to drop out of the middle class and become what he wants to become, a mechanic.

The novelists' shared conclusion is, not that money is the only value, but that urban society esteems it too much in relation to other values. Urban society must be reformed to admit other values (love, kindness, respect for one's fellow man) and to stifle its destructive tendencies (racial and ethnic hatreds). Then we shall have a world in which ordinary humans may survive and find some happiness.

All students and critics of urban society, whether sociologists, anthropologists, novelists, or whatever, hoped that cities could be made more humane. For better or worse, people were in cities, and it was in cities that their problems would be met. Urban dwellers would have to find the understanding and the means.

CHAPTER SIX
_____

Moles and Skylarks

Whether realists or utopians, city planners from 1915 to 1945 were most successful when they planned comprehensively or built specifically. Realistic building comprised parkway systems and similar projects that were geographically inclusive but conceptually narrow. Utopian schemes involved totally planned, spatially restricted undertakings such as public housing or greenbelt suburbs—islands afloat in seas of unplanning. Metropolitan areas continued to grow, usually without the benefit of more than the flimsiest control. This should not suggest that all planning was futile. It does mean that a study of city planning is quite different from a study of planned cities.

THE REALISTS

The realists' planning attitudes and activities of the early twentieth century cast long shadows. By 1915 City Beautiful plans were gathering dust, and City Beautiful planners were mostly aging landscape architects. Younger planners often scoffed at the City Beautiful legacy, charging its creators with a narrow concern for superficial and meretricious urban decoration in the midst of unplanned squalor and decay. The younger men prided themselves on their toughminded empiricism, their comprehensive view of urban problems, and their ability to merge their encyclopedic knowledge with their salesmanship in committing the public to the reconstruction of American cities. Their zest for fact-gathering and feasibility studies found expression in the phrases "city functional," "city scientific," and "city efficient." Everything urban—housing, education, public health, recreation, and mass transit—was within their professional ken.

The resulting grand plans suffered stillbirths despite their authors' optimism and certitude. The movement for "Boston—1915" begun in 1909, was the first thrust for a comprehensive metropolitan plan.

124

Youthful planners promised a blueprint for strengthening the complex interrelationships of urban living. What emerged was a metropolitan improvement scheme to be financed partly by Boston, partly by levies on the suburbs, partly by the state. It failed because of suburban indifference and hostility toward Boston's taxes and the lower-class elements in its population.

Planners already had taken up the fight for beliefs that would later become conventional wisdom. By 1915 most had been converted to zoning. Philip Kates, an attorney interested in urban problems, already had proposed an investigative federal Municipal Commission in a speech to the 1911 Conference on City Planning. The prospect of federal intervention horrified many planners. Yet the conviction that urban problems were national problems requiring federal involvement had begun to gather momentum. Planning already had become a profession, in the eyes of planners at least, with all that meant in the way of organizations, annual meetings, publications, special training, and expanding institutional relationships. The National Conferences on City Planning were (since 1909) drawing together planners, social and settlement-house workers, housers, architects, and sympathetic professionals in other fields for searching discussions of the urban crisis. In 1909 Harvard University offered the first course in planning, a harbinger of the departments of city planning to follow a generation later.

The 1913 planning conference anticipated the mushroom growth of city planning commissions with its model enabling act for a municipal "Department of City Planning." Planning commissions were the spawn of the same quest for efficiency and order that produced the city manager movement. They implied a similar bureaucratic development, with the model "department" employing "engineers." The American City Planning Institute (later the American Institute of Planners) would be formed in 1917.

Planning literature mushroomed. The *Survey* magazine, *American City*, and other periodicals carried news of planners' activities and aspirations. Published plans such as *The Plan of Chicago* (1909) were a well-established means of disseminating planning ideas. A wealth of "how-to" books complimented the plans. They conceded greater social sophistication to European, especially German, cities with their careful land-use controls (zoning), their reservation of grounds for public purposes, and their restrictions on urban land speculation. Discussions of the problems of state enabling legislation and legal snares foreshadowed the time when impatient urban bureaucrats and civic leaders would rebel against statehouse control and constricting court decisions. Frank acknowledgment that many major improvements would cost more money than the cities' residents had previously raised forecast the day when urban projects would require federal financing. Benjamin C. Marsh's *An Introduction to City Planning: Democracy's Challenge to the American City* (1909) discussed the European successes while later books concentrated more on immediate problems, legislative and legal. They included John Nolen's *Replanning Small Cities* (1912) and Flavel Shurtleff's *Carrying Out the City Plan* (1914).

All these planners were realists, that is, they planned for the existing order. Their visions of the future embraced a society based on free enterprise, still individualistic and democratic if somewhat more malleable. Their realistic planning impinged on most of the physical growth of cities during the interwar period. Their victories, in the short run at least, were many. The zoning movement towers among the realists' great achievements. It also typifies their shortcomings.

Efforts to establish zoning, that is, to separate and restrict urban areas according to function, were ancient. The hyperdevelopment of industrial cities intensified the urge to control. City Beautiful planners of the nineteenth century, forced to work without serious limitations on land use, designed some parks and boulevards to divide retail from residential districts, inhibit industrial expansion, and segregate racial neighborhoods. Cities turned to nuisance regulations, but the courts sometimes limited them to prohibiting flagrant assaults on the senses. A relatively smokeless and noiseless factory, for instance, might be allowed in a residential neighborhood even though it violated the doctrine of separation of functions.

Deed restrictions on residential lots were a solution but only for higher priced developments. Besides, the Supreme Court was more friendly to municipal controls, approving Boston's heights of buildings ordinance in 1909 and Los Angeles' industrial zones in 1915. Professional planners, their eyes fixed on European cities, mostly ignored these domestic solutions. In 1913 the legislatures of New York, Minnesota, Wisconsin, and Illinois passed bills enabling cities to designate residential areas closed to industry. The governor of Illinois vetoed the bill presented to him but the other bills stood. Clearly urban citizens were desperately determined to halt the blighting of residence districts. But the legislation did not even hint at the need for comprehensive zoning, to say nothing of comprehensive planning.

Zoning did not emerge from the plight of the citizen-as-resident, however much it might shape his future homebody role. Instead it was a response to threats against commercial and retail property in one place, New York City. The threatened property owners' economic and political power forced a solution, a solution rendered with such skill that it became the panacea for pell-mell urban growth. That a solution designed for one locality could be generally accepted may seem absurd, but its acceptance has a rational explanation.

Commercial and retail property owners on Manhattan Island faced property losses as threatening as any confronting the most harried middle-class homeowner. In lower Manhattan the skyscraper loomed as the monstrous offspring of technological wizardry. Astronomical land values, structural steel, and a sophisticated life support system combined with egotism to shove buildings ever higher. In 1913 the dynamic merchant Frank W. Woolworth sent his gothic skyscraper to 60 stories, 792 feet above the pavement. It was a huge structure by the standards of any time and place. The Woolworth and other tall buildings robbed their lesser neighbors of light and air, though their tower construction mitigated the damage.

Even while Woolworth opened his tower, General Thomas Coleman duPont was planning something more ominous, a new Equitable Building at 120 Broadway. When completed in 1915, the Equitable's 42 stories no longer were spectacular. But its dimensions were. Forecasting later slab-sided monsters, the Equitable covered a city block, crammed 13,000 workers into its 1,250,000 square feet of office space, and forced the surrounding streets and sidewalks to accept the 100,000 people who entered and left the building each day. Worse, the Equitable cast a noontime shadow four blocks long, sealing off buildings up to half its height from direct sunlight. Owners of buildings wrapped in the new gloom suffered a loss of tenants and received reduced tax valuations. Tenants who remained reported that their office workers were absent on account of illness more often than before.

Farther up Manhattan another land-use battle raged. Since the late nineties an expanding cluster of stores and specialty shops catering to the carriage trade had steadily shoved aside the millionaire's mansions on Fifth Avenue north of Thirty-fourth Street. The millionaires fought the encroachment. The Avenue's soaring land values, its proximity to store and shop customers, and its safe distance from warehouses, loft factories, and immigrants were against them. By 1907 the battle between millionaires and stores was over and the defeated rich were in retreat up Fifth Avenue to make another stand on the margin of Central Park. Now the store owners turned to face a new foe—the garment industry with its thousands of poor Russian Jewish workers. The garment factories were moving north and west from the inefficient, overcrowded tenements of the lower east side to newer buildings nearer the major railroad stations. In 1907 the Fifth Avenue Association was formed by merchants determined to hold their conquest for themselves.

A few years after its founding the Fifth Avenue Association began pressuring Manhattan's borough president, George McAneny, to persuade the city to set low maximum building heights on Fifth Avenue. No overt regulation could keep out the garment industry, but low buildings would be too small, forcing the industry to look elsewhere for space. Nothing came of the height regulations, but McAneny was the right man to pressure. A newspaperman and reform politician, he was later to be a member of planning agencies both public and private. At the same time that the Fifth Avenue Association was at work, another reformer, Edward M. Bassett, was discussing with McAneny the interrelated problems of building height, congestion, and chaotic land use. Bassett was the father of zoning in America. He had been influenced by various European schemes to deconcentrate urban areas, and had already decided to devote his substantial legal talent to the cause of city planning.

McAneny led the city council in establishing, in February, 1913, a Heights of Buildings Commission to study the problem of size limits on commercial buildings. The Commission was to examine all aspects of the matter, including zoning the city by function, and report to a specially designated committee of the city council. Four circumstances surrounding the Heights of Buildings Commission were especially noteworthy. First, its creation did not commit anybody to anything. Second, its 19 members were mostly real estate men or members of the Fifth Avenue Association; therefore any recommendations were almost certain to reflect what the dominant owners of commercial and retail property wanted. Third, although zoning was, strictly speaking, only a demarcation based on the functional *status quo,* McAneny termed the commission "a wedge into the problem of city planning." [1] In later years zoning rarely came within shouting distance of true planning for the future. Yet McAneny had called zoning a part of planning, an identification that grew until, in many minds, the part was mistaken for the whole. Fourth, Bassett was chairman of the Heights of Buildings Commission. With a dogged determination worthy of his name, Bassett set about drafting a zoning ordinance that would serve property owners while it survived legal assaults. Bassett was no tool of the rich. He was a reformer, one of those men who likes to think of himself as a practical idealist.

The committee's report of December, 1913 suggested that height

---

[1] Seymour I. Toll, *Zoned American,* Grossman, New York, 1969, p. 147.

regulations on buildings, stated as multiples of street width, would admit sufficient light and air. Unfortunately there were no existing standards of sufficiency for either. Above the maximum height (300 feet was the highest) buildings would be set or stepped back, revealing their neighbors to the sun and preventing any more unconscionable overcrowding. Or so the theory went. Outside of the heavily congested districts there were more severe building height and volume limits. The next step after the report was to secure a zoning enabling act from the legislature, done in 1914. In the summer of that year the council appointed a second commission, the Commission on Building Districts and Restrictions, to hold hearings and draft a zoning ordinance. Bassett was chairman once more, and the membership was little changed from that of the first commission.

The difference between the titles of the first and second commissions—Heights of Buildings *versus* Building Districts and Restrictions—indicated an increasing concern for the functional segregation of urban activities. In hearing after hearing the indefatigable Bassett promoted that concern. He reassured owners that their property values would be maintained, indeed enhanced, that broadly conceived zoning was legally secure, and that his careful, block-by-block ordinance would ratify the *status quo*. Bassett was convincing. With the New York commercial and financial community solidly behind it, the commission's draft became law on July 25, 1916.

In some ways the law was without predecent, in the United States at least. The ordinance divided New York into commercial, residential, and unrestricted districts; into five types of heights-of-building districts, and into five types of area districts that regulated the size of courts and yards. The height and area requirements really regulated the *volumes* of tall buildings by requiring in crowded districts, for example, either a set-back design or a tower that left a portion of the air above its lot unoccupied. Detailed maps showed the boundaries and extent of each type of district.

The ordinance was a beginning. If it had been used with a lively sense of its shortcomings and of the need for its improvement, its regulations might have been beneficial to New York and other cities. It was not so used. The second commission regretted the lack of comprehensive planning, and some shortcomings were confessed. But in the minds of Bassett and most of his associates their unprecedented labors outweighed any defects.

There were defects. The use, height, and area maps overlapped in confusing ways. Many builders of large speculative office buildings sought the maximum allowable volume for their structures. The result, in the maximum height districts, was a building "envelope" of ziggurat shape, like an awkward staircase for giants. The ziggurats were not always unlovely, although most of them were. In either case they stole light and air from surrounding buildings as before. A ziggurat could be avoided by sending up a slender tower, but tower construction sacrificed huge hunks of rentable office space to esthetics. Towers were possible only when their owners wished to satisfy desires for recognition and display.

The ordinance permitted—or omitted to control—much that begged for restriction. The report of the Height of Buildings Commission verged on the hysterical when it described the possibilities of a serious fire in a tall building. It conjured up horrible visions of the panic that would occur if a disaster disgorged the human contents of skyscrapers upon Manhattan's narrow streets. Such fancies were farfetched but they did dramatize the real problem of congestion in lower Manhattan. The obvious solution was to limit the heights of buildings in crowded areas. But only heights up to the first setback, not absolute heights, were regulated. Anyone with the money and the will could send a building up as high as he wished so long as he complied with the regulations.

The ordinance failed to limit any type of residence in commercial districts. Neither did it exclude all manufacturing. The city took no action against the garment industries crowding nearer to the fashionable stores along Fifth Avenue. Only the year before the Supreme Court had vindicated Los Angeles' ejecting factories from newly established nonindustrial areas. The timid New Yorkers were content to forbid any more factories near Fifth Avenue.

In the case of Fifth Avenue, indeed, the private action of the Fifth Avenue Association accomplished what the ordinance could not—it rid the area north of Thirty-Fourth Street of garment factories. The Fifth Avenue Association supported zoning, but it had three other, stronger strings to its bow. First, it persuaded the city's major lending institutions to withhold loans from the builders of loft buildings north of Thirty-fourth Street. The action made it clear to factory owners that they could not extend their beachhead in the fashionable retail district. Second, in March, 1916 the Fifth Avenue Association ran full-page ads in the major dailies to announce a boycott of all garment manufacturers who refused to move by February of the following year. Third, the Association sweetened the pill. It offered help in relocation and promised not to enforce the boycott against firms agreeing to move when their leases expired. The result was a near-unanimous capitulation by the garment industry, even before the zoning ordinance became law.

Zoning contained no incentives to "upgrade" an industrial or commercial district to residential use, only a mechanism of "adjustment," or "rezoning" to open a residential neighborhood to commercial and industrial encroachment. Zoning, then, was narrow, partial, and socially defective. But its very shortcomings made its success. Enlightened real estate developers, store owners, and industrialists in city after city favored zoning because it officially endorsed their past activities and promised them more of the same. A few intelligent New Yorkers warned against the blind adoption of an imperfect scheme for one city, but to no avail. The largest, most sophisticated city seemed to be the most innovative. To harassed city planners, anxious for allies, zoning was an issue on which they could unite with forward-looking businessmen.

Enlightenment and progressivism produced zoning's ultimate folly, rigid segregation of districts by function. *Some* segregation, such as banning new single-family dwellings in industrial developments, was justified. It was left to the advanced intellectual community of Berkeley, California—on the suggestion of some local manufacturers—to ban *all* new residential construction in industrial districts. In contrast, the utopians of the day believed that workers' domestic and productive lives needed reintegration, not further separation. The utopians may not have hit upon a universal solution but at least their ideas were worth heeding. Suppose Berkeley's planners, industrialists, and landlords sat down together to refashion factories into clean, quiet places that could nestle side by side with humanely replanned workers' housing. That would have been a truly enlightened act, whether or not an entirely successful one. Nothing of the sort was considered. Instead, the Berkeley solution increased the psychic and physical distances between home and work, not to mention the cost of transportation. Suggestions that cities should establish semirural greenbelts by zoning out all building on their peripheries were equally ignored.

By the end of 1921 city planners and local elites had secured zoning enabling acts from almost half the state legislatures in the country. No less a personage than the indefatigable Herbert Hoover gave their efforts a boost during that year. Hoover, as Secretary of Commerce, appointed an advisory committee to draft a model state zoning enabling act. Hoover's passion for system, order, and planning through voluntary cooperation led him to proven methods. He appointed Bassett to head the committee, thereby insuring the transfer of New York's wisdom, or unwisdom, to the nation. The other members of the committee were realists in housing, planning, and real estate, men ready to follow Bassett's lead.

The committee was ready with a preliminary draft by September,

1921; by early 1924 the Government Printing Office was distributing the finished document, the Standard State Zoning Enabling Act. The model act gave the merest nod in the direction of comprehensive planning. There was nothing in it to prevent a city from making its zoning ordinance a substitute for a comprehensive plan. The energy of zoning's backers and the ease of its adoption sped acceptance. In his introduction to the model zoning ordinance Hoover boasted that 22 million people lived under zoning, with their number growing month by month.

Even though Hoover had blessed zoning, it was not entirely secure until the United States Supreme Court had passed upon its constitutionality. By 1926 more than 400 cities and towns had zoning ordinances, and several state supreme courts had upheld zoning as a proper exercise of municipal police power. Only courts in states without state enabling acts had overturned zoning. The reiterated police power doctrine and the sheer number of zoned municipalities seemed to place zoning beyond danger. Bassett wanted it that way—to make Supreme Court justices blanch at the thought of unsettling the lives of the tens of millions of people who lived on zoned land.

Urban police power was safe from direct assault but not from an astute introduction of some equally valued principle in opposition. The lawyers for a Cleveland real estate firm hit upon such a principle—the loss of rights guaranteed by the Fourteenth Amendment to the federal constitution. Euclid, Ohio, a suburb of Cleveland, was the other party to the suit. In 1922 Euclid adopted a zoning ordinance placing land owned by the Ambler Realty Company in a residential category. The Ambler firm was holding the property for commercial and industrial development, and was dismayed by the loss of values. It argued that its property, that is, the difference between the lower residential values, and the higher commercial and industrial values, had been taken from it without the due process of law guaranteed by the Fourteenth Amendment.

There was really no defense against Ambler's argument, except to say that it was irrelevant. The danger for zoning was that the conservative courts of the day zealously guarded property rights, especially those infringed by newfangled regulations. The United States District Court upheld Ambler, and Euclid appealed to the Supreme Court. The high court vindicated zoning in a landmark four-to-three decision, a decision owing much to a brilliant brief by Alfred Bettman, a Cincinnati lawyer and city planner. Bettman focused his attack on a secondary statement in the Ambler brief, that urban growth was too dynamic and spontaneous to foresee or control. Zoning, Bettman replied, "represents the application of foresight and intelligence to the development of the community." [2] He marshaled mountains of evidence and supporting briefs to show that zoning involved assigning various needed urban functions to their proper places, or as he expressed it, keeping the furnace out of the living room. He was careful to include the Bassett argument: if the high court undid zoning in this instance the results would be catastrophic and nationwide. His arguments probably persuaded one of the court's conservatives, Justice George Sutherland, to abandon his beloved Fourteenth Amendment in favor of municipal police power.

Ironically, infatuation with zoning began to fade just as the Supreme Court affirmed its validity. Zoning had not abolished human nature. Reform groups in New York City attacked the Board of Standards and Appeals for corruption in the granting of variances. The full scandal was not revealed until 1931 and 1932, when it became an issue in the reform movement that triumphed in the mayoral election of Fiorello H. La Guardia. Often the bribery (usually accomplished by kickbacks and excessive fees) did not harm anyone in any tangible way. Sometimes, as when a block in a fine Manhattan residential district was opened to business over the residents' opposition, it did. Either way, the public became less enamored of zoning as other cities followed New York, not only in adopting zoning, but in establishing boards to grant variances.

Planners lost faith, too. At first they confined themselves to reiterations that zoning was not a substitute for planning. Bettman sounded the warning. So did Thomas Adams, a gifted British planner who frequently worked in the United States during the twenties and thirties. Zoning was the end of the planning process, not the beginning, Adams told the national planning conference in 1920. Adams proposed a two-step planning exercise. First, he would have extended city planning to encompass regional planning. Second, he would have worked from the region back through general plans for population centers, through specific plans for housing, industries, and other basic elements, with zoning used to fix the final decision. The Standard City Planning Enabling Act of 1927, prepared under the aegis of Hoover's Department of Commerce, reflected the new concern. The zoning enabling act of three years before had nearly brushed planning aside, but the later act paid it exclusive attention. Without rigidly defining a master plan, the act's most influential authors— Bassett, Bettman, the younger Frederick Law Olmsted—suggested five areas of planning. These included streets, public grounds, public

[2] *Ibid.*, p. 238.

buildings, public utilities, and zoning, which brought up the rear in a distinctly subordinate position.

Planners' initial caution had become widespread disillusionment by the thirties. They complained of unsound zoning changes based on nothing more than the ignorance or venality of adjustment boards and city councils. They attacked overzoning, or the reserving of vastly more land for commercial and industrial purposes than could be used. Some of these projections for business use would have brought a gasp from the most sanguine of boosters. In this the zoning laws followed New York's famed 1916 resolution, which permitted, under full utilization, working space for some 300 million employees. (The population of New York City in 1920 numbered fewer than six million souls.) Los Angeles zoned enough business land for a population larger than the country's. Modest-sized Duluth established land uses and office building envelopes to house a highly improbable 20 million workers.

All this might have been dismissed as innocent Babbittry except for some pernicious results. The other side of the overzoning coin was the underzoning of residential property. In 1923 single-family residences occupied 12 percent of Chicago's land area. So did industry. The zoning ordinance doubled industry's allotment to 24 percent; it cut the area reserved for single-family residences to three percent. Commercial, two-family, and apartment uses all received bigger slices of the land pie than they occupied at the time. The zoning ordinance left three-fourths of Chicago's single-family residential land unprotected against encroachments. It also encouraged property taxation based on future, not present, uses. Heavier taxation sped the destruction of residential areas in favor of "more intensive uses," a euphemism for crowding. Those tendencies were not confined to Chicago but were nationwide.

So-called "spot zoning" developed during the twenties. Spot zoning involved rezoning lots here and there, usually for some nonresidential purpose in a residential area. It was one result of the over-refinement of zoning classifications. Permissive adjustment boards conferred these ultra-refined classifications on patches of land all over cities. The result was practically the same as the granting of variances.

How much in favor of zoning may be rescued from this sordid tale? Not much. In some instances zoning probably saved investments, in others it provided landowners with windfall profits to offset higher taxes. In many aging residential areas it probably retarded helter-skelter conversions to nonresidential use. These gains scarcely overcame the deficiencies.

Comprehensive or "master" planning resulted in no more definite improvement and even less superficial activity than did zoning. Much so-called master planning occurred in the understaffed offices of city planning commissions. Many commissions lacked the numbers and knowledge to construct comprehensive plans. They took refuge in an interpretation of the Standard City Planning Enabling Act (repeated almost verbatim in many state statutes) permitting the piecemeal development of comprehensive plans. Thus urban citizens of the late twenties and thirties were treated to one-at-a-time "master" plans of the single elements in a comprehensive plan— parks, streets, public transportation, and so on.

Independent professional planners often produced genuine comprehensive plans. Typically a city or some well-financed citizen group within it would hire a professional consultant and some of his staff to make surveys, draw maps and perspectives of projected improvements, and write up analyses and cost estimates. Frequently the outside planners worked with the local planning commission if there was one. Usually the plans incorporated revised versions of past proposals. New portions almost always included radial and circumferential highways for traffic relief.

Sometimes the plans were true supraurban schemes, such as Russell V. Black's inspired plan for the Philadelphia region. Harland Bartholomew authored a perceptive study of the San Francisco Bay area. Like most city plans, the regional schemes foundered on the rock of expense; huge levies would be required to transfer the finger parks and the multilane highways from paper to ground. There were other problems. Because most regional plans seemed to work outward from their dominant cities, residents of the region feared urban imperialism. Then too, important interests might oppose or mishandle the plans. Black found his efforts frustrated because at least one businessman-member of the sponsoring organization attacked elements of the Philadelphia plan that clashed with the interests of his firm. Bartholomew's San Francisco plan was in the hands of a dedicated, sympathetic businessman who was genuinely concerned for the bay area. He failed, however, to approach the jealous, somewhat fearful leaders in the smaller communities with the required diplomacy and tact.

A street cut through here, a parkway built there, were the noticeable results of almost all such city and regional plans. But there were important if less tangible increments. The plans promoted thinking about class interdependence, about housing, about the separation or mixing of urban functions, about transportation, and about the symbiosis of city and region. They incorporated past ideas in park extensions, zoning, streets and housing, bringing them abreast of the current situation. If the older proposals were not realized in their revised form, they were available to still later planners.

The noblest of the era's comprehensive plans was the great Regional Plan of New York and Its Environs. "Monumental" is a tired word but the only adjective adequate to this interdisciplinary effort by the outstanding urbanologists of the day. Their cooperative labors cost more than a million dollars, lasted 10 years (although the full-scale effort took about seven years), and produced 10 books. The plan was a success in realistic terms, for many of its proposed highways, rail routes, parkways, and air terminals were built.

The RPNY sponsors and managers formed a roster of leading lights. Charles D. Norton, an enlightened banker, sold the Russell Sage Foundation on the regional scheme. Unofficially begun early in 1921, the RPNY was formally announced the next May with an initial $25,000 grant from the foundation. Luminaries including Herbert Hoover and Elihu Root graced the send-off banquet. Norton was the first chairman of the guiding Committee on the Regional Plan. Thomas Adams, early an advisor, became the general director of plans and surveys in 1923. Top professionals in planning, architecture, engineering, sociology, housing, economics, and other specialties joined the staff.

If realism and professionalism was the RPNY's strength, it was also its weakness. Three limitations marred the work of its dedicated planners. First, such men, working under such auspices, were not likely to consider plans requiring the modification of any existing economic and social arrangements. This is not a harsh criticism, for it implies neither that the RPNY was a spineless sellout to The Interests, nor that it should have been composed of bug-eyed radicals with brains on fire. It does suggest that the planners might have speculated on, say, the possibilities in the continued growth of special-purpose metropolitan districts and in new uses for the district idea. They might have suggested what changes in housing or transportation could be foreseen, given huge, if improbable, federal outlays for those purposes. They might have dwelt on the disadvantages of jealous localism and the possible gains from consolidating some of the over 500 incorporated cities and towns in the region. All of these "mights," and more, would have been compatible with a hardheaded statement of what could be done (and could not be done) given the existing situation. The RPNY looked only at what was, not at what could have been. Its failure to speculate, to cut itself adrift from its own present (except in certain population and economic projections) was an unfortunate limitation, no less arbitrary for being self-imposed.

Second, the RPNY was a scheme to save New York City by preserving its economic and cultural viability. Norton's thinking had begun with restoring the city's commercial areas—naturally enough, given his banking background—and had extended to transportation, recreation, and civic art. Adams and his co-workers accepted Norton's premises. According to Adams, the RPNY included three major purposes: (1) to promote lower densities through "diffused recentralization of industry" and planning for new industrial centers; (2) to reunify home and work by planning for new residential areas near industry; and (3) "sub-centralization" of business for greater consumer convenience.

Some of the plans derived from these principles were practical and sensible, such as the residential superblocks equivalent in size to four or six standard city blocks with their intervening streets. The word "superblock" later became associated with dehumanized skyscraper housing, but in the twenties it included even single-family residences. The land not given over to streets in the superblocks could be used for parking, for playgrounds, for houselots with garden spaces, and for wider, safer through streets on the perimeter. The irrationality of the village street pattern in an urban setting—giving some 40 percent of the land over to streets and jamming the people onto the remainder—was recognized in the nineteenth century. The RPNY intelligently planned a corrective within the metropolitan framework.

When all was said and done, however, the RPNY's three purposes boiled down to one: to decentralize and decongest New York enough for it to continue functioning in traditional ways. The humane intelligence of some specific plans did not alter the fact. The planners of the RPNY did not oppose all congestion and overcrowding; they opposed only the extreme agglutinations that carried the threat of death to the city's commercial, financial, and cultural institutions. Some traffic diversion, some retail decentralization was necessary to keep Manhattan from strangling to death. But the revivified Manhattan was not to be fundamentally altered.

For example, the RPNY's proposal for lower Manhattan consisted of a Washington Monument-type obelisk at the water's edge, with a semicircle of heavily wooded parkland beyond. The scheme was undoubtedly expensive, and was attractive, even allowing for its overblown formalism. But it was little more than a cosmetic application. Nothing basic changed in or about the forest of skyscrapers looming above the forest of park trees.

Third, the RPNY was really a plan for "New York and Its Environs," and not a true regional plan. The plan assumed the overriding importance of New York and its continued domination of its hinterland. Indeed Norton believed that planners would have to confine themselves to a radius of 40 miles from the center, a convenient commuting distance. The committee thrust out as far as 130 miles, but Norton's principle remained intact. The RPNY planned for the area palpably dominated by New York City. Of course there were verbal genuflections to local interests in the planners' essays. In 1929 the committee, its work largely done, was replaced by the proselytizing Regional Plan Association. The RPA sent emissaries to village and county boards by the dozen. They distributed copies of the RPNY volumes, exhorted their listeners to accept planning, and measured their success in planning boards established and zoning ordinances adopted.

The RPNY's limitations were hopeless defects in the eyes of Lewis Mumford, the utopian replanner. In two articles in the liberal *New Republic* during 1932 Mumford laid bare the sins, great and small, of the RPNY. Its manifold evils stemmed from its acceptance of the *status quo,* so that its talk of garden cities, land-use controls, farms nestled comfortably in the semiurban landscape, and so on were mere camouflage for continuing centralization. While Mumford's criticism was captious and possibly mistaken in some particulars, it did touch the basic flaw in the RPNY and in all such regional plans. For the RPNY was devoid of alternatives to the existing arrangements. It based its cautious projections upon "reasonable" expectations of public opinion or government policy.

In reply Adams quarrelled over details, but he could offer no real refutation of Mumford's main attack beyond restating the RPNY's original purpose. What Mumford wanted, Adams wrote, was an economic and social revolution in the states of New York, New Jersey, and Connecticut, or else a "despotic" government to carry out a radical decentralization scheme. But Mumford was really criticizing Adams for doing half a planner's job, for providing many acceptable (and therefore obsolescent) plans but failing to supply a vision of a more just, equitable future.

Books and articles on planning more than kept pace with the plans themselves. The result was an expansion of knowledge beyond even an expert's ability to assimilate. Much of the literature was ephemeral or arcane, appearing in newspapers, newsmagazines, or in specialized publications including the *National Municipal Review,* the *Architectural Record,* and the *Journal of the American Institute of Planners.* Scholarly and semischolarly journals accepted articles on city and regional planning. The cascade of books included Harland Bartholomew's *Urban Land Uses* (1932), an early volume in the Harvard City Planning Series, Thomas Adams' erudite *Outline of Town and City Planning,* published by the Russell Sage Foundation in 1935, and Robert A. Walker's astute *The Planning Function in Urban Government* (1941).

Educational expansion continued. The 1928 Conference on Research and Instruction in City and Regional Planning at Columbia University asked for planning to be recognized as a profession requiring the usual educational reinforcement, full-blown schools on university campuses graduating young people trained in professional canons and techniques. The conference deplored inadequate preparation and narrow specialization in a field requiring both breadth of knowledge and integration of separate disciplines such as landscape architecture and sanitation. Harvard University was already preparing a School of City Planning. It opened in 1929, with a grant from the Rockefeller Foundation and an endowed Charles Dyer Norton Chair of Regional Planning. In that year more than 30 colleges and universities in the United States offered courses in city planning. Through the years to World War II they would expand their offerings into professional curricula within established schools of architecture or, in some cases, into new schools.

Somehow, 30 years of realistic planning, zoning, construction, writing, and schooling seemed to make less difference than they should have. Plans of the twenties and thirties got no further, with some exceptions, than had "Boston—1915." Zoning in 1945 seemed much less a savior than it had in 1915, although communities without zoning ordinances were considered by outsiders to be cultural Possum Trots. Demands for professional recognition had brought more conferences, courses, and textbooks. Whether the apparatus of professionalism was responsible for any results on the ground, or whether it merely served careerism, was a question not objectively answerable. Despite government intervention in two world wars and the New Deal, planners had no more than scratched the surface of dealing with the housing problem.

At the same time, realists succeeded in bringing many grand if specialized projects from the drawing boards. The realists' excellent quantitative showing depended on five related developments that they turned to good account. First, millions of people were willing to pay heavy taxes and suffer many direct and indirect burdens if only they could operate private motorcars wherever they wished. Second, to meet the demands for urban services, governments at all levels began increasing taxes, expanding their taxing and bonding limits, and devising new ways of separating the citizen from his coin. Third, people were ever more willing to assign complex and serious problems, such as water supply, to the experts on special metropolitan district boards or to increasingly powerful municipal governments. Fourth, thoughtful businessmen came to understand that a lot of realistic planning aimed at saving retail and industrial cores that were losing customers to suburban competitors, relatively if not yet absolutely. Fifth, more sophisticated techniques of advertising and propaganda enabled planners and their business allies to convince the public of the need for spending money to realize the plans.

The RPNY committee's careful cultivation of local interests was an example of sophisticated propagandizing. In New York City itself, a group of privately financed "quiet-lovers" organized against noise pollution. They succeeded in making the public aware of the problem through skillful publicity of scientific noise-measurement studies and research on the physiological effects of noise. Antinoise ordinances of 1930 and 1936, little enforced, were the chief legislative victories. Crusaders against the "din of iniquity," like those against dens of iniquity, had to count their gains mostly in growing public understanding. In Philadelphia during the twenties and thirties, parkways, subways, bridges, and many other public improvements were related to downtown and the maintenance of its property values. Outlying centers, the retail lifeblood of many residential areas, received only incidental attention. Such was the stuff of realistic planning in the interwar years.

Many improvements centered on New York City, not because the city was large, but because it was the home of the greatest realist of them all—the brilliant Robert Moses. Moses' accomplishments as city park commissioner included a professional parks and recreation staff; expanded recreation areas; reconstructed zoos; and the construction of the 1939 World's Fair. Had he done only those things he would deserve a high place in New York's history. But he did so much more that he became known in New York and among planners the country over as "the man who gets things done." Any man who gets things done has enemies, but Moses garnered more than his share, largely because of his calculated vituperation against those who deplored his methods and his aims. His pen sometimes cut a wider swath than his parkways.

Moses was born in 1888 at New Haven, Connecticut, where his father was a well-to-do merchant. His background was Jewish although his parents did not practice the traditional faith. His family moved to New York before young Robert was nine, but he fulfilled a boyhood ambition to matriculate at Yale. In 1913 he took an Oxford M.A., and earned a Ph.D. at Columbia University by examination and submission of a manuscript on the British Civil Service. By his midtwenties Moses appeared much as he would in later years: tall and handsome, with the powerful build of a champion swimmer, which he had been at Yale.

Although Moses was diffident about family finances, his father and his mother's family had accumulated enough to relieve him of money worries. He earned good salaries and consulting fees throughout his career, but they were nominal for a man of his ability. His first job, with the New York Bureau of Municipal Research, led to meetings with Alfred E. Smith. Later, as secretary of the private New York State Association, he worked with Governor Smith at various plans for statewide improvements. Moses' interest in athletics led him to concentrate on park and parkway planning, and in 1924 Smith appointed him chairman of the State Council of Parks. Robert Moses was on his way.

Moses continued to come forward with projects, appropriations bills, bond issues, and shrewd publicity. Smith meanwhile established the pattern for Moses' public career by piling title after title upon him, including the presidency of the Long Island State Park Commission and the chairmanship of the Jones Beach State Parkway Authority. La Guardia continued the practice, naming him to a growing list of jobs, the most important of which (other than Park Commissioner) was the chairmanship of the Triborough Bridge Authority. The authority was an independent government agency selling bonds for public works, supervising the works, and redeeming the bonds through charges on users. The Triborough Bridge Authority, for example, constructed, operated, and collected tolls from drivers on its bridges.

It is not possible to give an adequate picture of Moses' great achievements without more visual apparatus than a book allows. Recitals of dollars spent, miles of parkway constructed, and acres of parks laid out do not help much in perception or valuation. What he strove for and in large measure achieved was an integrated park, parkway, and recreational system reciprocating between New York City and the state's lesser cities, and between the cities and the recreational sites themselves. His vast undertakings within New York City tied into the outer network of parkways and parks. Moses' beliefs and methods, as well as his personality, explain his amazing success.

First, Moses believed in dedicated public service as firmly as he believed in anything. Public service involved long hours, hard work, sacrifice, and scrupulous honesty with public funds. Anyone who failed to deliver on any one of those criteria had a brief career with Moses' staff. The same went for everybody in any department under his supervision, including common laborers. He recognized the value of partisan politics; indeed, he ran for the governorship in 1934, only to lose overwhelmingly to Democrat Herbert Lehman. Moses did not, however, see any virtue in patronage appointments. He alienated Franklin D. Roosevelt when he refused to appoint Louis Howe, Roosevelt's confidant, to a sinecure in the state park system. Later, when he was president, F.D.R. unsuccessfully tried to withhold federal funds from the Triborough Bridge Authority until Moses resigned as chairman. Moses also had words with the Works Progress Administration because of his conviction that WPA employees should be workers first and reliefers last.

Second, despite his public service ideals, Moses was at pains to disassociate himself from the old-style efficiency cult represented by the bureaus of municipal research. He was anxious to spend money aplenty if, in his opinion, the public weal justified it. He prided himself on acquiring more than the necessary right-of-way for bridge approaches, then converting the extra land into parks and playgrounds. He was willing to spend money to save money, as in antilitter and antivandalism campaigns. On rare occasions he ordered parkways redesigned to more expensive locations, to escape exhausting haggles over right-of-way acquisition.

Third, Moses acted extralegally (and resourcefully) when his assessment of the situation warranted corner cutting. One example was his overacquisition of bridge approaches. At times he deliberately underestimated costs to make them more palatable to the politicians. He could always return later with requests for supplemental appropriations. He was at the center of the bitter disputes of the twenties over park and parkway construction on Long Island. On one occasion an official attempting to serve papers halting a Moses project was dumped into Long Island Sound, and his papers set adrift. Another time Moses borrowed $20,000 from his mother to see some construction through before a legal deadline. At no time did he profit financially from any of it. The public good was the great end that always justified the means.

Fourth, Moses was well aware that New York and other cities would have to find the wherewithal to finance their survival. He did not express the problem in those terms, but he acted to get the most from the urban dollar. After the New Deal began, he kept Mayor La Guardia's office well supplied with projects eligible for federal funds. He created authorities, with their revenue bonds, to avoid overstraining city budgets and to generate income for still other projects once the bonds were retired.

Fifth, Moses used his various state and city positions to plan and build unitedly. He had held seven major official positions and a scad of minor ones by the late 1940s, although he drew a salary for only one of them, City Park Commissioner. Certainly by the early 1930s, and possibly before, he was using his multifarious jobs to coordinate recreational and highway developments impossible to integrate by any other means. It was not the best method, but Moses, ever the realist, understood how necessary it was. In the early days, at least, no legislature would have granted one man the power that Moses gathered piecemeal but wielded comprehensively.

All this makes Moses out to be a great man, which he was. It scarcely explains why his name was a swear word to many thoughtful planners who might be expected to forgive his tactical ruthlessness and vituperation. The explanation lies in three of Moses' controversial assumptions. They were, first, that New York could be saved by making it more livable for its middle class; second, that meeting its recreational and automotive demands was the way to keep the middle class contented and, third, that regional planning meant the exploitation of the region by the metropolis.

To save New York Moses worked to make it possible for middle-class people to enter the city, move about in it, and leave it in reasonable comfort. As a member of the middle class, though near its upper limits, he best understood its needs and desires. He had no patience with the rich people who often fought the parkways that he built through their estates and preserves and who in any case could take care of themselves. He struggled to break up the clubby atmosphere on the boards of the city's public museums and galleries. Those institutions relied too heavily on the patronage of people who had, or wished to acquire, status. His proposed changes were careful and reasonable, designed to encourage intelligent, aware middle-class people to exploit their cultural opportunities more fully.

When it came to the needs of poor people, Moses was less comprehending. He built recreational areas in Harlem, a decent and humane thing to do, but he refused to designate Harlem as a special area with needs more pressing than those in some other sections of the city. He did not become involved with public housing until the late 1930s, when it was evidently going to run into big money. Then he became involved because housers, in his opinion, were often impractical visionaries who gave inadequate attention to the recreational needs of the residents. Public housing and recreation, he said, had to be planned together from the beginning. Moses' criticism of the housers and his perception of linked housing and recreational needs were apt. He was not, however, so much interested in public housing because poor people needed it as he was concerned about the proper combination, under his direction, of housing and recreation.

Moses shared a narrow, class-oriented view of urban problems with many other public officials. It is as effortless as it is fatuous to criticize a man for being a child of his time, yet his limited conception of the public weal must be called by its right name. Neither New York nor any other city could be saved by a combination of recreation, uplift, and coordination of a few essential construction activities.

When Moses concentrated on recreation and roads for wheeled traffic he planned well but again, too narrowly. Most middle-class people spent most of their time at work, or at home, or commuting, or shopping. As the utopians insisted, it was essential to arrange the whole of life humanely, not merely to plan recreational escape hatches for the middle class. Because New York and all large cities were overcrowded, comprehensive planning should have involved decongestion and increased reliance on mass transit, so much more economical of space than automobiles. Yet Moses piled on the parkways, bridges, and tunnels in a frantic effort to keep wheeled traffic moving into, out of, through, and around New York. By building with such extraordinary vigor, he helped to inculcate the notion that highway construction of epic proportions was a basic solution to the urban crisis. Even before World War II the utopians were predicting an urban arteriosclerosis brought on in part by the insatiable space demands of the private car. Some realists, such as those in Los Angeles, had long since recognized the need for "mixed" transit facilities. Moses, however, was wedded to what was possible, and it was always possible to float more bonds for more highways.

One of the sadder aspects of Moses' commitment to the car was that he spoke more understandingly than he built. That was true, at least, of his pre-World War II career. In an address published in 1939 he depreciated the Manhattan skyline. Skyscrapers, he announced, "symbolize thoroughly bad planning, crazy land values which cannot in the long run be sustained, overcrowding, deprivation of light and air, concentration where there should be decentralization, inhuman transportation and traffic arrangements, and a dozen other monstrosities." [3] Trenchant talk. Yet when he illustrated a 1944 article with photographs of his deeds, he chose projects devoted to recreation and the car: the great Triborough Bridge system with its complex of

[3] Robert S. Rankin, ed., *A Century of Social Thought*, Duke University Press, Durham, North Carolina, 1939, p. 137.

playgrounds and parks; the West Side Improvement, a park containing the Henry Hudson Parkway; and the Corlears Hook Park with the East River Drive running through.

Moses also raised critics' wrath because he was an urban imperialist. He believed in satisfying New York's transportation and recreational needs by grabbing off huge chunks of land outside the city. Nobody could criticize him for his adroit realization of Jones Beach, dedicated in 1929, and for other far-flung recreational projects. His efforts might have been better directed toward making the city itself more livable, so that its residents would not need his great projects quite so desperately.

Certainly New Yorkers required some extensive beaches and natural environments, no matter how humane their city. But Moses proceeded to engulf rural land with gross disregard for its inhabitants, with arrogance, and with an hypocrisy as unconscious as it was stupefying. To defeat the people who stood between him and land for middle-class city dwellers, he worked unremittingly at condemnations, negotiations, and searches for defective titles. His opponents all were, according to him, unlovely: the idle rich who wanted to keep their rural solitude inviolate; snobs who hated the urban hordes escaping from their confines; greedy descendants of original patentees; and immoral people of various sorts including an ex-Klansman. Of course a person arrayed against baddies like that could justify any amount of vicious infighting, and Moses did. But it sounded odd, coming from a man who often waxed sentimental over New York City's hallowed traditions. To ambitious replanners Moses usually replied (in his mellower moments) that the city was rich in history, that New Yorkers loved both the city and its traditions. Only some sort of monster in human shape could entertain serious thought of tearing down whole blocks or neighborhoods of the beloved old town. The New York countryside was another matter. It and its people had no particular history or traditions or ways of life that Robert Moses was bound to respect. City dwellers needed the land, and that was that.

Finally, Moses' vituperative attacks on his critics added a personal dimension to controversies already bitter enough. He commonly indulged in generalized criticisms, such as his reference to "partisans, enthusiasts, crackpots, fanatics, or other horned cattle," in his 1939 address at Duke University.[4] Rexford G. Tugwell, a prominent New Dealer, felt his verbal shafts. When Tugwell became head of New York's City Planning Commission in 1938, Moses fought the Com-

[4] *Ibid.*, p. 128.

mission's master planning with every political weapon including the epithet "Planning Reds."

Moses went further in 1944, when he indulged in the wholesale personal vilification that would become part of his theatrical stock-in-trade. The choice in planning, he declared in the *New York Times Magazine*, was between people like himself who worked in the real world and "the subsidized lamas in their remote mountain temples" who subtly influence public opinion in favor of their outrageous schemes. Many of these visionaries were "Beiunskis," foreigners who fled their homelands only to criticize the United States "beiuns" how things were done differently in Europe. He then denounced several great architect-planners, including Eliel Saarinen for advocating municipal land ownership as an aid in defeating overconcentration; Walter Gropius for declaring that new ways of thinking about city problems must precede an attack on urban "anarchy"; and Eric Mendelsohn for wishing to eliminate all wheeled surface traffic from congested areas.

Next Moses took up the utopians' charge that they were strategists, he a mere tactician. Where were the strategists, he asked, when he put through Jones Beach and the Long Island parkway? Nowhere around, for rough-and-tumble was not to the taste of "the Vestal Virgins of long-haired planning." It required too many battles with politicians, with avaricious real estate interests, with uppity owners of sprawling estates. Then he trained his guns on some native planners. He called Frank Lloyd Wright the "brilliant but erratic" inventor of the Broadacre City. Moses summed up his reaction to Wright's plan: "you would get further if you tried an experiment on a reasonable scale, frankly called it an experiment, and refrained from announcing that it was the pattern of all future American living." Tugwell's cooperative ideas came in for criticism, as did Lewis Mumford's six stages of urban growth and decay.[5]

The best that could be said for the article was that it was lively, clever, and funny. But it also revealed a Moses who was impatient with abstract ideas, who tarred a variety of men with the same brush, and who was unforgiveably superficial, as when he ripped Mumford's stages of urban development from their context. Finally, Moses took too much license with his "beiunski" characterization of several brilliant exiled Europeans. It was some time before the howls produced by his article died away. Moses, who could damn an opponent by name and then shake hands when the fight was over,

[5] "Mr. Moses Dissects the 'Long-Haired Planners,'" *New York Times Magazine*, June 25, 1944, pp. 16–17, 38–39.

never understood why others were offended.

It was Moses' private friend and public critic, Frank Lloyd Wright, who best summed up New York's Park Commissioner. Wright remarked that the city, defined as a pre-World War II retail-commercial node, was dying. But Moses had kept New York alive by his brilliant improvisations. What would be a suitable reward? Wright answered: "New York should be given outright to Robert Moses." [6]

THE UTOPIANS

While Moses built, others built less and dreamed more. They dreamed of new and better cities and societies, and for that Moses ridiculed them. Perhaps the plans devolving from their dreams were ridiculous in their own time. Yet it takes but one turn of the wheel for utopians to seem utterly practical and the works of the realists to appear fantastic. Of all the utopians, three have been chosen because they were representative of the larger group while possessing unique qualities themselves. They are Lewis Mumford, Frank Lloyd Wright, and the planners in the Suburban Division of the Resettlement Adminstration who built the New Deal's greenbelt towns.

The utopians held four ideas in common. They believed that mankind possessed dignity and worth. They believed that the commercial-industrial cities of the twentieth century degraded man, exploiting his worth rather than cultivating it. They believed that urban decentralization and regional settlement were already well advanced and were definitely the living patterns of the future. Existing cities could not be saved in their present form, no matter what the expedients. And they believed that men would have to abandon their individualistic, competitive society for one cooperatively organized before deconcentration could develop in socially constructive ways.

Lewis Mumford, a gifted social critic and brilliant stylist, was born in 1895. His utopianism took shape early. Before he was 20 he had been influenced by the Scottish ecologist and planner Patrick Geddes, and through Geddes, a host of other European thinkers and planners. From Geddes and his other teachers, and from his own spacious intellect, Mumford developed the principles guiding his voluminous writings. By 1945 he had published many articles and a dozen books. Those best known to students to architecture and planning were *Sticks and Stones* (1924), *The Brown Decades* (1931), and the massive *The Culture of Cities* (1938).

[6] Jeanne R. Lowe, *Cities in a Race with Time*, Knopf, New York, 1967, p. 52.

Mumford's principles, though not always articulated in every work, permeated each of his books. First, he believed that all civilizations and cultures were organic, retaining some past habits and forms while developing new modes of thinking and acting. Second, because cultures were the sum of their past developments, true scholarship consisted of discovering and presenting the origins and paths of those developments. Of course the study of culture required specialists who hacked culture apart and examined the pieces carefully. In the process the specialists gained manageability and depth but lost essential breadth. It was the business of the generalists, the Mumfords, to reassemble the pieces into broad, interdisciplinary studies.

Third, he believed, cities had two purposes: to collect, reinforce, and develop their cultures; and to provide the good life for their inhabitants. The "good life" was not materialistic in the sense of the technological abundance associated with North American middle- and upper-class lives in the late twentieth century. Mumford argued for material sufficiency, but his emphasis lay elsewhere. Cities could function successfully as reservoirs of culture, he wrote, by freeing their inhabitants to develop their own potentials. Thus individual contributions would reinforce the culture. People lived full lives when they experienced interaction with one another in neighborhoods small enough for them to identify with and to understand entirely.

Fourth, Mumford believed that the commercial-industrial city failed to provide the good life. For one thing, it existed primarily to produce and distribute goods and services for a profit. For another, it robbed its region to produce glitter for the advantaged few at the heart of the metropolis, but impoverishment for the unfortunates who were failures by the canons of a capitalistic society, or who lived "in the sticks" away from the metropolitan core. Fifth, he hoped for a renascence based on the death of the economic and social forms of the imperialistic metropolis, and the rebirth of true regionalism built up from neighborhood units. The renascence would occur when men triumphed over technology and turned it from profit making to humane ends.

Mumford's principles shaped his understanding of urban development in the western world. In the tenth century, he believed, men lived in humane cities. Medieval cities were relatively small, were in close connection with their surroundings, were based on human relationships of neighborhood and craft, and were the cultural centers of their countries. From the twelfth century, capitalistically controlled technology began to disrupt medieval patterns of life and the easy symbiosis betweeen city and region. In destroying the medieval city, technology undermined its sense of community and common purpose. From the eighteenth century cities expressed increasing mechanical refinement, at least whenever mechanical refinement made a profit and, simultaneously, growing social chaos. The process reached its nadir in the "paleotechnic" age, roughly the middle to late Victorian period. Paleotechnic culture submerged humanity and its values in an orgy of filth, overcrowding, clatter and environmental destruction.

Even while most western urban dwellers suffered the horrors of the paleotechnic age, men were perfecting their machines. They were suggesting ways and means for the people who could afford it to escape the city, and inventing all the wondrous contemporary technology that would make it possible. Then came the "neotechnic" megalopolis, that marvel of mechanization, of sprawl, of fantastic skyscraper palaces. But the neotechnic age was fading away in its turn. The "biotechnic" age represented the forseeably final development. Biotechnic society heralded man's victory over technology, or the control of machines for social ends. It would come about when men acted upon their knowledge of what capitalistically controlled machines had done to them.

Although this is the barest sketch of Mumford's assumptions and his historical thinking, it is enough background for judging his ideas and some of the strictures against him. First, there was an uneasy relationship between his evolutionary view of technological culture (plus man's ability to shape that culture) and his conviction that human history reaches some sort of plateau with the biotechnic era. Mumford was careful to write that nothing human was ever final or complete but his references to the biotechnic age—if his words are taken at their plain meaning—wrap the biotechnic in a cloak of finality. Furthermore, Mumford's attack on "capitalism" as an independent force did not quite square with his belief that man was the master of his fate. Men, after all, directed capitalistic development.

Other criticisms of Mumford, in and out of academic circles, were mostly hooey. Some critics including Robert Moses ridiculed Mumford's belief in the organic development of cultures and cities. Cities are not organic, so the criticism ran, because men shape them. But men consciously (and unconsciously) shape many organisms, as they do in the selective breeding of domestic animals, the hybridizing of plants, and the spraying of pesticides. The charge that Mumford disliked cities is refuted by his praise of cities in medieval times. Neither was he lost in a romance with the medieval city, for he had little sympathy with its undifferentiated, poorly heated houses, and the consequent restriction on adult lovemaking. Medieval culture's primitive etiology and the massive deaths from plague or other causes were even more appalling to him. That Mumford was in the throes of a cultural revolt against Victorianism there is no doubt. He did, however, appreciate the creative efforts of Henry Hobson Richardson and John W. Root, two nineteenth-century pioneers in architecture. Nor did his revolt against bric-a-brac and overstuffed chairs blind him to the work of the Roeblings in bridge construction, Albert Pinkham Ryder in painting, Frederick Law Olmsted in landscape architecture, and Montgomery Schuyler in architectural criticism. His writing was as subtle and sympathetic as it was intelligent.

Above all, Mumford's attack on contemporary cities and his plea for humane regionalism were uncannily brilliant. His analysis began with the gargantuan commercial-industrial city of the multimillions. Megalopolis, he wrote, was simply too large to be efficiently or economically operated. More and more human intelligence and effort were diverted to keeping the city going, in finding water for its growing population, and in devising expedients for circulating its sluggish traffic. Megalopolis was depersonalizing because it was too huge for the human mind to grasp. The virulent pathology of urban dwellers was alarming but understandable. Wanton violence could be explained as the only possible response to a horrible environment. Because contemporary cities were organized to inflate property values, they put a premium on crowding and still more crowding. So people jammed buildings to the bursting point, wearing them out, discouraging effective maintenance, finally abandoning them. Then there were no more property values, no monetary values, and certainly no human values except when cities condemned the worthless land and converted it into a park.

Junk the present-day city and plan on a true regional basis, Mumford insisted. That was the only hope for salvation. His proposal seemed wildy radical to critics of the Moses persuasion. In truth it would have required a lot of physical reconstruction to carry through his ideas. Whether it would have required much more than the sum of the post-World War II pulling down and putting up is doubtful. His ideas were really quite cautious and conservative.

Mumford argued that regions were historical and cultural entities serving human purposes, not financial or capitalistic ones. Although not autonomous, they were sufficiently complex, diverse, and balanced to supply many of man's economic and cultural needs. Thus they were neither metropolitan playthings, nor were they synonymous with arbitrary political boundaries. Because they had grown up as the products of human need and human imagination, they were large-scale environments requiring comprehensive treatment. They could not be planned from a mere metropolitan or state point of view.

This was reasonable enough, but most realists jumped Mumford's ship when they read his basic requirement for a true regional plan: scrap power-seeking politics, and "getting things done" as a means of personal advancement and control over other's lives. Mumford meant all such politics, local, state, national, international, because in seeking power it recognized no interests other than its own. That was more than enough for most realists, but Mumford had only begun to raise the hackles of those who were still reading him. Proper regional development required common land ownership, he maintained. He carefully explained that communal ownership was not an end in itself, but simply a means to controlled, rational land development. Because men yearned for security in their lives, individuals would be secure in their land tenure during their lifetimes. When present politics and landholding systems ceased, so would public developments of the Moses type.

Anyone who thought Mumford a communist, an egalitarian, or a dreamer simply did not follow the meaning of his assaults on Moses' recreational developments. For in Mumford's assessment, Moses erred by opening up all the wilderness to everybody, or, at least, to everybody with a car or the price of a train ticket. In reality, not everyone could properly appreciate or conserve every natural environment. To bid culturally underequipped people to invade nature was to invite the destruction of nature. Mumford was no more a cultural snob than he was a Red, but he did believe that not all people enjoyed the same types of nature in the same ways. Men who had dwelt in narrow urban confines so long that their sensibilities were blunted would have to be carefully introduced to nature.

Mumford's blueprint for regional planning was the Garden City idea as developed by the Englishman Ebenezer Howard and first presented in *Tomorrow: a Peaceful Path to Real Reform* (1898) revised in 1902 as *Garden Cities of Tomorrow*. Howard envisioned compact residential settlements surrounded by a permanent buffer of unsettled land in orchards, farms, and parks. The garden cities included all the services, retail shops, and industry required to support their residents. For major cultural services, industrial requirements, and the like they would draw on somewhat larger central cities. Their transportation arrangements would emphasize inter-city rail transit and highways but allow few through streets for heavy traffic within the cities themselves. Their land policies would preclude speculative investment and enrichment. Howard refused to commit himself to absolute population maxima but he suggested 32,000 as a comfortable upper limit.

Mumford, his associates who formed the loosely knit Regional Planning Association of America, and many others were captivated by the vision of this English law court stenographer. Howard's conception inspired the two English garden cities of Letchworth and Welwyn, the greenbelt towns of the New Deal, and many suburban developments, though the greenbelt towns and the suburbs were but truncated renditions of the original idea. For Mumford the virtues of Howard's plan lay, first, in its adaptability to regional planning on a human scale; second, in its controlled growth; and third, in its functional balance between commerce, industry, agriculture, and residence.

The ideal of greenbelt decentralization within a region would be achieved, Mumford believed, in four stages. A thorough survey of the region's total resources was the first step. Next came a "revaluation" of common assumptions and ideas about the region, bringing them into line with newly discovered realities. Third, experts drew up the plan. Finally came implementation and the necessary modifications, necessary because no plan could foresee all circumstances and because people would resist some changes no matter how desirable in the abstract.

Most of all Mumford hoped for regional planning that accomplished two purposes. It would develop a region as a whole, not as the slave of some metropolis. And it would try to anticipate the future. Intelligent planners perceived the future, not as the glorified extension of the dying present, but as the development of forms and trends only emerging. In identifying and encouraging the emergents of a better tomorrow lay the challenge and the danger of Mumford's thought.

Frank Lloyd Wright's Broadacre City scheme generated more controversy than the remarkably similar Mumford-RPAA ideas, in rough proportion to Wright's calculated outrageousness and his gift for self-publicity. Wright's prose—bitter, ironic, rambling, repetitious, with its cabalistic vocabulary, punctuation, and capitalization—obscured some shallowness as well as some almost incredible profundity.

Broadacre City was a thin slice from the rich creative life of a colossal genius. Had Wright died in 1910, instead of in 1959 when he was almost 90, he would still have been ranked among the greatest of American architects, if not the greatest. To cite but one example of his greatness, his so-called "prairie houses" built in the first decade of the twentieth century were so advanced that 60 years later they appeared contemporary to unpracticed eyes. Nothing Wright did could ever be considered apart from his personality. He made certain of that. He broke up a good marriage for a series of well-publicized, disastrous love affairs. He was sartorially impossible, affecting capes, belted jackets, wide, wide lapels, canes, and porkpie hats over his long white hair. His criticisms of other architects were always scabrous if not always fair. His staggering egotism was a stance he preferred, he said in a typical wisecrack, to "hypocritical humility." All this lodged in some minds the conviction that Wright was unstable and utterly out of touch with the real world.

In truth Wright was an incurable nineteenth-century romantic with deep faith in the goodness of man. Broadacre City, with its acre for each family, was his anodyne for the inhuman cities that were crushing out mankind's essential goodness. His understanding of cities' historical development and present crisis is quickly told. Cities, Wright believed, grew from man's desire for security and for the evident advantages of multiple face-to-face contacts in an era of crude transportation and communication. But now (1932), he argued, the centralizing process of cities was out of control because the system of capitalism was itself out of control. Man lived either to pay capitalism's rent exactions or to coerce other men so that he and they might pay. The exactions were three: land rent, money interest, and most iniquitous of all, profits from machine production and invention. Profits from the machine especially offended because the machine should be used for man, not man for the machine, and because they were mostly the result of "good fortune," of being at the right place at the right time.

Happily the big city was on its way out, first, because man's wanderlust was once again asserting itself over his quest for security and, second, because of a rebirth of democracy. These two developments occurred as soon as machine technology radically altered the basis of life. Electronic communications eliminated man's need to bunch up while performing complex tasks and being entertained. In 1932 Wright even referred to the birth of "teletransmission," a development—here came one of those infuriating Wright remarks—as infant as the minds in charge of it. Rail, auto, and air transportation freed man from any one place, and endowed him with amazing mobility. Mechanical heating, refrigeration, and lighting placed the pasha's life, potentially at least, within the reach of all. New materials including steel and stressed concrete made possible a cheap, light, airy "organic" house architecture, built low to the scale of man and his immediate environment. Mass production, if properly organized, would make both necessities and luxuries available to all. Taken together these developments had lifted the burden of degrading heavy labor from the backs of men.

Since the city was slowly dying from its own poisonous wastes and from suburban decentralization of living and work, why not rejoice and let well enough alone? Wright could not, for he believed that the transition was thoughtless. People, numbed to the good life by urban environments, were misusing the land, violating the proper spatial relationships, and building new but inhumane houses, factories, and stores. The United States had no culture and esthetics comparable to its great political ideal of democracy.

Broadacre City was the answer. Although his critics called it everything from insane to plain dull, Wright's purposes were entirely rational and humane. First, he proposed to lower living costs by abolishing rent, interest, and profits. Since the savings would be so great, they would more than compensate for the higher costs of small, decentralized factories and farms. (This was not Wright's argument, at least not directly. He maintained that smallness itself involved overlooked efficiencies.) Second, he wished to reestablish the lost symbiosis between man and nature. He intended to achieve it by allotting one acre in secured tenure to each family for house, garden, and fruit trees. In this blessed environment people would once more learn to nurture and be nurtured by growing plants. Whether there was enough arable land for Wright's purposes is conjectural, but the proposal was not ridiculous given his grudging admission that some people will not wish to fool with nature and must be provided with apartment houses.

Third, Wright wanted to restore citizen awareness of rural primacy. No longer, he wrote, would farmers be despised "hicks" in thrall to the city. Broadacre Cityites would see small farms all about them and would know where their sustenance came from. Fourth, he intended to exploit machines for people by, among other things, building compact, unitized, prefabricated bathrooms and kitchens for every family. Fifth, he hoped to reintegrate living and working. Factory workers would travel but short distances to small, pleasant, pollutionless factories. Shoppers would whisk their cars to decentralized, small-scale shopping centers. Professional people would have offices at home.

Sixth, Wright required a radical deemphasis of government and politics. They, together with capitalism, were responsible for the enormous public and private bureaucracies battening on the people. Seventh, he hoped to make Broadacre City an architectural jewel box. Indeed his perspective drawings of Broadacre City are beautiful, with examples of his arresting architecture placed in lovely natural landscapes. Factories, apartments, stores, houses, all built according to Wrightian principles, would rebuild popular notions of beauty to the point at which people could for the first time enjoy tasteful luxuries.

Finally and most importantly, Wright yearned for society's renascence through the contributions of liberated individuals. Broadacres would provide both freedom and stimulation to individual efforts. Individuals would use their talents to enrich the whole, a sublime individualism when compared to "rugged individualism," which was merely self-indulgence.

Such a place might be dull for a few, but Wright understood that most people beyond adolescence are uninterested in much more entertainment than an evening at home with friends or an occasional night on the town. Certainly they are not panting after symphonies, the opera, or poetry readings at sidewalk cafes. electronic communication had done away with the need for most cultural getting together, anyhow. The unsatisfied few probably could have made their cultural arrangements within the Broadacre City framework. Wright knew from his own experience that anybody with marketable talent, particularly if it carries implications of snobbery, can write his own ticket.

There were gaps in Wright's design for his new order, and the critics delighted in romping through them. Wright was vague about the politics of Broadacres, and about the relationship between government and the noncapitalistic economics of Broadacre City. But these were areas he had always treated with disgust or amused contempt. They were not his strengths. Possibly he understood that detailed political and economic blueprints from a nonspecialist would invite criticism and deflect attention from his main message.

Wright's conception of quasi-governmental "design centers" or "style centers" was less realistic, and more disturbing. In theory at least the design centers were to be decentralized, spirited, and free. Yet Wright projected the style centers' virtual dictatorship over the cultural and esthetic life of Broadacre City. Graduates of the centers would call the shots in industrial design and the arrangement of public works. Supposedly they would be welcomed as the technician-beauticians of the new order. Wright never supposed that someone else might have his own ideas. Indeed, he came close to arguing that most problems were not really social or political, but esthetic. Problems would be solved by the expert manipulation of man's environment. The proposition may be true, but it is certainly not democratic by most definitions, Wright's included.

Wright also played fast and loose with the problem of poverty, a rather persistent problem in most human societies. According to Wright, the poor man would earn his house piecemeal by piling up work credits at his neighborhood factory. First would come the pre-fab bathroom, next the kitchen, then a bedroom or two and an end to camping out. A finished house, fruit trees, and whatever else was required could be earned by work credits, too. Unfortunately the work-credit system was suited only to someone already in touch with the ethic of work and the rudiments of factory labor. Wright had no plan for the mass of acultural people attuned to neither. It is doubtful whether he was even aware of their existence. Wright was really designing for white, middle-class Americans, the people who com-missioned his houses, the people whom he understood.

Finally, Wright leaned too heavily on the car for transportation. His greatest error, functionally speaking, was to sneer at railroads as archaic, and to defend his view with a photograph of a crowded freight marshaling yard! His mistake was at least understandable, for Wright was mature when the practical car came along in the first de-cade of the twentieth century. His generation experienced personal liberation by car as none other ever could. But it was unwise to pro-ject his love of cars onto the drawing boards of Broadacre City. Some of Wright's cars were weird tricycles with a tiny steering wheel at the end of a long, sloping snout and a bubble for the driver set high at the back above rear wheels some five feet tall. His superhighways (if one takes his table models seriously) boasted primitive in-terchanges and pavement lighting that would send any sane highway engineer into shock.

These are serious charges against Broadacre City and its creator, but they scarcely disqualify Broadacres or Wright's humane ideals from consideration. Robert Moses sometimes ridiculed Wright, a dis-tant cousin by marriage, in their witty if acidulous "Cousin Bob" and "Cousin Frank" exchanges. But Moses understood how desperately society needed visionaries with Wright's dynamic intelligence. Moses once received a medal from the Society of Moles, an organiza-tion of construction men. Showing the medal to Wright, he ex-claimed, "See, I am a Mole. You are a Skylark." [7]

The planners of the New Deal's famed greenbelt towns came to resent the word "utopian," at least as anti-New Deal ideologues ap-plied it to them and their work. They were utopian nonetheless. Because they were such a diverse lot, it would be rash to declare that all of them believed in the death of the big city. Almost all of them were convinced that America's residential future lay with its sub-urbs. They were shaping the future, staking out the path of subur-

[7] Cleveland Rodgers, *Robert Moses, Builder for Democracy,* Holt, New York, 1952, p. 250.

ban development from their own time forward.

The greenbelt towns enjoyed precedents aplenty. Federal intervention in housing came with World War I and the well-designed war workers' units built under the auspices of the Emergency Fleet Corporation and the United States Housing Corporation. The wartime housing had little if any direct influence, but it was a part of the gigantic federal involvement so inspiring to New Dealers. The lineage from Ebenezer Howard's garden city was more direct, even if filtered through the earnest group of thinkers in the RPAA. Three members of the RPAA had actually realized a segment of the garden city idea on the ground, albeit in the shape of a middle-class housing development. Clarence Stein and Henry Wright designed Radburn, New Jersey with superblocks, interior courts, and bypass traffic streets. The City Housing Corporation of Alexander Bing, who combined wheeler-dealer and visionary in one personality, provided the funds. The first families moved into Radburn in 1929, just in time for the stock market crash and the opening scenes of the Great Depression. Radburn was never completed.

Precedents do not entirely explain the greenbelt towns. Rexford G. Tugwell, the greenbelt's overall administrator, shared the belief that future populations would live in the suburbs. He dismissed as wishful thinking the back-to-the-land movement and the hope of rebuilding slum areas into spacious housing. Both the farmstead and the overcrowded inner city were archaic, and were losing population to the suburbs. "Rex" Tugwell—brilliant, handsome, a natty dresser, and an academic with a burning vision of the future cooperative commonwealth—was an early member of the New Deal "Brain Trust." He convinced President Franklin D. Roosevelt to make the greenbelt experiment part of the New Deal's resettlement program.

Tugwell formally administered the greenbelt project from the inception of his Resettlement Administration in April, 1935 to his resignation at the end of 1936. However, the active day-to-day administration was in the hands of John S. Lansill, the head of the RA's Suburban Resettlement Division. Lansill, a wealthy, courtly, engaging Kentucky Republican, smoothed over disputes and coordinated land acquisition, design, and construction. Frederick Bigger, a member of the RPAA, was brought in as chief of planning for the Suburban Division during an organizational crisis in October, 1935. Bigger was a first-rate designer in the Radburn tradition as well as a smooth administrator. As Tugwell was responsible for the inception of the greenbelt idea, so were Lansill and Bigger responsible for its execution.

The Suburban Division established a number of location criteria dovetailing with the New Deal's pro-labor bias and with the RA's plan for low-income, garden-type cities. RA researchers studied urban centers to discover those having the steadiest employment and payroll growth, the most enlightened labor policies, the greatest industrial diversity, and a potential greenbelt site on the outskirts. Most selections were made from the list compiled, but a site at Bound Brook, New Jersey was chosen because the distinguished city planner Russell V. Black prevailed on the RA to select it. Since the list was too long for the funds available, many cities had to be dropped: Los Angeles was too far away from Washington, St. Louis officials too quarrelsome, and so on. Finally the list was narrowed to four: Greenbrook at Bound Brook in the New York metropolitan region; Greenhills, just north of Cincinnati; Greendale, on the southwestern fringe of Milwaukee; and, the most important, Greenbelt, Maryland some seven miles northeast of Washington, D.C.

Land acquisition—in the hands of local real estate agents in each area—encountered the usual number of embattled farmers who did not wish to sell their land. Opposition was especially strong in Bound Brook, where family landholdings sometimes dated back to pre-Revolutionary times. To these historic and emotional considerations were added fears of the "scum of the earth" moving into the quiet old area. Two opponents were especially determined and effective. One, a wealthy Republican industrialist, was bitterly anti-New Deal. The other, a local tax assessor, was miffed because the RA would not buy his farm for double its value. The upshot was a federal court injuction against the construction of Greenbrook. The RA abandoned the project rather than risk a Supreme Court ruling against it and the other greenbelt towns as well. Because Greenbrook would have included an industrial park, it was the closest thing to a true garden city planned by the New Deal. Whether Greenbrook, as a working community, would have spawned imitators across the country is purely conjectural. Its sacrifice on the altar of vanity, ill-will, and emotionalism was sad indeed.

Meanwhile work went ahead at the other sites. There was a lot of initial confusion that Bigger resolved partly by creating three semi-autonomous planning and architectural staffs, one for each community. The first families moved into Greenbelt (near Washington) in September, 1937, into Greenhills (near Cincinnati) in May, 1938 and into Greendale (near Milwaukee) during the following month. What greeted them in each instance was a representation of the Radburn idea, with extra land in superblocks given over to gardens, with play and work spaces in interior courts. Each town had a large number of multiple-unit dwellings to hold down costs, a compact shopping center, and (especially at Greenbelt) severe restrictions on through automobile traffic plus a system of protected pedestrian walkways. Greenbelt was arranged in a giant fishhook curve and sported a large lake. Greenhills' streets followed its rugged topography, many of them ending in cul-de-sacs, while at Greendale the layout was close to that of any conventional farming community.

For a time the new residents shared the eagerness of the builders of their towns. They considered themselves pioneers on a suburban frontier. They were enthusiastic about their new living quarters, were delighted with their children's larger, safer play spaces, and were excited about cooperative ownership of the stores in their shopping centers. The youth of the first residents—the adults averaged a little more than 30 years of age—contributed to the initial interest.

The first blush of enthusiasm faded fairly quickly for reasons both internal and external to the projects. The internal reasons were, first, resident selection and income limitations that made for a high turnover. Depending on family size, potential greenbelt residents could earn as little as $800 or as much as $2200. By later standards these salaries seem minuscule, but they were "low to moderate" incomes in the late thirties. The RA early gave up the idea of having really poor people who could not afford even the $21 to $45 per month rent. Incomes at the towns averaged from about $1600 to $1800 in 1938. Whenever a family's income bumped against the ceiling, it had to move. This arrangement lent a temporary aspect to life in the greenbelt towns. They became a warm, friendly place to live, better for the money than anything else available, until one could afford a home of one's own. The air of impermanence remained even though allowable incomes rose under inflationary pressure.

Second, the greenbelt towns were overorganized civically and socially. The pace of meetings was so rapid at first that stay-at-home weeks were declared. Less organized socializing became the rule within a year after residents resolved most of the basic civic issues and turnover had split the towns into "old settlers" and "newcomers." Third, cooperative marketing prospered only at Greenbelt, which held 855 families to Greenhills' 676 and Greendale's 572. In 1941, 1000 units of defense workers' housing at Greenbelt sent coop sales soaring even though they disrupted the community socially. Finally, international events weighed more heavily on residents' minds after World War II began in September, 1939, making local matters seem less important.

External pressures effectively limited the towns to three, and to the first units built, except for the added defense housing at Greenbelt.

The limits related to a significant shift in the national mood between 1935, when the towns were planned, and 1938, when they were occupied. By the latter year there was little public sympathy for innovation and experiment. Most of the criticisms, from real estate interests, and other ideologues, pandered to the new mood. They focused on the socialism involved in government housing, a supposed threat to land values in the neighborhoods of the greenbelt towns, a set of regulations no more severe than those imposed by many private landlords, and costs.

Many criticisms were either emotional, or arguments from first principles, but costs were the project's Achilles heel. The unit costs ranged from about $15,400 at Greenbelt to $16,600 at Greendale, fairly expensive housing by prices then current. Apologists for those figures, then and later, argued for an average unit cost of less than $10,000. They pointed to the expense of relief labor and the unfairness of saddling the units built with the costs of utilities systems designed for twice as many residences, with the expense of farmland buffer areas, with the cost of furniture and other items. Viewed in either way, however, the greenbelt towns were not inexpensive housing. At 1941 rentals, it would have taken 300 years to pay for Greenbelt, even with interest forgiven. Tugwell boldly admitted needing the subsidy, cited the hidden subsidies involved in slum housing, and declared that the country required 3000, not three greenbelt towns. He was right, probably, but costs were against it.

Another criticism, the esthetic, was borne out by time. Critics attacked the severe, slab-sided, flat-roofed houses at Greenbelt and some of the barracks-like row houses at Greenhills. In truth the styles of the thirties have not worn well. The flat-roofed houses were kin to the International Style, scarcely a fresh approach to housing design by 1935. The architectural *cognoscenti* of the day defended them over the neocolonial designs also used in the greenbelt towns. They forgot that the neocolonial, though derivative, is gracious and adaptable. The flat-roofed houses instead are period pieces, well-designed and functional, but too stark to be attractive.

For all the enthusiasm, the greenbelt towns did not amount to much as demonstrations or indications of the future suburbia. The government sold most of the land, houses, and buildings in 1952, the rest by 1954. The original towns remain the physical expression of a utopian vision. The national mood, the expense, the deepening international crisis all precluded any further development of the greenbelt idea. Nor did the towns indicate how either public or private building might house the poor. The RA excluded blacks without really justifying the policy. RA administrators probably decided that they were taking enough ideological flack without having to deal with racist accusations of a plot to infiltrate blacks into suburbia.

Ironically, the practical utopians of the Suburban Division built the most but inspired the fewest followers. Their real legacy is more general and more enduring than their vision of the future suburbia. For they showed how concrete responses to urban problems could develop within the federal government, sometimes more effectively than within the cities themselves.

CHAPTER SEVEN

The Nationalization of Cities

The nationalization of American cities involved, basically, the realization that urban and national problems were inseparable. The truth had dawned in some minds by 1915. Other minds as yet uncommitted, knit together organizations, plans, and publications operating on the principle whether consciously or not. The nationalization of cities necessarily assumed federal money grants to ease national predicaments that happened to be in cities. The idea of direct federal aid was counterpoint to the reigning belief in cities' ability to solve their own problems.

Cities appeared to be financially viable until the Great Depression. That calamity dispelled once and for all the myth of urban economic self-sufficiency. The unprecedented collapse of urban governments was as awesome as the New Deal's energetic attempts at recovery. Depression and New Deal experiences forged new federal-urban relationships, but their novelty obscured a network of older, important, less remarked intergovernmental ties. The web of relationships grew closer when World War II repeated on a grander scale the crises in housing and industrial relocation of the first global conflict. The war helped lay to rest surviving notions of urban independence. Postwar plans drawn in wartime were not city plans but almost always metropolitan or regional plans, grounded on assumptions of growing federal aid for housing, highways, and airports.

PROFESSIONALISM AND CITIES

Urban-based organizations continued to grow and to spread the news of urban developments nationwide. The National Municipal League (founded in 1895), a collection of urban reform organizations, published the *National Municipal Review*. Older professional societies including the American Institute of Architects (founded in 1857) and the American Institute of Planners (founded in 1917) gave attention to urban issues in their journals and conferences. The Russell Sage Foundation continued its financial support of educational and reform projects, while the durable National Conference on City Planning maintained a forum for ideas.

Other groups influenced urban policies even though they were not organized to confront urban problems. The National Association of Real Estate Boards was a powerful voice for free enterprise, private rights to the increment of urban-suburban lands, and (until the late thirties) federal noninterference in housing or redevelopment. The NAREB's semiautonomous Urban Land Institute (established in 1936) produced thoughtful studies of suburbanization and deconcentration. The progressive League of Women Voters (founded in 1920) was concerned with various political issues including urban reform.

Accelerating professionalism and specialization produced new organizations to represent their members and to circulate information and ideas among them. The veteran administrator Louis Brownlow, once a commissioner for the District of Columbia, founded a special superorganization, the Public Administration Clearing House, in 1930. Brownlow argued that city managers and other people concerned with municipal administration had established national (and international) organizations dedicated to their special interests. The municipal research movement had spawned organizations equipped to investigate stubborn civic problems. Yet there was no one organization exclusively concerned with improving administrative effectiveness. There was no central agency devoted to collecting and disseminating successful methods of administration. There was no central library in which all the organizations could deposit their publications, and on which they could draw for reference material. As conducted by Brownlow the PACH stayed out of politics and expressed no overt preferences for one form of urban government over the others. Financed by various foundations, it continued its work without independent sources of income until 1956. Rather than assume research or advisory functions in competition with its cooperating organizations, it closed its doors.

In January, 1934 the National Association of Housing Officials opened for business with private financial support. It set about educating urban housing officials in the opportunities for federal assistance under the New Deal, in the correct methods of housing surveys, and in the superior design of proposed projects. Toward the end of 1934, Brownlow and other people anxious to spread planning information founded the American Society of Planning Officials. The ASPO tried to draw others besides professional planners into its net, for lay members of planning commissions and nonplanners in city administration needed educating, too. The ASPO attempted to widen its members' often segmented views of planning, to wean them from thinking of land-use planning in terms of mere zoning, and to encourage their efforts for truly comprehensive urban plans.

Organizations designed to speed the solution of specialists' common problems were needed, as were efforts to inform politicians, general administrators, and specialists of shared concerns. They were not enough, however. The mayors of larger cities with depression-exhausted treasuries needed some organizational voice at Washington. In February, 1933 they met in the shadow of national collapse to plan an appeal to the incoming Roosevelt administration. The resulting United States Conference of Mayors was a frank pressure group lobbying on behalf of the nation's cities. Wisely, for reasons political and humane, New Dealers such as Rexford Tugwell and Harold L. Ickes, the Secretary of the Interior, promised massive aid to cities. Just as wisely, the Conference soon elected indefatigable Fiorello La Guardia to be its chairman. La Guardia's standing with the White House was known to be high.

In the midst of all these special concerns some publications tried to keep in focus a common, unified view of the urban kaleidoscope. The *National Municipal Review* was one. The *American City* magazine was another. Under the editorship of Harold S. Buttenheim, *American City* ran nuts-and-bolts articles on a wide range of subjects including traffic control, park development, recreation, and planning.

The *Survey* magazine left an extraordinary legacy of achievement when it expired in 1952. The *Survey* originated in the *Charities Review*, the publication of the New York Charity Organization Society. Almost from its inception in 1891 the weekly *Charities Review* served social workers across the country. In 1909 it was retitled the *Survey*, the name it carried (with variations) through the rest of its life. The *Survey* expanded its coverage and absorbed related publications, under the direction of a series of able editors.

After Editor Paul U. Kellogg directed the famous Pittsburgh Survey, both he and the Charity Organization Society recognized the need for a magazine dedicated to reformist, preventative social service. In 1912 the *Survey* severed its connection with the Charity Organization Society. It was later published by a group of special contributors, the Survey Associates, Inc., from which a smaller advisory board was named to oversee the journal. The *Survey*, always a subsidized publication, survived because of institutional gifts, principally from the Russell Sage Foundation in the early years, and individual contributions and bequests. It became a monthly, supplemented during the prosperous twenties, the challenging thirties, and the bewildering forties by a *Midmonthly*.

Editor Paul Kellogg came to the magazine in 1902 from a middle-class background in Kalamazoo, Michigan. He was in his thirties when the *Survey* became an independent publication. By then his ideas and personality were fixed. He was a dynamic, enthusiastic, gregarious, blond man who believed in the basic goodness of mankind. During a mature lifetime in New York he liked to escape to the woods for reasons spiritual as well as physical. He retained, may even have cultivated, an unspoiled midwestern folksiness. He believed that people would act as their better natures directed if only they had the facts. Regarding his editorial tasks, he believed that social workers could never afford to become narrow specialists who ignored the other branches of their discipline nor the larger world about them. Kellogg's motto, "nothing alien," led him to some strange enthusiasms, for a journal of social work, including a series on Mexico. Most of his editorial talent, however, went into making the *Survey* lively and graphically inviting to his social service audience.

Kellogg's greatest contribution to an understanding of things urban, apart from a preponderance of articles on social work in cities, was a number of special issues on urban problems and urban life. The 1925 issue on Harlem was the most famous of all. Alain Locke, a young, black Howard University professor, edited the number. Rejecting the hackneyed "Negro problem" approach, Locke pulled together stories on black achievements and black contributions to the national culture. Kellogg's final editing of Locke's prose was merciless (as it was with everyone's) but he did not tamper with Locke's provocative analysis of the "New Negro." The result was an issue remarkably free from the usual white stereotypes of deviant black behavior. In an age when "darky jokes" appeared in newspapers and "coon songs" were popular with whites, it was a daring piece of work. The success of the Harlem issue (40,000 copies sold *versus* the usual 20,000) confirmed Kellogg's vision.

Kellogg has received less credit for devoting an issue to regional planning during the same year. His initial judgment was to forgo an analysis of a topic so abstract and unrealized as regional planning. Members of the Regional Planning Association of America kept talking, and at last Kellogg relented. His acquiescence was all the more remarkable because realistic planners entertained low opinions of the editor, Lewis Mumford, and the contributors. So it was that Clarence Stein's provocative article on the snowballing investment in urban "social overhead" saw the light as "Dinosaur Cities."

Early in 1928 Kellogg began to receive disturbing squiggles on his informal social seismograph. Unemployment, so it seemed, was rising. In a notable special issue that March, he analyzed the prevailing economic insecurity of a "prosperous" year. He predicted a financial and social crisis, although he did not forecast its form. He ran follow-up articles on unemployment after the special issue. When severe unemployment came, thoughtful readers of the *Survey* were forewarned.

During the 1930s the *Survey* consistently supported the New Deal, giving lots of space to federal programs impinging on urban social work. At the same time it began to show signs of the institutional illness that killed it in the early 1950s. The death, in 1934, of Kellogg's brother Arthur was a serious upset. Although warm and compassionate, Arthur possessed more surface crust and much more realism than did Paul. He was in fact, if not in title, the joint editor as well as the real manager of the enterprise. About the time of Arthur's death, financial benefactors faced with depression-trimmed purses and competing demands for their dollars cut their contributions to the magazine.

The *Survey* attracted a few talented and ambitious young people to its small editorial staff. Fewer remained. Kellogg seemed incapable of facing up to training his successor. Opportunities appeared elsewhere, first with returning prosperity, then with World War II. Nobody really replaced Arthur. Although Kellogg would occasionally rouse himself for a good issue, he was badly overworked and his intellectual rallies were fewer and fewer. His magazine drifted into the postwar era in the shadow of financial failure. Yet the *Survey's* decline should not obscure the service it rendered in helping to make the urban scene intelligible to an important national audience.

CITIES AND GOVERNMENTS

Intergovernmental relationships played a vital role in nationalizing the cities. But the place of the states in the intergovernmental equation was distinctly nonvital, and when direct urban-federal relationships became important the states were all but brushed aside. The states' place was insignificant because the rural-based state legislatures refused to admit their burgeoning cities into full partnership in the political process. The knife cut both ways. The cities developed no loyalties or obligations to state governments, and gladly short-circuited their statehouses when the federal manna fell. For refusing to recognize legitimate urban aspirations, legislatures stand accused of bigotry against urban ethnic groups and indifference to the problems of cities. City-watchers are especially inclined to sound off on bigotry or indifference when discussing malapportionment in state legislatures, surely the most glaring example of statehouse disdain.

Malapportionment resulted from the legislatures' refusal to allow urban areas their fair proportion of state representatives as the cities grew. The population of Birmingham rose from 178,806 in 1920 to 326,037 in 1950, yet the Alabama legislature, in violation of the state constitution, refused to allow the city more representation. The legislature had refused to reapportion in favor of urban areas since 1901 and would continue to do so until after 1962, when the federal supreme court finally intervened in the matter of malapportionment. If the federal courts were reluctant, the state courts were deciding in favor of the legislatures. Illinois lawmakers, like Alabama's, were contemptuous of a constitutional injunction to reapportion every 10 years. In the 1926 case of *Fergus v. Marks* an Illinois judge refused to infringe on legislative sovereignty and order reapportionment. The same year California voters adopted a constitutional amendment designed to perpetuate rural control of the state senate—no county could have more than one senator and no more than three counties could be combined into one senatorial district. Thus Los Angeles County and its millions sent one senator to Sacramento, as did rural counties with their thousands.

This was grossly unfair to the one-man-one-vote principle, but it was not necessarily bigoted. True, some provincial downstate Illinois representative might express his refusal in terms of denying a larger voice to Chicago's blacks, boss politicians, Czechs, and other riffraff. The trouble is, a nationwide phenomenon such as malapportionment cannot be explained by the cultural divisions and bigotry in one or a few states. Bigotry does not help much in explaining the situation in California, where ethnic minorities were significant in the cities (but not as significant as in eastern cities), and where minorities also dwelt on farms. Bigotry existed there, of course, but it had little antiurban content. The problem in Alabama was akin to California's. Therefore the apportionment problem was a problem of power, even though it had racial overtones. Simply put, the rural legislators had the power, and like most people with power they intended to keep it.

The indifference to urban problems was more serious. Rural and small-town legislators were not very interested in traffic congestion, deteriorating slums, and inadequate recreation. They were reasonably willing to allow cities somewhat more scope to their own problem solving, provided that the new arrangements placed no extra burdens on state governments. Thus they acquiesced in the continuing movement for "home rule" charters. Home rule usually removed administrative agencies—local health boards, police, and the like—from the list of gubernatorial appointments, placing them under mayors or city councils. Sometimes the new charters allowed increased taxing and bonding powers.

Similarly, the states passed enabling acts encouraging new functions such as planning and zoning, or permitting cities to share in the federal largesse. All this undermined the legal fiction that sizable cities were mere creatures of the states, subject even to corporate destruction by an act of the state legislatures. In addition the states' "let George do it" attitude toward urban problems took the bloom from the rose of area representation. Area representation was malapportionment in the perspective of one-man-one-vote. That was a good thing, so its defense ran, because it preserved historic and community interests, and these were as important to democracy as representation based on population. The problem was that the disproportionate representation of rural areas may have saved *them* from horrible fates at the hands of the urban masses. It did precious little toward saving the cities.

State indifference and inaction smoothed the path of growing urban-federal cooperation. The process involved in that cooperation, while well known, was less well understood. In the late twentieth century most students of intergovernmental relations accepted one of three views of its historical development. One group—the continuity school—argued for the presence of local-federal relationships from the dawn of the republic. The principal change over time was in the number and complexity of federal programs, which increased as federal activities and objectives expanded. Granting the existence of federal programs in the eighteenth and nineteenth centuries, and granting the existence of critical "watershed" dates in the continuity approach, the argument rang hollow. There had been simply too many changes in the nature and scope of federal programs for cities. For instance the massive New Deal WPA and PWA projects would have boggled the minds of earlier generations—boggled enough minds during the New Deal as it was.

The second school argued for two periods of important change in urban-federal relations, the New Deal's welfare and employment programs, and the massive, urban-oriented programs of the post-World War II era. The problem here is that many federal operations—the post office, work in rivers and harbors, and military installations—have had continuing importance for cities. The third, or "revolution" camp believed in the overwhelming importance of urban-federal changes in the 1960s. According to this way of thinking, the latter enormous federal funding and close control had made all previous activity quite unremarkable by comparison. This assumption too severely downgraded continuing federal services of the post-office type, and belittled federal public works of an earlier age merely because they were relatively inexpensive.

All of these views agreed in two important respects: they admitted the long duration of urban-federal relationships, and they saw important changes in the nature of those relationships over time. That agreement is a base for building another version of federal aid to cities in the interwar period. Properly understood, urban-federal relationships developed in three phases, each new phase supplementing rather than displacing the work of the previous phase. The first phase, from 1915 to 1921, saw traditional federal services to cities (such as harbor improvements) increasing rapidly. During the second phase, from 1921 to 1933, traditional services expanded, but federal officials emphasized direct, voluntary cooperation between the national government and the cities. From 1933 until the end of World War II the New Deal expanded existing intergovernmental relationships, but the spotlight fell on its unprecedented programs of unemployment relief and national reconstruction. Many of the New Deal's new programs focused on the cities, where the needs were most obvious.

Few federal officials working in any of these phases viewed the city in the same light as did their successors in the late twentieth century. Most men of an earlier day did not think of cities as having special difficulties crying for solution or different populations in need of salvation. Instead they thought of national problems and needs. Because those problems and needs were located in cities, they would have to be met in cities. In the short run, how people perceived problems mattered less than what they did about them.

During the first phase, largely a continuation of traditional aids, federal river-and-harbors work was critically important to many cities, including Sacramento, California. Although inland some 95 miles from the Pacific Coast, Sacramento was the head of navigation on the Sacramento River. The Corps of Engineers had been authorized to maintain a seven-foot channel since 1899. In 1917 it began an independent flood control project that helped preserve the river's navigability and protect property in and around the city. Congressional action in 1919 had a profound impact on Houston, Texas. In that year it authorized a deepwater dredging (30 feet) for the Houston ship channel. The move opened the way for an enormous commercial expansion in Houston just at the time when Congress decided to build an American merchant marine. In 1925 Houston became a full-fledged ocean port even though its center lay 18 airline miles from the shore of Galveston Bay.

During World War I San Francisco (among many other cities) received enormous federal benefits. These were not primarily from war workers' housing. The federal wartime housing effort has been overrated, both for its immediate results, which were meager, and its value as a precedent, which was minor. More significant federal activity centered around Bethlehem Steel's Union Iron Works. Wartime shipbuilding contracts drove the labor force from a prewar 7000 to more than 35,000 workers in 1918. The Navy not only outfitted the Bethlehem plant for destroyer construction, it allotted money to build a huge cafeteria seating 1600. It loaned money to the streetcar company to improve service. When influenza struck the San Francisco Bay area late in 1918, the Navy sent 125 medical specialists to serve in civilian hospitals. It opened its own sick bays for civilians early the next year. When manpower shortages developed, the Navy trained skilled workmen. Cooperating with other agencies, it worked out recruiting programs, antistrike and antilockout policies, and wage rates. Together, these activities demonstrated federal effectiveness in relieving a series of difficult urban problems.

Of the traditional agencies influencing city development the post office played the most important role. By 1915 free city delivery was a traditional but vital part of urban education and communication. Special delivery, immediate delivery within specified hours at the point of destination, was an extra, more expensive urban service. Even rural free delivery (RFD), generally thought to be a lamp of enlightenment in the bucolic darkness, had important urban consequences. City-based businesses enjoyed closer communication with rural customers, of course. But urban post offices had to handle the growing volume of rural mail, over one billion newspapers and magazines by 1911. As RFD grew, village post offices closed, throwing letters and packages formerly sorted at the crossroads into the laps of urban mail clerks.

City dwellers had to pay more than their postage to receive expanding post office services. By 1920 the post office department would enlarge its urban carrier routes only if cities made "civic improvements, such as good, continuous sidewalks, crosswalks, streetlights and signs, house numbers, and [household] receptacles." [1] It

---

[1] Carl H. Scheele, "The Post Office Department and Urban Congestion, 1893–1953," paper read at the annual meeting of the American Historical Association, Toronto, 1967, p. 8.

would have been unthinkable for the federal government to throw such burdens on urban budgets by the late twentieth century, but cities then cheerfully shouldered the expense in return for the service. Then, civic appropriations were supposed to meet all the demands on the community. Probably most of the improvements would have been made, although not so rapidly, even without pressure from the post office. Besides, there is plenty of evidence that postal service amounted to a huge grant of "federal aid" to cities in the twentieth century.

Although postal officials have been accused of being hopeless fuddy-duddies, they tried to meet the growing mail volume with innovations in two areas: collecting and transporting the mail, and processing it. Their efforts were especially noticeable in urban areas. By 1915 the department had already experimented with variously sized and shaped collection boxes. It had toyed with zoned address schemes. It had established the Railway Mail Service with its in-transit sorting, which kept huge piles of unsorted mail out of urban post offices and saved space for intracity letters. To answer the demands of urban businessmen for better local service, the department tried new systems. The fate of one system, a tunnel under Chicago's Loop, foretold the doom of others. From early 1907 to mid-1908 electric trains carried tons of mail between post offices and railroad depots. When the contractor wanted more money, the post office let the contract expire, returning to less efficient but less expensive surface transportation.

In 1915 two other intracity mail systems, tubes and trolleys, were in operation. The pneumatic tubes were the most innovative and the most controversial. The tubes ran 56½ miles in five cities, with almost half of that mileage in New York City. Boston, Philadelphia, Chicago, and St. Louis were the other cities served. In New York alone the tubes moved six million letters each day at an average of 35 miles per hour. They cut the time between some post offices by 45 minutes. There were disadvantages, including the rough ride (usually fatal to fragile contents in unmarked packages) and the small diameter of the tubes (eight to 10 inches). The greatest drawback was the cost: $961,707, huge for those days.

Almost from the beginning of tube service (Philadelphia, 1893) there were complaints about its expense. The tube's small diameter was a greater disadvantage after 1913 and the introduction of an expanded parcel post. Because the tubes could not accept the new, large packages, proportionately more mail had to be carried on the surface. Postal patrons valued the tubes more than the post office department did. In 1918, in the name of wartime economy, the department allowed the tube contracts to lapse. Businessmen complained of shifting the mail to already crowded streets. The department finally bowed to the pressure, reopening most of the New York mileage in 1922, restoring Boston's lines in 1926.

Although the tubes became more appreciated as the crush of traffic grew above them, they remained vulnerable to the trucks. Trucks could always handle the tube mail, less expensively if not so well. Plans for larger and better tubes were drawn but were shelved during the Great Depression. In 1953 the post office ended the last tube service, a victim of costs and the car.

Streetcar Railway Post Offices were a familiar sight at one time or another in 15 large cities. They offered direct service between crosstown points, the mail bypassing the central post office altogether. Because out-of-town mail was cancelled and sorted along with the rest, some streetcar routes carried mail directly to outbound trains. The post office department set up letter-drop boxes painted white, the same color as the Railway Post Office streetcars. Letters deposited in the special boxes were whisked away on the next white streetcar. Many of the cars came equipped with letter drops on their sides. Efficient though it was, the streetcar Railway Post Office (RPO) was on the way out by 1915. Most city service had been established in the nineties, none was inaugurated after 1910. Of the 15 cities served by the white cars at one time or another, six had lost the service before 1915; another five saw it discontinued that year. The streetcar RPO was another sacrifice to the ubiquitous motor vehicle.

The "horseless wagon" enthralled postal officials as much as its passenger-carrying counterpart excited other Americans. In their early years, motortrucks rated higher as technological wonders than streetcars or pneumatic tubes. They collected and distributed mail much more rapidly than horse-drawn wagons could. They were useful in dashing out for smaller quantities of mail, which was then fed piecemeal into post offices, rather than in great gluts. Motors could carry mail swiftly to suburban factories.

The truck had its advantages, true, but the post office department irrationally favored it over other forms of mail transportation. The department complained only of the costs of early contract city trucking, eliminated in 1918, and of maintaining the 28 separate makes of trucks transferred as war surplus in 1919 and 1920. On the other hand, expense was no bar to building up fleets of trucks, garaging, maintaining, and repairing them. In defense of the post office, it did innovate, it did try to move the mass of urban mail more quickly. Unfortunately it shared in the widespread failure to recognize the virtues of a diversified transportation system.

Mail processing demanded at least as much ingenuity as transporting it, for most of the 20 *billion* and more pieces per year were funnelled through urban post offices at some point in their travels. The department attacked the problem on two fronts, mechanizing the mail flow within the offices while encouraging the use of precancels and postage meters to deflect bulk mailings from post office processing. By 1915 automatic facing and cancelling machines were widely used, and post offices had experimented with overhead conveyors and with sorting tables. A distributing and cancelling machine was tested in 1918, but was set aside to gather dust along with other innovative equipment. The department's introduction of new devices was fairly progressive if less than perfect. After about 1910 new urban post office construction recognized the need for adequate light, ventilation, and workspace.

After the turn of the century metered mail machines developed rapidly. Their purposes were to speed the stamping of commercial mail and to avoid jamming it through all of the steps in post office handling. The technical problem was to develop a "foolproof" machine that could not be tampered with. Machines using coiled stamps were unsatisfactory because the stamps could be stolen. Abandoning stamps, Arthur H. Pitney developed practical electric metered mail machines that stamped envelopes with the date, place, and permit number of the machine. Because the Pitney-Bowes machine was set with a given amount of prepaid postage at the post office, then locked, it was difficult to defraud its user. Nor could the post office be easily defrauded, for the machine shut down after it had "metered out" the prepaid postage. It would not make more imprints until the post office reset it. The department first authorized a Pitney-Bowes machine in September, 1920, and its use spread rapidly after that.

The chronicle of one federal department's efforts to keep pace with growing demands of an urban population demonstrates how open the post office was to innovation. Despite a few blind spots it used technology to advantage, at least until it joined the national craze for the motor vehicle. It did require cities to provide expensive services before it would extend mail deliveries, but in return provided a service making urban existence possible. The postal service was extensive, complex, and sophisticated because the department heeded demands from importunate city dwellers.

The post office and other traditional aids to cities continued after 1920, but more spectacular federal activities overshadowed them. From 1921 to 1933 Herbert Hoover's "voluntary cooperation" and "associational activities" dominated urban-federal relationships. As

Secretary of Commerce (1921–1929) and as President (1929–1933), Hoover orchestrated conferences, reports, and publications on children's health, zoning, planning, housing, and social trends. In so doing he helped to nationalize cities, emphasizing common solutions to shared problems.

Herbert Hoover was one of the greatest men ever to hold the presidency. His mind ranged widely and brilliantly. He was a master organizer. He had won the devotion of millions with his famine relief and food conservation programs during and after World War I. His reputation as a mining engineer was unmatched. Daniel Guggenheim of the great mining syndicate offered Hoover a minimum salary of $500,000 a year and a share in the business if he would leave government service. Hoover refused.

The round-faced, youthful Hoover obviously cared nothing about piling up a great fortune. Already a millionaire, he donated his government salary to charity. What he did care about was applying his tremendous abilities to coordinating American life, so that individualism might flourish. Usually his efforts emphasized the voluntary and the cooperative, and only occasionally would he find controls necessary, as in the federal licensing of radio broadcast stations. Hoover's purpose boiled down to creating a social environment in which each individual could develop his fullest potential in constructive ways. Then the individual would use the fruits of his own development for his, and others', material and spiritual well-being. Individual health, safety, security, and home ownership all were essential to this vision of society.

Hoover's contributions to urban development have been largely overlooked. This is so because his detractors and his defenders have fired most of their ammunition attacking or supporting his philosophy and his handling of the Great Depression. Furthermore, Hoover himself did not see the cities as entities; rather, he saw them as parts of the social landscape. He implicitly believed in the nonmetropolitan basis for American uniqueness and individuality. Yet the American people were where one found them and, if many of them happened to be in cities, they were not thereby disqualified for assistance in realizing their individualism. Hoover's work in regulating the airlines and radio improved communications and transportation among cities. Radio, as regulated by the Department of Commerce until the Federal Radio Commission was established in 1927, spread urban values and concerns across the country. Much of Hoover's labor in the health care field benefited urban children. His road safety conferences stimulated urban planning.

Hoover's concern for adequate housing and slum clearance drew the federal government inexorably toward the subsidized housing of the New Deal and post-New Deal years. He established a Division of Building and Housing within the Commerce Department to improve, through research and publicity, all the phases of house and apartment building. The Housing Division published studies of site selection, building plans, and financing. Impressed with the antique provisions of some building codes, the sharp seasonality of the building industry, and the lack of standardization in construction, Hoover labored to change the situation. Hoover-sponsored conferences and private committees created a standard building code, smoothed out seasonal business cycles, and standardized building materials. Characteristically, Hoover established a parallel private association to promote home ownership.

While president, Hoover arranged a White House conference on housing. His opening address (December 2, 1931) assailed slums and the lack of adequate house financing. In a subsequent series of studies the conference laid bare the problems of housing in the United States. Once the Great Depression spurred him to direct federal action, he moved to save defaulting homeowners and the holders of their mortgages. Even before the conference on housing convened, he asked for a system of Home Loan Discount Banks. In essence Hoover proposed federal guarantees of mortgage loans to responsible borrowers. Congress passed a bill with more restrictions than Hoover liked during July, 1932, and the banks were functioning by early September. In 1932 Hoover secured Congressional authority for slum-clearance loans from the depression-born Reconstruction Finance Corporation. The loans were to be repaid by income generated from whatever public works replaced the slums.

Hoover's depression expedients had little effect on the housing situation. They came too late in his administration. Unfortunately they lend an air of tokenism and ineffectiveness to his entire housing program. Actually Hoover's Housing Division in the Commerce Department and his later conference on housing left valuable studies behind them. He had to eat a lot of words to ask for them, but his Home Loan Banks set a precedent for federal involvement in middle-class housing.

Hoover thought of his labors on behalf of zoning as merely an extension of his housing activities, but they assumed an independent significance. Zoning was an idea whose time had come. When Hoover's committee on zoning issued a standard state zoning enabling act in 1924, 22 million people lived under zoning. That was double the number in late 1921, when the committee began its work. Its publicity and interim reports probably helped push zoning along.

What is certain is that within a year after the committee ended its labors, 11 states had used the standard enabling act as the basis for their enabling legislation.

A second Hoover committee issued a preliminary standard city planning enabling act in 1927. This model act has been criticized for encouraging cities to plan in terms of the present, not possible future, situations. It has been charged with encouraging piecemeal planning under the false colors of "master" plans. The criticisms are well taken. However, they should not obscure Hoover's expressed concern for people who suffered from inadequate space and light because of failure to plan.

CITIES AND THE GREAT DEPRESSION

Hoover helped the cities during his battle against the Great Depression. Actions especially beneficial to urban areas were: encouraging private contributions to charitable organizations; distributing federal surplus materials and commodities at little or no cost; aiding businesses and banks through the Reconstruction Finance Corporation (RFC); and encouraging governors and mayors to increase their spending on public works. For his own part President Hoover actively sought federal public works funds from Congress.

Critics sometimes misunderstood or misconstrued Hoover's attitudes toward RFC loans. The beleaguered president has been accused of safeguarding the individualism of the poor by refusing to administer direct relief to them, while doling out money to the rich through the RFC. The criticism is wide of the mark. First, the RFC did much to save the metropolitan banking system. Second, Hoover cared little for banking executives as such. What he did care about was preserving the country's institutions, including its financial institutions. RFC largesse saved several urban banks, including Chicago's in the summer of 1932.

The Hoover approach to public works was less attuned to urban needs and of little help to the cities' staggering welfare loads. Hoover believed in the stabilization function of highways, dams, and bridges. That is, he conceived of public works spending taking up the slack in private construction during hard times. In his eagerness for increased municipal public works spending he failed to understand how deeply the cities were indebted. Most had bonded themselves to the hilt for public improvements during the sanguine twenties.

Hoover also was trapped by his insistence on productive public works. To him the only good public work was a self-liquidating public work, such as a toll bridge. Projects built for esthetic reasons, to create work, or for any other nonmonetary consideration violated his sense of economy and efficiency, which were his idols next to individualism itself. Unfortunately for Hoover's theory, cities were well endowed with productive, or self-liquidating, public works. Unfortunately, too, many men and women without building skills lost their jobs. Stimulating the construction industry might lead to their reemployment, or it might not.

For his own part Hoover increased federal public works spending from $307,000,000 in 1929 to $556,000,000 in 1932. He even swallowed his philosophy under extreme pressure from Congress. In July, 1932 he signed the Emergency Relief and Construction Act. This law provided $300,000,000 for loans through the RFC to states for direct relief and work relief. No state could claim more than 15 percent of the total funds authorized. Fewer than $20,000,000 could go directly to cities or counties, a proviso that made no significant contribution. In any case a state would have to show that it had exhausted its construction and relief funds, or that the community for which the money was destined was broke. The law's limitations, squabbling between the states and the RFC, and the usual bureaucracy added up to small accomplishment by the end of Hoover's term.

Detroit's depression agonies during the Hoover years exemplify the plight of industrial cities. Ironically Detroit was a kind of wonder child among metropolises. In 1910, when Henry Ford's revolutionary Model T was yet a fledgling, its population stood at 465,766. It was a large city by the standards of the day, but smaller than Boston, St. Louis, Pittsburgh, and several other places. By 1920 it just missed having a million souls and was the fourth largest city in the country. Ten years later it boasted a population of more than one and a half million, a gain of a million and more in a generation, drawn to Detroit by the giant automobile industry. By that time, too, the automobile industry was stagnant and Detroit was in deep trouble.

In 1930 the motor city's mayor was Frank Murphy, a handsome, curly-haired bachelor with towering political ambitions. Murphy was a dashing lady-killer. He led a bizarre night life featuring appearances at banquets and meetings with an entourage that included four police bodyguards and a wisecracking ex-prizefighter. He had a genius for publicity and made several grandstand plays involving municipal relief and debt refunding. He was not always appreciated. His tender regard for civil liberties in an era of increasing disorder led him to ask for spaces on public property where orators could denounce injustice without police interference. An exasperated city council placed one oratorical oasis on the lawn beneath Murphy's City Hall office.

For all his self-publicizing, Detroit's mayor sincerely cared for the disadvantaged and the dispossessed. His accomplishments in the face of plummeting revenues, an enormous fixed debt, recalcitrant bankers, and the absence of adequate outside assistance were remarkable. From the beginning Murphy had to make the most of his extremely limited maneuverability. When he took office Detroit's bonded debt was a huge $378,000,000, mostly the result of a public works program begun in the twenties to care for the booming population. Interest and debt retirement ate up so much of the budget that Murphy could not have begun any massive program of relief. At the beginning neither he nor anyone else thought it would be necessary. He asked the council for $25,000 for relief, especially work relief; asked city departments to study how they could use the unemployed; and established a Mayor's Unemployment Committee to coordinate the registration and placement of anyone out of work. He raised money for the needy privately, he urged the utilities to keep light and gas connected to the homes of the unemployed, and he gave as much business as possible to local firms to maintain employment.

By January, 1931 Murphy was reduced to a series of expedients. He cut back expenditures. He requested the aid of bankers in trimming expenses and loaning the city $5,000,000 to get by. Another $5,000,000 loan from the Ford Motor Company was needed before the end of the fiscal year. Unfortunately for Murphy, the city welfare department was shoddily run, and an investigation revealed petty welfare chiseling as well as serious misapplication of funds. In July, 1931 the city council responded to criticism, and to civic poverty, by cutting the welfare budget from $14,000,000 to $7,000,000. The unemployment committee helped to piece things out by maintaining homeless men in unused Fisher Body and Studebaker factories. It also allotted garden plots on vacant land.

With the Community Chest drive falling short of its goal the city was obviously in serious trouble as the fall of 1931 approached. It was then that Senator James Couzens, a brilliant, driven man, an ex-partner of Henry Ford, made a bombshell offer: he would grant $1,000,000 to welfare if other rich Detroiters would put up a total of $9,000,000. Although Murphy was a Democrat and Couzens a Republican, the two saw eye to eye on relief. Murphy called a meeting of the wealthy to explore Couzens' offer, but the wealthy let it be known that the Senator's suggestion was most unwelcome. Couzens donated $200,000 to an independent drive for funds to supplement the Community Chest and the Mayor's Unemployment Committee. There was grumbling over Couzens' show of independence, but Murphy counted the money ahead of bruised egos and set up the supplemental drive as Couzens wished. Murphy was amply rewarded when Couzens made other donations and bought street railway bonds at a time when they were a dubious investment at best.

By wintertime Murphy knew that the most diligent private fund raising and the most sincere conventional economy measures would not be enough. He then cut salaries and released workers from nonessential jobs, the art institute losing all of its expert staff in the process. He reduced jobs formerly considered essential to the point at which his health commissioner warned against further reductions in that department. Still it was not enough. Even though the city had lost about 10 percent of its population, Detroit's unemployed numbered 223,000. Only a quarter of these could be given relief payments. Money simply was not coming in. Murphy pushed up the tax rate but tax delinquencies—mostly unpaid property taxes—soared from $1,354,466 in fiscal 1929–1930 to just under $19,000,000 in fiscal 1931–1932. Heavy state-financed public works temporarily provided jobs and eased the situation that winter.

In the spring of 1932 the awful reality of Detroit's bonding spree of the twenties came home. More than a year before a syndicate of New York banks had agreed to pay all the city's obligations. Now Detroit owed the syndicate $27,000,000 out of a total $76,000,000 budget. Because of tax delinquencies only $57,000,000 was collectible. Deducting the money owed to the bankers left $30,000,000 to operate the city. Under pressure from the banks Murphy and the council, after some recrimination, cut city salaries again, this time by 50 percent for May and June. Other expedients, including advance tax payments and deep cuts in welfare, helped keep the city afloat.

By this time Murphy was convinced that cities and states could not cope with the depression and that the federal government would have to aid the cities directly with as little folderol as possible. To put pressure on the reluctant Hoover, he called a conference of Michigan mayors to meet in May, 1932. The conference appealed for a $5,000,000,000 federal grant to restore prosperity, then endorsed a national conference of mayors to meet in Detroit the next month. Murphy's invitations went to the mayors of all cities with populations exceeding 100,000. The second conference, which was the foundation of the later United States Conference of Mayors, also endorsed federal depression relief.

The Detroit conventions contributed to the pressure forcing the Hoover administration to propose what became the Emergency Relief and Construction Act of July, 1932. Murphy had already drawn up a budget presuming on a heavy contribution from the RFC. After some wrangling with the Republican governor, Murphy won his endorsement of Detroit's needs. From September, 1932 the RFC virtually picked up the check for Detroit's welfare expenditures. The city might have pulled through on the strength of federal and state aid, but Michigan's banks were tottering. In February, 1933 the governor closed them rather than undergo a wave of bank suspensions. The immediate effect was little better. Everybody's bank assets were frozen. Detroit could not pay its employees. It defaulted on its bonds. It issued scrip. Tax delinquencies were 40 percent and rising. Unemployment topped 40 percent. Murphy, an exceptionally resourceful mayor and a game man, had played out his string.

Throughout his unequal struggle with the Great Depression the doughty Detroiter clung to his liberal principles. In March, 1932 the police of suburban Dearborn fired on a group of hunger marchers at the gates of the Ford Motor Company. Murphy sympathized. The march had begun in Detroit, escorted in a friendly manner by Detroit police. The Detroit police guarded the funeral cortege of the four dead marchers, too, this time without clubs to emphasize nonviolence. There was occasional violence in Detroit involving the police, but the police did not fire into crowds. Murphy, although pressed by a thousand things, worked hard to keep violence from breaking out in difficult law enforcement situations.

Murphy stood by black municipal workers although it would have been easier to fire them. When unemployed whites demanded the firing of black garbage collectors, Murphy replied that whites refused to collect garbage in good times, leaving the job to blacks. In return for doing a dirty job the blacks received security, and Murphy would have it no other way. The mayor's action took on added significance because of the poignancy of Detroit blacks' depression situation. Blacks were four percent of the population but one-fourth of the welfare cases. Black municipal workers were dismissed during economy drives, but those job losses were related to financial hardship, not race.

Murphy's efforts were creditable. He was simply overwhelmed. So were most other mayors. Only some massive national action would save the situation for them. The new Democratic administration was pledged to both saving and reconstructing the cities and their populations, although in the early thirties the commitment was not phrased in those words. The New Deal's aid to cities spread over many areas but three—relief and reconstruction, housing, and the study of urban problems—were unusually significant.

Before we examine the Roosevelt administration's contributions in these areas, a word about the criticisms of the ebullient president and his New Deal. It is true that the New Deal programs were sometimes insufficient and sometimes ineptly designed. It is true that Roosevelt, an exceedingly complex man, was sometimes as calloused and deceitful as he was candid, sympathetic, and humane. Such criticisms matter more in retrospect than they do in an emergency. In 1933 something like one-fourth of the country's work force was unemployed. Stories of people grubbing for food in garbage pails usually produce impatience or boredom in readers, for after all, somebody somewhere is grubbing for food in a garbage pail right now. But in 1933 hundreds of people subsisted that way in every industrial city of the country. The magnitude of the thing was disheartening. So was the plight of an individual sufferer, the woman who telephoned Frank Murphy to ask how or where should she have her baby, now that Detroit could no longer pay for welfare maternity cases at the hospital.

It was true that Roosevelt's solutions did not differ so much from the position that Hoover had assumed by the fall of 1932. Yet there were crucial differences between the two men. Beneath his insouciance Roosevelt was determined to prevail over the Great Depression, while Hoover had exhausted his personal resources. Roosevelt was unafraid of using government power for humane ends while Hoover stuck at what were, for him, grave philosophical and national questions. Roosevelt was a superb leader in a crisis; Hoover longed for normality. Roosevelt was eager to govern; Hoover yearned to administer.

The temperamental differences made for distinctions of substance as well as of style. Thin, wisecracking Harry Hopkins headed three agencies that were better funded and more openhanded than anything created under Hoover. The Federal Emergency Relief Administration (FERA) was established in May, 1933 with $500,000,000 in grants, not loans. Half of this money was to be funneled through the states to cities and towns wherever Hopkins saw the greatest need. The other half was to be granted on a matching basis, one federal dollar for every three from states and localities. Because of animosity toward the tough hyperactive Hopkins, or because of state obstructionism, politics, or other reasons, the FERA administrations did not always hit it off with state relief agencies. Hopkins carried a generous heart in his emaciated frame, and he hated to see the unemployed caught in the middle and not receiving aid. Sometimes he federalized the relief process within a state to bypass recalcitrant governors or legislatures. In one way or another the unemployed were helped. From 1933 until its expiration late in 1935, the FERA provided direct relief (and some work relief), much of it in cities.

Hopkins was unhappy with the basic thrust of the FERA program from the beginning. He opposed direct dole relief programs no matter how well they were dressed up to preserve individual dignity. Relief granted without work in return, he believed, eventually undermined self-respect. Besides, the Public Works Administration under cautious Harold L. Ickes was moving too slowly toward its goal of reemployment through federally financed construction.

To head off an unemployment calamity during the winter of 1933–1934 Hopkins persuaded Roosevelt to establish a second agency, the Civil Works Administration, by executive order. The CWA was entirely federally controlled although most of the FERA staff and state relief officials worked for the CWA in a dual capacity. The CWA paid a minimum wage, hiring half reliefers and half unemployed who were not at the moment on the relief rolls. It built, among other things, 40,000 schools and 1000 airports. It assisted with other construction, educational, and artistic programs. At Christmas the infusion of CWA funds set off a mild urban retail boom. By the middle of January 4,230,000 workers were signed up with the CWA. Roosevelt, afraid of costs and a permanent make-work army, liquidated the CWA in the late winter and spring of 1935. The FERA finished out the CWA's work relief projects. By the end of 1935 organized federal relief, including administrative expenses, had cost more than $2,904,000,000 under the New Deal. State and local contributions were almost $1,200,000,000 more.

Hopkins' third and most extraordinary agency was the Works Progress Administration, established by the Emergency Relief Appropriation Act of April, 1935. With that act the federal government retired from the field of direct relief, leaving it to cities and states. In its stead the WPA inaugurated a massive work relief program for unemployed, ablebodied people in many fields, with many levels of skill. The WPA carried on construction projects of the CWA variety, the so-called "light" public works requiring little equipment investment. The Federal Theatre (voted out by Congress in 1939) produced a variety of shows in cities, towns, and rural areas. Most of the more sophisticated drama appeared in urban theaters. The projects for unemployed writers gathered local, state, and regional history, folklore, and memorabilia of all sorts. Unemployed writers fanned out across the country in search of materials but were almost always headquartered in cities.

The WPA's record in public works is more easily cataloged than its theatrical productions, its archival labors, its several artistic and musical activities. It built, improved, or repaired more than 125,000 public buildings; 650,000 miles of roads, streets, and highways, 8000 parks and a large miscellany of other improvements. Some of these were substantial construction projects scarcely distinguishable from the PWA's "heavy" construction. From its inception until its termination in 1943 the WPA spent some $11,000,000,000. It employed 8,500,000 people, spending 85 percent of its money on their wages and salaries.

The Public Works Administration, also directly involved with the urban scene, never became embroiled in the charges of waste and inefficiency that swirled about the Hopkins programs. This was partly because of its different character. Committed neither to relief nor to rapid reemployment, the PWA was designed to stimulate the construction industry and the industries linked to construction. It would entail growing employment and would replenish a public estate becoming shabbier with each passing depression year. PWA projects were contract projects, and that meant laborious screening, checking, and accounting.

The PWA moved slowly, too, because its administrator feared waste, corruption, and the attendant scandals. Harold L. Ickes was a suspicious, irascible, hardworking man who believed that much of humankind overflowed with deceit and ill will. He acted accordingly. Although his caution slowed the PWA, when it did get underway it gave a creditable performance. While spending four and a quarter billion dollars, Ickes oversaw the construction of important projects. New York's Triborough Bridge, Kansas City's fine municipal auditorium, and the buildings for the University of Washington (at Seattle) were among its urban projects.

A look at Detroit's experience with the relief and reconstruction agencies puts the New Deal's vast effort in focus. When FERA funds moved into Detroit they were, as elsewhere, channeled through the state upon the governor's certification of need. The need required little proof. During the second half of 1933, FERA funds went to a total of 379,325 separate cases in Detroit and surrounding Wayne County. The caseload peaked in November, 1934 at 72,629. Nineteen thirty-four also saw the largest number of separate cases, 589,987, with a monthly average of 209,843 people receiving relief. The impact of the FERA may be gauged by the agency's contribution to the Detroit-Wayne County relief budget, more than $52,262,700 of a total just under $64,600,000.

During the winter of 1933–1934 the CWA pumped almost $14,000,000 into Detroit, about $10,200,000 for wages alone. By employing 41,803 in the city and another 14,000 in the county, the CWA took up some serious unemployment slack. A brighter economic picture in the spring of 1934 enabled some CWA workers to return to private jobs even before the program ended in March. As the CWA passed from the scene, FERA work relief increased, rehabilitating the electric utility and the street railways, and repairing libraries. White collar projects included a housing survey. Since wages were low, the FERA sometimes had to continue direct relief to workers with large families.

Although the FERA operated in Detroit through December, 1935, the WPA took over more and more work relief responsibility after July of that year. As it did elsewhere the WPA hired employables, returning unemployables to state and local care. By 1938 the WPA and its predecessors were responsible for 63 miles of new sewers, 21 miles of new sidewalk, 100 miles of new street lighting, and thousands of new trees in the park system. Art, music and theater projects were popular, as was the Detroit WPA Sewing Project. In 1940 the Sewing Project employed 2600 women who made 5000 garments daily for Wayne County's welfare recipients.

None of this ought to suggest that the New Deal relief and reconstruction agencies solved urban problems. Underemployment continued. The WPA carried 13,239 on its Detroit rolls as late as March, 1942 despite the military draft and a roaring war boom. Detroit was as strapped financially at the beginning of 1942 as it had been at the end of 1932. Indeed it cared for its own welfare cases after the spring of 1938 only because the WPA waived the city's 15 percent contribution to work relief projects. In 1940 federal construction shifted to defense facilities. Under the new emphasis the WPA refurbished or rebuilt still more urban airports and defense-related facilities, but the concern for civilian improvements was past.

What the New Deal did accomplish was to keep some of the urban labor force in place and working. It greatly improved the urban capital estate while helping millions retain a sense of dignity and usefulness. More than that, it usually strengthened local governments because it pumped so much money through them. Urban officials who were in charge of work relief hiring discovered a new source of patronage. To get a good job or a contract it helped to know somebody. The New Deal funneled its money through boss-ruled urban machines, assisting them along with the rest.

The idea that the New Deal actually aided urban machines would have been fantastic to city-watchers of the post-World War II generation. They adhered to what has been called the "Last Hurrah thesis," after its statement in Edwin O'Connor's poignant novel, *The Last Hurrah* (1956). The urban machine, so says the "Last Hurrah" argument, was really a social welfare system. The New Deal displaced the traditional machine boss by conferring federal welfare favors, especially social security and unemployment insurance, upon his constituency. While the aged clung to the boss from loyalty, the young turned their eyes toward Washington. In a few years mortality diminished the boss's following to a shadow. Scholars have seconded the novelist, adding that perhaps the machine still performed a minor role—steering the ignorant to the proper federal welfare office.

The "Last Hurrah" argument simply does not touch the real world at any point. Its chief value lies in demonstrating how little some people know about the way the New Deal worked. The critical New Deal welfare programs were not unemployment and social security anyway; they were the FERA, the CWA, and the WPA. Next, they were adminstered on the state and local level by state and local people. The funds came from the federal government, true, but they were dispensed through the existing machinery of urban government. This was so even in a wholly federal program such as the CWA. In the case of the CWA, for instance, state and local officials already involved with relief and construction were given federal titles and federal money. Few state and local officials forgot that they owed their positions, not to the New Deal, but to the state or local political organization to which they belonged. And they made certain that the men and women who enjoyed relief benefits saw their relief coming from local government, and not from far-off Washington. Hiring and firing, after all, occurred at the grass roots.

Far from destroying a machine, the New Deal helped to create a powerful Democratic organization in Pittsburgh. Before the New Deal the steel city Democrats composed a shadow party. Their major function was supporting the machine Republicans in their factional disputes with reform Republicans. In return the Democrats garnered a good share of the patronage. In 1933, however, Pittsburgh Democrats rode to victory on the Great Depression issue and Roosevelt's coattails.

Sadly for the budding Democratic organization it had chosen an eccentric, erratic single-taxer for its mayoral candidate. William N. McNair's arbitrary appointments and dismissals and worst of all, his antagonism toward federal work relief, quickly alienated organization support. The mayor's hatred of New Deal welfare sprang from a belief in the sterner virtues and limited government, and from jealous opposition to any program he could not control. McNair regularly vetoed the ordinances required for Pittsburgh's participation in the New Deal programs, while impatient councilmen just as regularly overrode the vetoes. In 1936 McNair and his council reached an impasse. The volatile mayor resigned.

From then on the regular Democratic organization used the WPA for patronage. Insignificant jobs might be given to anybody in need of work, but many supervisory positions went to Democratic ward committeemen. Owners of trucks and construction equipment had to clear through the organization before they could rent their machines to the WPA. Some WPA workers were almost certainly assessed for Democratic election funds. Others electioneered on behalf of the Democrats. Although the WPA alone does not explain the triumph of the Democratic machine, the sudden appearance of thousands of Democratically controlled jobs gave it an invaluable impetus. Under the astute David L. Lawrence the new Democratic organization controlled Pittsburgh politics for the next 30 years.

New Deal programs were highly useful to the established Pendergast machine in Kansas City. From the beginning Thomas J. Pendergast sensed Roosevelt's grass-roots popularity and was with him. Pendergast maintained his early interest in F.D.R. behind a facade of support for a favorite son. The Missouri delegation to the 1932 Democratic national convention went for the favorite son on the first ballot. The boss then began to dribble votes to Roosevelt, helping F. D. R.'s total rise from ballot to ballot.

Roosevelt recognized his obligation to Pendergast. The paunchy boss secured a pardon for an associate who had been convicted on a federal lottery charge. Important appointments, including Harry S Truman's as state director of Federal Re-employment, were made from Pendergast's political friends. The CWA and the WPA offered Pendergast-controlled jobs and local opportunities to use Pendergast's Ready-Mixed Concrete. Moreover, the WPA enabled the Kansas Citian to consolidate his hold on the Democratic party in Missouri. Harry Hopkins appointed Kansas City's director of public works, a loyal Pendergast man, to be the director of federal public works in the state. The appointment opened highly desirable jobs to Pendergast supporters on a statewide basis. WPA district directors and other supervisors urged WPA employees—in some cases coerced them—to vote for candidates endorsed by Pendergast.

The New Deal aided Democratic machines in Kansas City and Pittsburgh certainly, and elsewhere, probably. But before we rush to embrace a new wisdom—that the New Deal revivified urban machines—some qualifications are in order. First, Roosevelt's recognition of Pendergast was because both men were Democrats and that Pendergast was a Roosevelt man. Roosevelt would not have done personal and patronage favors for Pendergast had he been a Republican. The president did not endorse urban machines as such, for he had battled Tammany during his New York political rise. Party, not a common view of government, bound the aristocratic New Yorker to the Middle Western son of Irish immigrants.

Second, the New Deal welfare programs worked with state and local organizations whatever their politics. Hopkins, a realist and humanitarian, handed patronage to Democrats when he could, and when they handled federal funds with reasonable efficiency. But he did not insist that Republicans become Democrats before receiving federal aid. Republicans played politics with WPA, too. Lorena Hickok, one of Hopkins' field representatives, recorded the anguished cries of Democrats out of office who saw juicy plums going to entrenched Republicans. In a word, the New Deal strengthened local politics whatever its morality or political coloration.

Third, the New Deal represented the drastic growth of the central government. It would be too much to say that the power of subordinate government and of individuals diminished in proportion to the growing power of the federal government. Yet the federal government exercised control and oversight of people's lives unprecedented in peacetime. Personally and politically corrupt as he was, Pendergast held sway in Kansas City and probably would not have been overturned despite the efforts of a small, militant band of local reformers. What downed Pendergast was a federal investigation of his income tax evasion and other illegal activities. In 1939 the boss was tried, convicted, fined, and sent to federal prison. In 1940 his machine buckled under the weight of the amazing corruption revealed during the federal investigation and trial. A reform slate swept into office, although the federal government helped to put the reformers in power just as surely as it had helped Pendergast.

Fourth and finally, the existence of machines seems to be tied to urban circumstances relatively constant from 1915 to 1945. Immigrants had to be acclimated, utilities had to be extended, the destitute and unemployed cared for, and important economic interests appeased or at least not antagonized. Merely electing good men to office or tinkering with governmental machinery was never enough to do the job. A hard-working, loyal, and (to some degree) self-interested organization was required in every city: to cut red tape, to enforce departmental cooperation, to mobilize votes in council or at the polls. The New Deal strengthened all such organizations, whether, like La Guardia's, they were fundamentally honest or, like Pendergast's, they were not.

Compared with relief and welfare programs, New Deal housing had a lesser but significant impact on cities. Its chief value was in building the foundation for the great housing boom of the post-World

War II period. National legislation proved a boon to urban middle-class homeowners, to housing contractors, and to mortgage lending institutions such as insurance companies, banks, and savings and loan associations. The Home Owners Loan Corporation, created by the Home Owners Refinancing Act of June, 1933 exchanged its own bonds for existing debts on houses. The HOLC refunded a million mortgages before its program ended in mid-1936. It also advanced money for taxes, maintenance, and repair of homes.

The Federal Housing Administration, offspring of the National Housing Act of June, 1934, insured residential mortgages. The process by which the FHA and related agencies insured home mortgages was somewhat complicated, but the effects of their operations were unmistakable. After a slow beginning the FHA was insuring some 35 percent of all new house mortgages between 1938 and 1941. FHA insurance amounted to guaranteed incomes for lending agencies, encouraging lower interest rates, lower down payments, and lengthier, amortized mortgages. Before the FHA would insure a loan, it required the mortgaged property to meet certain minimum requirements regarding construction details, room size, and materials. The agency's standards were generally well enforced.

The FHA's influence extended beyond the mortgages it insured. FHA housing requirements helped to raise construction standards for all houses. Low interest rates on FHA mortgages discouraged high rates on other mortgages. Long-term mortgages under the FHA encouraged long-term conventional mortgages. They relieved many homeowners of the necessity of a second mortgage at sometimes exorbitant rates of interest.

All this, however, was for people who could afford houses to begin with. For those who could not, the National Industrial Recovery Act of 1933 placed the "construction, reconstruction, alteration or repair . . . of low-rent housing and slum clearance projects" under the PWA. The PWA built 21,769 public housing units under the NIRA provisions. Despite the government's direct involvement in low rent housing, professional housers were far from pleased. First, the PWA program emphasized economic recovery and reemployment, not housing. Housing was merely a means, not an end in itself. For years progressive housers including Edith Wood and Catherine Bauer had argued against the old reformist priorities in housing—sanitary regulations and enforced codes. Private enterprise was uninterested in housing that returned little or no profit; since local governments lacked the resources, only the federal government could do the job.

Second, the PWA's 20,000 units scarcely mattered when measured

against the housers' 1935 estimate—nine million federally subsidized homes required to decently house low-income families during the next 10 years. There were several reasons why the PWA built
so few units. Ickes was cautious, careful, and slow with housing as
with other construction projects. Adverse federal court decisions
forced the PWA to shift its legal gears and work out new relationships with the local housing authorities actually in charge of the projects. President Roosevelt, anxious for a good showing on the unemployment front, shifted funds from the PWA to Hopkins' more
active agencies.

Private study and pressure groups such as the National Public
Housing Conference found a champion in Senator Robert F. Wagner
of New York. Wagner, himself a slum product, was a tireless, undog-
matic urban liberal involved with a broad range of humane concerns.
From early 1935 through the summer of 1937 Wagner fought for a
federal housing bill. He struggled through a thicket of opposition
including the National Association of Real Estate Boards and other
private groups, rural-based Congressmen who saw nothing for their
constituents in urban slum clearance and housing, friends of federal
housing who wrangled over procedural and administrative details,
and (for most of his fight) lukewarm backing from President Roosevelt.

As finally enacted, the National Housing Act of 1937 created the
United States Housing Authority in the Interior Department, empowered to loan 90 percent of the cost of slum clearance and housing
projects to local housing authorities. Rents were to be held to low-income levels through a system of federal and local subsidies. By the
end of 1940 the Housing Authority had 161,162 units under contract;
from then on most of its effort involved defense housing. The
Wagner housing act and the work done under it were limited, of
course. But the federal government had made a basic commitment to
housing for its own sake. Decent dwellings for urban populations
were from that time forward a recognized, if unfulfilled, national
goal.

The relief, reconstruction, and housing activities of the New Deal
directly assisted one group that the Roosevelt administration has
been accused of slighting—urban blacks. Both Hopkins and Ickes
were concerned about the especially depressed condition of blacks,
and made special efforts to help them. Hopkins did not solve the
problem of blacks, any more than he solved any other problems. He
did issue an order banning discrimination on any grounds, and pres-
sured local authorities to comply. Hopkins and his top aides, white

and black, were able to enforce his order well enough to give blacks WPA jobs in greater numbers than their proportion in the whole population.

Blacks did especially well in highly urbanized states, as in New York where 18 percent of the WPA workers came from a black population only 4.5 percent of the total. Even in southern cities blacks did well. In Baltimore the WPA hired 53 percent of its workers from a black population of 19 percent; in New Orleans it hired 56 percent black from a population 30 percent black. Before we grow too ecstatic over these figures we should know that rural blacks and black women, especially in the south, found WPA jobs difficult to obtain. Although he tried, Hopkins was unable to stop the southern practice of turning blacks off WPA rolls at harvest time. Nor did he halt discrimination on major urban projects in the north and middle west. Discrimination there was sometimes insidious, as permitting the hiring of blacks while keeping them at menial tasks unrelated to their skills.

Of course Hopkins *could* have stopped discrimination. The price he would have paid for the organizational shakeups in the politically sensitive WPA may easily be imagined. It would have been possible for affronted bigots and demagogues to join with conservatives to undermine the WPA. Hopkins' impetuosity could have destroyed his mutually beneficial relationships with local politicians. Hopkins was no coward, but he was always the realist. On balance he did as much for blacks as any terribly overworked, politically vulnerable white man could have been expected to do.

Harold Ickes was both more alert to blacks' problems and more able to aid them than was Hopkins. Ickes controlled the contract work under his WPA; therefore he could enforce nondiscrimination by writing compliance clauses into those contracts. Just how this could be done was at first something of a problem. It was one thing to issue an order against discrimination, quite another to enforce it. One contractor protested that a single Negro bricklayer out of 122 working on a post office building was evidence of his nondiscrimination! As Robert Weaver, one of Ickes' black aides, described it, the solution lay in discovering "a criterion which is *prima facie* evidence of discrimination." [2]

The solution proved to be this: requiring a contractor to pay black workers a proportion of his total payroll that bore some relationship to black representation in the labor force at large. The requirement

[2] Raymond Wolters, *Negroes and the Great Depression*, Greenwood, Westport, Connecticut, 1970, p. 201.

was enforced in public housing projects because the PWA was directly a party to the contracts. The proportion an individual contractor was required to pay varied from 50 to more than 100 percent of the proportion of blacks to total laborers. Local conditions determined the percentage of pay going to blacks.

In Montgomery, Alabama, the ratio was 50 percent. The occupational census of 1930 showed 42 percent of skilled workers to be black; therefore Montgomery contractors were required to pay 21 percent of their skilled payroll to blacks. In Washington, D. C., 12.5 percent of skilled workers were blacks, and contractors had to pay 12.5 percent of their payrolls to blacks. The United States Housing Authority continued the practice when it assumed the PWA's housing work. It also continued to build housing projects for blacks.

Ickes' ingenious aid to black laborers was certainly no panacea. Not only was it limited to housing projects, it was confined to keeping black employment near a predepression ratio to white employment. Ickes did not attempt to expand minority employment. That would have been foolhardy at a time when unemployed white workers were insisting on the right to displace working blacks.

In sum, neither Hopkins nor Ickes saved blacks from the depression. They could not, or at least did not, compensate for an unemployment rate three times as high among blacks as among whites. But they did do more than help blacks simply because they were helping poor people and blacks happened also to be poor. They realized that blacks had special problems and they tried to meet them. That they succeeded in even a small degree, and especially in cities, warrants a measure of praise.

Ickes' and Hopkins' aid to blacks raises a larger question of the relationship between the votes of urban minorities and the programs of the New Deal. Urban America voted Democratic in most national elections during the thirties and forties, a phenomenon well known to New Dealers who cut several of their programs to fit the electoral cloth. Nor was the urban vote lost on scholars, who pointed to the importance of city votes in articles written during the thirties and forties. By 1950 political scientists accepted the fact that the Democrats would have lost the elections of 1940, 1944, and 1948 had their pluralities in the 12 largest cities gone against them instead. Or, to put it another way, the city vote stayed firmly Democratic when the nonurban vote began drifting to the Republicans after 1936.

In his brilliant *The Future of American Politics*, published in 1952, the journalist and political analyst Samuel Lubell gave a captivating explanation of the "Roosevelt Revolution" in American politics. The huge Democratic urban votes of the thirties, Lubell wrote, were preceded by an "Al Smith Revolution" in 1928, when the submerged ethnic voters of the big cities gave a plurality to Smith, a consummate ethnic politician. Smith's appeal to the ethnic minorities, mostly politically apathetic eastern and southern Europeans, brought them into the Democratic party ahead of the Great Depression. The depression was a shock piled on the ethnics' continuing trauma of low-paid, sweaty jobs and severely limited opportunity. Roosevelt capitalized on both the depression and Smith's earlier appeal to swing even more ethnics into the Democratic column.

Only after 1933 did the true "Roosevelt Revolution" begin. Lubell singled out 1935, a year of extraordinary social legislation, as the "year of decision." In 1935 two more urban groups joined the Democratic coalition—the poorer native whites and the blacks. Ethnic antagonisms and a commitment to individualism explained the native whites' aloofness. But hard times, rising class consciouness, and the Rooseveltian reforms brought them around in 1935. Blacks were traditionally Republican, but the Democratic commitment to social reform in the midthirties brought them into camp. Expressed numerically, the shift in the 12 largest cities was from Republican pluralities of 1,638,000 in 1920 and 1,252,000 in 1924 to Democratic pluralities of 38,000 in 1928; 1,910,000 in 1932, and 3,608,000 in 1936. For the remaining Roosevelt elections the Democratic plurality stayed comfortably above two million.

Lubell's persuasive reasoning stood unchallenged for several years. In the meanwhile scholars studied the complex partisan responses of urban voters to issues and candidates, both local and national. They used computers and sophisticated analytical techniques. The returns from their quantitative studies are not all in, but it is fair to say that Lubell's conclusions have been modified or even disproven. Yet Lubell's book remains the baseline of urban political study, and generalizations from the new findings have to refer to Lubell.

The political apathy and herd voting that Lubell and other commentators have seen in ethnic minorities is more imaginary than real. From at least the time of World War I, Eastern European minorities voted in numbers comparable to the native whites'. They voted with as much discrimination, too. Urban Italians voted against Wilson, and not for Harding or against Cox, largely because of their unhappiness over the World War I peace settlement. Other ethnics voted for Harding because—although this hypothesis is yet to be tested— they were angry about the inflation, unemployment, and social disorder following the war. Historians have been so mesmerized by Wilson's internationalism and Harding's ineptitude that they have been slow to understand the operation, on low-income people especially, of Wilson's failure to plan for wartime homefront dislocations and for reconversion.

Once urban ethnics were in the Republican fold there was little except habit to keep them there. The Republican party's refusal to recognize its urban-ethnic support has to be one of the colossal failures of American politics. Thus the ethnics began drifting, slowly at first, to the Democratic party. The reasons for the gradual realignment were the Republicans' identification with Prohibition and immigration restriction, continued ethnic use of the Democratic party to achieve individual and group success, and the Democrats' dawning awareness of the new ethnic vote in the cities.

Although Al Smith did wrench some ethnic voters away from the Republican party, there are three important qualifications on Lubell's "Al Smith Revolution." First, Smith's revolution was geographically confined, to the heavily Catholic, immigrant northeast. Elsewhere Catholics and people of recent immigrant stock voted for him, but there was no sudden lurch to Smith. Instead Smith's candidacy masked another step in the urban masses' long, slow walk away from the Republican party. Second, in Pittsburgh, San Francisco, and possibly other cities, Robert M. La Follette's 1924 Progressive presidential candidacy lured some immigrants. La Follette helped to wean them from Republicanism on the national level, at least. Third, the Smith candidacy did not set up the urban masses for F. D. R.; the depression did that. In several cities people who were trending toward the Democrats nationally stayed with the Republicans locally through 1930.

The sluggishness of city Democratic organizations as compared with the national party helps to explain why urban blacks remained in the Republican party as long as they did. The political situation of blacks in those cities where they could vote was much more desperate than that of immigrant-stock whites. Although the incredibly smug Republicans increasingly ignored them, blacks received no encouragement from the Democrats. Some bolted for Smith in 1928, more for Roosevelt in 1932, but despite hard times most northern blacks stayed with Hoover.

Black bias for Republicans may be explained by Roosevelt's failure to commit himself to blacks during the 1932 campaign. But afterward black preference began to change. The relief programs helped blacks because they were poor, while Ickes and Hopkins recognized blacks' special problems. Urban black leaders had jumped from Republican to Democratic as early as 1928, but defections to the Democrats increased after 1932. Some time around late 1933 or early 1934 the Democratic party made a momentous decision: to go after the urban

Negro vote whatever the consequences.

This is not to say that the decision was fully rationalized, but the national Democrats recognized to some degree that they were changing their party's old-time biases forever. Either they decided that Southern Democrats would not bolt the party if it recognized blacks, or that if Southern Democrats did desert, their defection would not matter so long as the northern urbanites stayed Democratic. Local Democratic organizations could not long resist these pressures, nor, after having their eyes opened to the advantages of the Negro bloc vote, did they want to. Well before the social legislation of 1935, then, blacks began going Democratic. Roosevelt exploited the new ties in 1936 with special references to blacks, and by spotlighting Ickes, whose problack sentiments were well known.

How poorer urban native whites behaved electorally is not well understood. It may be true, as Lubell suggested, that they withheld their commitment to F. D. R. until 1936. In any case it is clear that by 1936 the Democratic party was the party of the urban masses. In several ways the New Deal had nationalized the cities: by recognizing urban problems to be national problems, by dealing with national problems in urban settings, and by appealing, nationwide, to the special interests of urban voters.

Apart from depression crises and partisan cannonading, the New Deal intensified the federal study of urban problems. The Federal Housing Administration, for instance, published guides to homeowning and examined successful suburbs. The United States Housing Authority publicized housers' findings about the heavy drain of slum areas on urban budgets for such items as police and fire protection and public health services. Much of the publication (and exhortation) about urban conditions and their possible improvement came from a curious, relatively little known agency, the National Resources Planning Board.

The administrative history of the NRPB is quickly told. It was originally established in 1933 as the National Planning Board of the Public Works Administration. In 1934 Roosevelt moved it from the PWA and rechristened it the National Resources Board. The next year, under authority of the emergency relief act, it became the National Resources Committee. From 1939 until Congress forced its expiration in 1943 the NRPB, again renamed, was part of the Executive Office. Among the reasons for the administrative convolutions were convenience and a desire to protect the board from charges of planning for centralized control of the nation's resources.

The NRPB and its subcommittees were the first federal agencies continuously surveying the total resources of the nation. They were the first to plan for their long-range conservation. The NRPB concentrated on water resources and land use, but it concerned itself with Americans and their environment wherever they lived, cities included. Its urban-related studies included publications on city government, slum clearance, and urban renewal. By far the most significant publication was the 1937 report of the NRPB's Urbanism Committee, *Our Cities: Their Role in the National Economy.*

Our Cities was the product of leading urbanists, Louis Brownlow and Louis Wirth among them. In its pages they explicitly stated that urban problems were national problems requiring consciously directed national efforts for their solution. The rapid urbanization of the United States, they argued, was coincident with its national maturity. Most goods, services, wages, and salaries were produced within the country's metropolitan areas, and that situation was likely to intensify in future years. Therefore saving the cities was practically synonymous with saving the country.

As a book *Our Cities* was a review, not just of the cities' economies, but of urban history, sociology, pathology, and land use. It noted the phenomenon of merging at urban fringes, later called conurbation. It concluded with recommendations for upgrading urban governments, services, and the quality of city life with national assistance. *Our Cities*, with its earnest prose and pictographs, now seems a little quaint. Its quaintness should not obscure the fact that in 1937 the federal government placed its imprint on a call to see cities in a new light, as a national responsibility.

During World War II the NRPB stimulated postwar urban planning. Some of its inspiration was indirect, its publications helping to fuel homegrown redevelopment projects. In three cities—Corpus Christi, Texas, Salt Lake City, and Tacoma, Washington, it had a direct impact. The three agreed to demonstrate a new planning technique for cities of 50,000 to half a million population. The technique boiled down to drafting a comprehensive, long-range plan in minimum time with the aid of a federal consultant. When drafted, the plan should reflect the desires of various civic, social, and economic groups within each city.

Its new technique, the NRPB believed, was suited to smaller cities lacking the staff organization for effective planning. The rationale was valid, but the results were ordinary. Just as planners had done in the past, the federal consultants worked with established interest groups such as the chambers of commerce. The procedure might have produced something startling in the long run. But Congress was increasingly dubious of federal activities not related in some way to the war effort, especially those activities capable of producing startling results. In 1943 it refused to fund the NRPB. The first continuous national planning agency expired.

The discussion of New Deal initiatives on the urban scene should not suggest an end to traditional federal aids. On the contrary, many of them were greatly expanded. The New Deal pumped new life into the federal airport program. Its increased intervention in labor-management relations impinged on urban life. The post office department turned more and more to air service as the answer to the interurban communications problem. Important as the traditional activities were, however, they were subordinate to a new spirit in federal-urban relations. Once and for all the New Deal was done with reliance on traditional federal aids and with sympathetically encouraging cities to solve their own problems. The New Deal, sometimes knowingly, sometimes willy-nilly, had committed the country to vitalizing the cities.

CITIES AND WAR

After 1941, when, in Roosevelt's phrase, "Dr. Win-the-War" replaced "Dr. New Deal" the nationalizing trend continued. During the war the basic responsibility for assuring racial peace and public order in large cities fell to the federal government. This is much clearer in retrospect than it was at the time, when immediate wartime concerns obscured the shadows of coming events. Indeed, the government appeared to flee from its new responsibilities, only to be overtaken in the end.

The domestic racial crisis of World War II was primarily located in the cities. Here black and white war workers jostled one another on the streets, for jobs, and for inadequate housing. Black soldiers from nearby military installations frequently came to town. Because most army posts were in the South, "town" was often a Southern city where local whites tried to enforce Southern codes of racial accommodation on northern blacks. After hundreds of incidents during the summer of 1942 the War Department took steps to improve the morale of black troops, although off-post discrimination continued. The wartime urban race problem was less tractable. The situation in the cities was a compound of white economic insecurity, black eagerness for jobs after blacks' especially severe depression experience, and irrational superstitions on both sides. During 1943 it surfaced again and again. In Los Angeles and elsewhere mobs of whites in uniform attacked black civilians wearing exaggerated "zoot" suits. In Mobile, Alabama white shipyard workers struck and rioted four days in protest against promoting black workers. Federal troops restored order, but the riot so cowed the Federal Fair Employment Practices Commission that it let Mobile's shipyards remain segregated.

Black organizations grew more militantly angry as the FEPC buckled under violence and threats of violence from the white supremacist organizations springing up in the war plants. Extreme pressure from blacks, including threats of a march on Washington, brought a May, 1943 Executive Order making nondiscrimination mandatory in war contracts. Roosevelt's order did not dampen seething Detroit. There, more than half a million white and black defense workers jammed into a city unable to cope with the influx. The races carried rumors about one another, traded insults, and fought minor skirmishes.

When a riot broke out at an amusement park on a June Sunday, there was plenty of emotional fuel to carry it across the city. Burning, looting, gunplay, and beatings continued into Monday. Firemen and policemen were overwhelmed. After some antic-tragic buck-passing between city, state, and federal authorities, troops arrived on Monday night to quell the riot. Horrible as 34 deaths, more than 700 injuries, and millions of dollars in property damage were, they were not enough to prevent another riot in Harlem that August.

Two developments stand out from this unhappy tale of racial animosity. First, the government flexed its muscle as a wealthy customer to force defense industries to end discrimination. Second, federal troops were employed as an urban peacekeeping force in a fashion that became commonplace a generation later. What obscured these federal solutions to urban problems was the extreme reluctance of everyone in government from Roosevelt on down to become involved.

As with racial strife, so with housing, public health, and schooling at defense industry sites. Hesitantly, under a Congressional injunction that no wartime housing should be permanent, the federal government began to provide living quarters for war workers. Socially conscious critics were better able to discover gaps and flaws in the housing program than to find successes. They were even less able to detect straws in the wind.

There were, of course, gaps and flaws aplenty. At Willow Run in the Detroit suburban ring the Ford Motor Company tore up woods and soybean fields to build a huge bomber plant for the government. Yet the government's first concern was for a fancy highway connecting the plant with the outside world! More than 42,000 people worked at producing B-24 bombers during the 1943 employment peak. During that time federal housing sheltered a bit more than 7 percent of the working force, and less than 2½ percent of the workers' families.

At Willow Run the government had to cope with wartime materials demands, opposition from local real estate interests, and the Ford Motor Company's hostility to federal improvement of workers' conditions. The result was living conditions that were overcrowded and frustrating at best, slum-like at their worst. A declining labor force and increasing construction improved the situation by mid-1944. Tarpaper shacks, converted garages, outside toilets draining into shallow wells, hostility between old residents and newcomers, and inadequate community facilities remained.

Given these and similar situations in Newport News, Los Angeles, and hundreds of other military-industrial urban concentrations across the country, it was difficult to see the outlines of a new federal commitment. But the commitment was there. The war was one more demonstration that individual communities could not, indeed should not, have to struggle singlehandedly with the local consequences of national crises. Depression then war fused urban and national problems. In the future an urbanized nation could not afford to distinguish between them.

Bibliography

This is a selected bibliography. Only books having a significant impact on this one are included, surveys excepted. Most books of readings and collections of documents are excluded. Articles are not listed unless they were used directly in the preparation of this book. Most books and articles considered in the text are not reviewed again. Anyone who wishes to investigate a problem in depth should consult the bibliographies in the relevant listed works.

Subtitles have been added when they help to explain a book's content, omitted when they do not. Some books were useful to more than one chapter of this study. They are listed under the chapter to which they were the most pertinent.

CHAPTER ONE: THE CITIES GROW UP

Eight general urban histories review the years 1915 to 1945. Charles N. Glaab and A. Theodore Brown, *A History of Urban America* (New York, 1967) begins with the colonial period and is richly interpretive but covers the years from World War I through World War II rather briefly. Constance M. Green's brief *The Rise of Urban America* (New York, 1965) is a miserly book from the hand of a master historian. It lacks analysis and is excessively concerned with national events. The concluding chapters of Blake McKelvey's *The Urbanization of America, 1860–1915* (New Brunswick, New Jersey, 1963) are a useful introduction. His second volume, *The Emergence of Metropolitan America, 1915–1966* (New Brunswick, New Jersey, 1968), is packed with data and is good on federal-urban relationships, institutional developments, and organizational growth. It is superficial in the areas of suburbanization, planning, and urban studies. *The Urban Wilderness: A History of the American City* (New York, 1972) by Sam B. Warner is a masterful blend of national developments in the areas of technology, transportation, and business with changes in the urban scene. The author's commitment to middle-class, left-wing activism intrudes frankly and honestly, but the book is much better as history than it is as a political tract. McKelvey's brief *American Urbanization: A Comparative History* (Glenview, Illinois, 1973) contains helpful references to urbanization in Great Britain and continental Europe. Zane L. Miller's *Urbanization of Modern America* (New York, 1973) is somewhat categorical in its early chapters but is also thoughtful, well written, and well illustrated. Janet Roebuck, *The Shaping of Urban Society* (New York, 1974) and Bayard Still, *Urban America: A History With Documents* (Boston, 1974) are recently published.

Histories of single cities, the so-called urban biographies, abound. One of the best, which ends with a superior synthesis of local, regional, and national developments from a twentieth-century urban perspective, is *Milwaukee: the History of a City* (rev. ed., Madison, Wisconsin, 1965), by Bayard Still. For a meaty, widely ranging review of urban developments in the twenties, see Charles N. Glaab, "Metropolis and Suburbs: The Changing American City," pp. 399–437, in John Braeman *et al.*, eds., *Change and Continuity in Twentieth-Century America: The 1920's* (Columbus, Ohio, 1968). *American Cities in the Growth of the Nation* (New York, 1953) by Constance M. Green contains some information on the 1915–1945 period.

Books of readings have proliferated in urban history just as they have in other subject areas. One of the best is Alexander B. Callow, Jr., *American Urban History: An Interpretive Reader with Commentaries* (second ed., New York, 1973). The first edition, published in 1961, includes articles not found in the second. Kenneth T. Jackson and Stanley K. Schultz, *Cities in American History* (New York, 1972) contains the work of several younger scholars.

Periodicals concentrating on interwar urban developments include the *American City*, the *National Municipal Review*, the *Survey*, and the *Municipal Year Book*. The *Annals of the American Academy of Political and Social Science* devote several issues to urban problems. The *Journal of American History* carries articles on United States urban history and lists those appearing in other journals in its "Recent Articles" section. The United States Census volumes contain statistics on cities, as does the highly useful *Historical Statistics of the United States: Colonial Times to 1957* (Washington, D. C., 1960).

CHAPTER TWO: OUT OF EGYPT

Among the studies of the blacks' Great Migration the most imaginative is *The Negro Family in Chicago* (Chicago, 1932) by E. Franklin Frazier, which is based on contemporary data from social service agencies and on interviews with migrants. One of the most thoughtful and careful is Louise Venable Kennedy's *The Negro Peasant Turns Cityward: Effects of Recent Migrations to Northern Cities* (New York, 1930). *The Mobility of the Negro* (New York, 1931) by Edward E. Lewis is another careful study. It demonstrates that the industrial "pull" was stronger than the agricultural "push." T. J. Woofter, *Negro Problems in Cities* (reprint ed., College Park, Maryland, 1969) draws in part on data gathered by methods that would not pass muster these days. But it contains shrewd judgments about urban black life based on the observations and experience of Woofter and his assistants. Henderson H. Donald, "The Urbanization of the American Negro," pp. 181–199 in George Peter Murdock, ed., *Studies in the Science of Society* (New Haven, Connecticut, 1937) is a useful analysis of census data about black migration since the Civil War, both North and South. June Sochen, in *The Unbridgeable Gap: Blacks and Their Quest for the American Dream, 1900–1930* (Chicago, 1972), writes thoughtfully about the problems of organizations designed to help blacks. Ira Katznelson, *Black Men, White Cities: Race, Politics and Migration in the United States, 1900–30, and Britain, 1948–68* (New York, 1973) is a pessimistic sociological-historical account.

Problems in black culture are analyzed in E. Franklin Frazier's *The Negro Family in the United States* (rev. ed., Chicago, 1966), which also considers the migrations and urbanizations of blacks. Melville J. Herskovits makes a case for important African survivals in black culture in his *The Myth of the Negro Past* (rev. ed., Boston, 1958). The introduction and the first two chapters of *Urban Blues* (Chicago, 1966) by Charles Keil form a first-rate commentary on black culture and its influence on white culture.

Few biographies of blacks bear on urban situations. One that does is *The Lonely Warrior: The Life and Times of Robert S. Abbott* (Chicago, 1955), by Roi Ottley. It is an undisciplined narrative but is good on Abbott's contributions to black journalism. Two studies of Marcus Garvey are important. E. David Cronon's *Black Moses* (Madison, Wisconsin, 1955), is scholarly and somewhat narrowly focused. *Black Power and the Garvey Movement* by Theodore G. Vincent (Berkeley, California, 1971) places Garvey in the context of worldwide black radicalism but is not meticulously done.

Black Chicagoans have received disproportionate attention from scholars. An excellent sociological-anthropological study of Chicago's black community, focusing on the late thirties and early forties, is St. Clair Drake and Horace R. Cayton, *Black Metropolis* (New York, 1945). Otis Dudley Duncan and Beverly Duncan produced a very good examination of shifting residential patterns and land uses in *The Negro Population of Chicago* (Chicago, 1957), which emphasizes the period after 1939. Although contemporary political scientists might find fault with its methodology, Harold F. Gosnell's *Negro Politicians* (Chicago, 1935) is an imaginative study containing valuable biographical information about Chicago's black political leaders. *Black Chicago: The Making of a Negro Ghetto, 1890–1920* (Chicago, 1967) by Allan H. Spear is a readable historical-sociological study. Arvah E. Strickland sympathetically reviews the *History of the Chicago Urban League* (Urbana, Illinois, 1966) as do Guichard Paris and Lester Brooks for the National Urban League in *Blacks in the City* (Boston, 1971). Neither study alters the conviction expressed in this book that the Urban League did little to help newly arrived migrants. The best study of the 1919 race riots is William M. Tuttle Jr., *Race Riot: Chicago in the Red Summer of 1919* (New York, 1970). It is an excellent review of race conflict in Chicago and the nation, its careful, controlled writing marred only by a strained effort at contemporary relevance in the last few pages.

Black residents of Washington, D. C. are given their due in Constance M. Green's *The Secret City: A History of Race Relations in the Nation's Capital* (Princeton, 1967). Mrs. Green traces the steady deterioration of race relations and declining opportunities for blacks from Reconstruction onward, plus black protest and white indifference.

Gilbert Osofsky's *Harlem: The Making of a Ghetto, Negro New York, 1890–1930* (paperbound ed., New York, 1968) is a classic of black history. Roi Ottley and William J. Weatherby edited *The Negro in New York* (New York, 1967), the manuscript prepared by the Federal Writers Project. The book covers the years from 1626 to 1940, and includes social life, the Harlem Renaissance, and the impact of the Great Depression. Indispensable for students of black culture and black New York is Nathan I. Huggins' scholarly, witty *Harlem Renaissance* (New York, 1971).

Elliott M. Rudiwick's *Race Riot at East St. Louis, July 2, 1917* (Carbondale, Illinois, 1964) covers its subject well. An illuminating article on blacks in the West is "The City of Black Angels: Emergence of the Los Angeles Ghetto, 1890–1930," *Pacific Historical Review* (August, 1970), pp. 323–352, by Lawrence B. De Graaf. Urban Klansmen, less racist and more concerned with enforcing "morality" than their country cousins, are depicted in Kenneth T. Jackson's *The Ku Klux Klan in the City, 1915–1930* (New York, 1967).

A monograph with a deceptively narrow title is Gerd Korman's *Industrialization, Immigrants and Americanizers: The View From Milwaukee, 1866–1921* (Madison, Wisconsin, 1967). Other aspects of "late" immigration and problems of assimilation are treated in Humbert S. Nelli, *Italians in Chicago, 1880–1930* (New York, 1970). Jane Addams, *The Second Twenty Years at Hull-House* (New York, 1930) and Louise C. Wade, *Graham Taylor* (Chicago, 1964) recount efforts to cope with the immigrant influx around settlement houses.

Jewish settlers in American cities are the subject of many books. Stephen Birmingham, *"Our Crowd": The Great Jewish Families of New York* (New York, 1967) is a lively, informal social history. *Jewish Community Organizations in the United States* (New York, 1938) by Maurice J. Karpf discusses the problems of Jews' relationship with the larger community, their safety, and their recognition as of the late 1930s. An excellent sociological study that uses history intelligently is C. Bezalel Sherman's *The Jew Within American Society* (Detroit, 1961). Louis Wirth's *The Ghetto* (Chicago, 1928) is a classic.

Individual Jewish communities have been studied in books of uneven quality. Two that revel in antiquarian detail and social narrative are Selig Adler and Thomas G. Connolly, *From Ararat to Suburbia: The History of the Jewish Community of Buffalo* (Philadelphia, 1960), and Albert I. Gordon, *Jews in Transition* [Minneapolis] (Minneapolis, 1949), although Gordon is frank about anti-Semitism and related problems. Sidney Goldstein and Calvin Goldscheider, *Jewish Americans: Three Generations in a Jewish Community* (Englewood Cliffs, New Jersey, 1968) is a good sociological study of Jews in greater Providence, Rhode Island. Louis P. Swichkow and Lloyd P. Gartner, *The History of the Jews of Milwaukee* (Philadelphia, 1963) is a solid social history that ties in the relevant national and international developments with Milwaukee's Jewry.

CHAPTER THREE: THE PROMISED LAND

Several ecological studies help in the understanding of interwar urban-suburban relationships. Two of these are by Donald J. Bogue: *The Structure of the Metropolitan Community: A Study of Dominance and Subdominance* (Ann Arbor, 1949) and *Population Growth in Standard Metropolitan Areas, 1900–1950* (Washington, D.C., 1953). *The Changing Shape of Metropolitan America: Deconcentration Since 1920* (Glencoe, Illinois, 1956) by Amos H. Hawley is a statistical study of population changes in most metropolitan areas through the 1950 census. It delivers less than the title suggests. Warren S. Thompson's *Population: the Growth of Metropolitan Districts in the United States, 1900–1940* (Washington, D. C., 1947) contains useful statistics.

There is no single study of the psychological and physical factors in suburbanization between the wars. Bennett M. Berger, *Working-Class Suburb* (Berkeley, California, 1960), and Samuel D. Clark, *The Suburban Society* (Toronto, 1960), are two of several post–1945 studies that found general stability and contentment among suburbanites. Useful background information may also be had from Benjamin Chinitz, ed., *City and Suburb* (Englewood Cliffs, New Jersey, 1964) and William M. Dobriner, *Class in Suburbia* (Englewood Cliffs, New Jersey, 1963).

Harlan Paul Douglas' *The Suburban Trend* (New York, 1925) is an optimistic review of the development of middle-class and upper middle-class suburbs. Douglas anticipates a blend of the best of city and country in suburbia. Homer Hoyt, *The Structure and Growth of Residential Neighborhoods in American Cities* (Washington, D.C., 1939) is descriptive, while George A. Lundberg *et al., Leisure: A Suburban Study* (New York, 1934) is a classic, the second chapter of which is valuable for "freezing" the Westchester County, New York suburbs in the early 1930s.

Chicago: Growth of a Metropolis (Chicago, 1969) by Harold M. Mayer and Richard C. Wade is an excellent source for photographs and line drawings of urban-suburban development. Victor Steinbrueck's *Seattle Cityscape* (Seattle, 1962) contains interesting graphics and helpful descriptions of suburban building styles. For a discussion of the cultural impetus to early suburbanization see Peter J. Schmidt, *Back to Nature* (New York, 1969). Graham R. Taylor's *Satellite Cities* (New York, 1915) is a prescient study of industrial suburbanization. Sam B. Warner's *Streetcar Suburbs: The Process of Growth in Boston, 1870–1900* (Cambridge, Massachusetts, 1962) is a disciplined, imaginative approach to suburbanization, and a model for any historical study of the subject.

Lewis Mumford's *The City in History* (New York, 1961) is wise, rich, and humane. Chapter 16 stakes out most of the critical lines of attack on suburbia. His earlier "The Wilderness of Suburbia," *The New Republic* (September 7, 1921), pp. 44–45, is discussed in the text, as is Edward Yeomans' "The Suburb De Lux," *Atlantic Monthly* (January, 1920), pp. 105–107.

There is a great deal of literature on cars, trains, and interurbans, much of it of strictly antiquarian interest. This is not true of "A Symbol of Modernity: Attitudes Toward the Automobile in Southern Cities in the 1920s," a thoughtful article by Blaine A. Brownell in *American Quarterly* (March, 1972), pp. 20–44. Robert M. Fogelson, *The Fragmented Metropolis: Los Angeles, 1850–1930* (Cambridge, Massachusetts, 1967) contains good discussions of the city's suburbanization and electric interurbans. Although it relies mostly on published sources, George W. Hilton and John F. Dué, *The Electric Interurban Railways in America* (Stanford, California, 1960) remains the standard source on its subject. It is sympathetic in tone and smooth in narrative. John B. Rae's *The American Automobile* (Chicago, 1965) is a lively, brief introduction with short but sound discussions of the automobile problem, Rae's pro-automobile *The Road and the Car in American Life* (Cambridge, Massachusetts, 1971) is mostly about the post-World War II period but includes excellent historical flashbacks. The most relevant chapter in John F. Stover's introductory *American Railroads* (Chicago, 1961) is the one about their decline.

CHAPTER FOUR: VARIETIES OF POLITICS

The indispensable book on urban politics is Edward C. Banfield and James Q. Wilson, *City Politics* (Cambridge, Massachusetts, 1963), which deals with historical trends. The classic description of the "latent functions" of the urban political machine is by Robert K. Merton in *Social Theory and Social Structure* (rev. ed., Glencoe, Illinois, 1957), pp. 70–82. For brief but perspicacious introductions to the historical problems of black politics, see *Negro Politics* (Glencoe, Illinois, 1960) by James Q. Wilson. Bruce M. Stave has edited a good book of readings with a recommended bibliography, *Urban Bosses, Machines, and Progressive Reformers* (Lexington, Massachusetts, 1972).

The literature on the council-manager form and on municipal reform organizations is voluminous. The booklets of the National Municipal League are valuable for the viewpoint of that organization, irrespective of subject. One of the most pertinent is Arthur W. Bromage, *Manager Plan Abandonments* (New York, 1964). Richard S. Childs reveals a great deal about himself and the reform mentality in *Civic Victories* (New York, 1952) and *The First 50 Years of the Council-Manager Plan of Municipal Government* (New York, 1965). *Municipal Research Bureaus* (Washington, D. C., 1944) by Norman N. Gill is descriptive and friendly to the bureaus.

Of all the revisionist writing about urban progressives, none has been more influential or widely reprinted than Samuel P. Hays, "The Politics of Reform in Municipal Government in the Progressive

Era," *Pacific Northwest Quarterly* (October, 1964), pp. 157–169. Hays finds most urban progressives to be upper-class centralists who wrapped their schemes in self-serving rhetoric. Gladys M. Kammerer, *City Managers in Politics* (Gainesville, Florida, 1962) is a good study of manager mobility and professional loyalties. Two intelligent studies of the actual operation of council-manager governments, favoring professionalism but open-minded and free from axegrinding are Frederick C. Mosher *et al.*, *City Manager Government in Seven Cities* (Chicago, 1940) and Harold A. Stone *et al.*, *City Manager Government in Nine Cities* (Chicago, 1940). Frank Mann Stewart's *A Half Century of Municipal Reform* (Berkeley, California, 1950) is useful for the internal development of the National Municipal League and its links with other urban-oriented organizations. A generally praiseful evaluation of managers against strictly professional criteria is Leonard D. White's *The City Manger* (Chicago, 1927). Lyle Dorsett's "The City Boss and the Reformer: A Reappraisal," *Pacific Northwest Quarterly* (October, 1972), pp. 150–154, emphasizes the similarities between the political practices of bosses and reformers.

The best study of La Guardia is Arthur Mann's, of which the second volume, *La Guardia Comes to Power: 1933* (Chicago, 1965), is pertinent. Until Mann completes his biography the standard work on La Guardia's mayorality will continue to be Charles Garrett's *The La Guardia Years* (New Brunswick, New Jersey, 1961). Less enamored of La Guardia than his scholarly biographers is Rexford G. Tugwell, who served under the peppery little politician and writes critically of him in *The Art of Politics* (Garden City, New York, 1958). *Charles Francis Murphy, 1858–1924* (Northhampton, Massachusetts, 1968) by Nancy Joan Weiss is an excellent AB thesis, a model of research and writing for students and their professors.

Chicago's politics, reform and crime have been well studied. A standard analysis, careful and sensible, is *Machine Politics: Chicago Model* (Chicago, 1937) by Harold F. Gosnell. Rich in background and insight is Alex Gottfried's *Boss Cermak of Chicago* (Seattle, 1962), an exhaustive study of a tough politician with all the warts on. John Landesco, *Organized Crime in Chicago* (Chicago, 1968) is good on organized crime and youth gangs. Forrest Mc Donald, *Insull* (Chicago, 1962) is worshipful but deeply researched, and includes passages on the utilities magnate's relationship to Chicago politics. *Big Bill of Chicago* (Indianapolis, 1953) by Lloyd Wendt and Herman Kogan is a lively narrative about a perversely appealing subject. The same authors' *Lords of the Levee* (Indianapolis, 1943) is a topflight popular history about two even more colorful characters, John Coughlin and Michael Kenna.

CHAPTER FIVE: CITIES ANALYZED

Much of the relevant literature is mentioned in the text. For reviews of the state of sociology at various periods, see George A. Lundberg *et al., Trends in American Sociology* (New York, 1929); L. L. Bernard, ed., *The Fields and Methods of Sociology* (New York, 1934); and Paul K. Hatt and Albert J. Reiss, Jr., eds., *Reader in Urban Sociology* (Glencoe, Illinois, 1951).

The extensive writing on the Chicago school sees its practitioners from many different perspectives. One of the most widely known studies on American thinkers, Morton and Lucia White's *The Intellectual Versus the City* (Cambridge, Massachusetts, 1962) treats Park in part of one chapter. The discussion of Park as an antiurbanite is highly selective and slanted, with coyly hedged conclusions. Herbert Blumer, *An Appraisal of Thomas and Znaniecki's The Polish Peasant in Europe and America* (New York, 1939) is an enlightening discussion of a path-breaking effort to describe community acculturation. Maurice R. Davie, "The Pattern of Urban Growth," pp. 133–161 in George Peter Murdock, ed., *Studies in the Science of Society* (New Haven, Connecticut, 1937) is strong when describing New Haven's physical expansion, merely fussy when attacking Ernest W. Burgess. Park Dixon Goist sees Robert Park's function as examining and comprehending the individual and collective transition from village to metropolis. See his "City and 'Community': The Urban Theory of Robert Park," *American Quarterly* (Spring, 1971), pp. 46–59. A wise book with an excellent discussion of the Chicago school's analysis of deviant individuals and communities is David Matza's *Becoming Deviant* (Englewood Cliffs, New Jersey, 1969). Robert E. L. Faris presents an inside view of the Chicago faculty and its ideas in *Chicago Sociology, 1920–1932* (Chicago, 1970).

Leonard Reissman's *The Urban Process* (New York, 1964), seeks to understand what parts of its past are valid for contemporary sociology. Reissman's astute criticism of Park and Louis Wirth repays reading. The introduction to James F. Short, Jr., *The Social Fabric of the Metropolis* (Chicago, 1971) is a useful discussion of Chicago-school contributions and their post-1945 influence. T. V. Smith and Leonard D. White, *Chicago: An Experiment in Social Science Research* (Chicago, 1929) is an interdisciplinary review of the urban studies done under the auspices of the Local Community Research Committee.

Robert E. Park, *Race and Culture* (New York, 1950) collects Park's writings on those subjects.

The Eclipse of Community by Maurice R. Stein (Princeton, 1960) includes a selective, descriptive review of Park, the Lynds, and W. Lloyd Warner. The last three chapters and the epilogue are more analytical. Stephan Thernstrom's *Poverty and Progress* (Cambridge, Massachusetts, 1964) is about nineteenth-century Newburyport. Chapter 8 and the Appendix concerning Warner's ahistoricism are essential to the development of the viewpoint presented in this book. Of the Yankee City series the first volume by Warner and Paul S. Lunt, *The Social Life of a Modern Community* (New Haven, Connecticut, 1941) should be consulted for a summary of findings, the background of the research, explicit and implicit assumptions, and methodology. Blanche H. Gelfant's *The American City Novel* (Norman, Oklahoma, 1954) is clouded by the author's conviction that the successful city novel must deal with human degradation and despair. Nevertheless it is very useful. A perceptive study of the American novel, focusing on the novelists' personal experiences as well as on twentieth-century social developments is Nelson Manfred Blake, *Novelists' America: Fiction as History, 1910–1940* (Syracuse, New York, 1969). Blake's first and final chapters, together with his discussions of Lewis, Dos Passos, Farrell, and Wright are recommended.

CHAPTER SIX: MOLES AND SKYLARKS

Mel Scott's *American City Planning Since 1890* (Berkeley, California, 1969) is a masterpiece of scholarship. Although it pays most attention to the professional planners, this monumental study ignores little. It is must reading for anyone who wants to understand the range of city planning in the twentieth century. Although Scott is quite good on zoning, his account should be reinforced by Seymour I. Toll's *Zoned American* (New York, 1969), a usually entertaining, sometimes idiosyncratic, always intensely personal history of zoning by a lawyer-planner. Robert Moses is the author of two autobiographical efforts, *Public Works* (New York, 1970), a discursive account, and *Working for the People* (New York, 1956), which is more tightly organized. Cleveland Rodgers supervised the earlier autobiography and also wrote *Robert Moses* (New York, 1952). Rodgers' book is praiseful but manages to see some shortcomings in its subject. Moses' "Plan and Performance," in Robert S. Rankin, ed., *A Century of Social Thought* (Durham, North Carolina, 1939) is pure Moses, a spicy, witty, highly intelligent statement of his planning philosophy. The chapter on Moses in Jeanne R. Lowe,

Cities in a Race With Time (New York, 1967) concentrates on his post-World War II career. City planning receives its due in Norman T. Newton's comprehensive, scholarly, sensitive *Design on the Land: The Development of Landscape Architecture* (Cambridge, Massachusetts, 1971).

Thomas Adams' *Outline of Town and City Planning* (New York, 1935), which discusses the RPNY, is one of the best surveys of realistic planning. Another valuable study is John C. Bollens, *Special District Governments in the United States* (Berkeley, California, 1957), which discusses metropolitan districts. Bollens concentrates on the period since World War II but includes useful historical sections. Robert A. Walker, *The Planning Function in Urban Government* (rev. ed., Chicago, 1950) also is important. Susanne Starling recounts one citizen effort at realistic planning in a 1970 North Texas State University seminar paper, "The Din of Iniquity: A Decade of Concern Over Urban Noise in New York City." There is an insightful discussion of the thrust and limitations of business-oriented planning in the 1920s and 1930s in Sam Bass Warner, Jr., *The Private City: Philadelphia in Three Stages of Its Growth* (Philadelphia, 1968).

The beginning point for interwar utopian planning is Ebenezer Howard's *Garden Cities of To-Morrow* (reprint ed., Cambridge, Massachusetts, 1965). Roy Lubove's *Community Planning in the 1920's* (Pittsburgh, 1963) is a brief study of the RPAA, which could be even briefer without the loss of essential material. The complete exposition of Lewis Mumford's thought on urban development, presented more judiciously than in some other books, appears in *The Culture of Cities* (New York, 1938). Two of Frank Lloyd Wright's expositions of his Broadacre City are in *The Disappearing City* (New York, 1932) and *When Democracy Builds* (Chicago, 1945). His *The Living City* (New York, 1958) is well illustrated. Paul and Percival Goodman's *Communitas* (rev. ed., New York, 1960) contains spirited if bigoted criticisms of Broadacre City and the Greenbelt towns. Two biographies of Wright discuss Broadacre City. Norris Kelly Smith's *Frank Lloyd Wright: A Study in Architectural Content* (Englewood Cliffs, New Jersey, 1966) is intelligent if arrogant, and places Wright in the context of Western thought. Robert C. Twombly's authoritative, superbly crafted *Frank Lloyd Wright: An Interpretive Biography* (New York, 1973) includes a fine summary of Wright's critique of the industrial-commercial city. Twombly ably relates Broadacre City to more recent proposals for solving urban problems.

Of the books on the Greenbelt towns three are most useful. Joseph L. Arnold, *The New Deal in the Suburbs* (Columbus, Ohio, 1971) is scholarly and thorough. Arnold rejects the idea that the Greenbelt towns were part of the back-to-the-land movement. One chapter of Paul K. Conkin's comprehensive study of the New Deal resettlement program, *Tomorrow A New World* (Ithaca, New York, 1959), is devoted to the Greenbelt towns. Clarence S. Stein, *Toward New Towns for America* (rev. ed., Cambridge, Massachusetts, 1966), includes a chapter on the Greenbelt towns in an optimistic statement of the Radburn Idea.

CHAPTER SEVEN: THE NATIONALIZATION OF CITIES

For the activities of one person who worked both sides of the nationalizing street, see Louis Brownlow, *A Passion for Anonymity* (Chicago, 1958). Clarke A. Chambers, *Paul U. Kellogg and the Survey* (Minneapolis, 1971) is a superior study. Unfortunately for urban historians Chambers is more concerned with Kellogg as a voice for social work than he is with Kellogg's handling of urban problems.

Most of the literature on intergovernmental relationships focuses on the period since World War II. Robert H. Connery and Richard H. Leach, *The Federal Government and Metropolitan Areas* (Cambridge, Massachusetts, 1960) is concerned with the situation in the late fifties but manages a few historical flashbacks. A widely ranging if somewhat categorical and simplistic review is Daniel J. Elazar's "The Shaping of Intergovernmental Relations in the Twentieth Century," *Annals of the American Academy of Political and Social Science* (May, 1965), pp. 10–22. Morton Grodzins, *The American System* (Chicago, 1966) discusses federalism in the 1950s and 1960s from a state-federal standpoint with some attention to local relationships. The historical sections lump "local" governments of all sizes together. James T. Patterson's *The New Deal and the States* (Princeton, 1969), a study of federal-state relationships, contains suggestions of the growing importance of urban-federal relations during the New Deal. Harry N. Scheiber overstates the case for a postwar revolution in federal-urban relationships in "The Condition of American Federalism," in Frank Smallwood, ed., *The New Federalism* (Hanover, New Hampshire, 1967), pp. 19–55. Howard D. Hamilton, ed., *Legislative Apportionment* (New York, 1964) is one of many studies of the problem.

There is little literature bearing on interwar federal-urban relationships. Two preliminary drafts prepared for the Conference on the National Archives and Urban Research, Washington, 1970 are useful. They are William H. Cunliffe, "Military Development and Urban

Growth in the San Francisco Bay Area Prior to World War II," and Edward E. Hill, "Records in the National Archives Relating to Public Works in the City of Sacramento." Carl H. Scheele is the author of two important studies concerned with traditional urban-federal relations: "The Post Office Department and Urban Congestion, 1893–1953," a paper read at the 1967 meeting of the American Historical Association, and *A Short History of the Mail Service* (Washington, D. C., 1970), which is chronologically inclusive and necessarily briefer on the period from 1915 to 1945. Marilyn McAdams Sibley's *The Port of Houston* (Austin, Texas, 1968) is utterly uncritical. Its failure to probe other than local sources is incomprehensible, but it does demonstrate how even far-visioned, clear-eyed captains of industry depended on federal largess.

Herbert Hoover vindicates himself in the two relevant volumes of his memoirs, *The Cabinet and the Presidency, 1920–1933* and *The Great Depression* (New York, 1952). One result of his deep concern for the study of social developments is The President's Research Committee on Social Trends, *Recent Social Trends in the United States* (New York, 1933), a massive compendium containing several chapters that impinge upon urban life. Paul V. Betters, *Federal Services to Municipal Governments* (Washington, D. C., 1931) is a department-by-department review of federal aids as they had developed by the time of publication. A shrewd critique of the idea of stabilizing the economy through public works spending, and a review of public works spending at all levels of government is in *Public Works in Prosperity and Depression* (New York, 1935) by Arthur D. Gayer. Gayer includes a chapter on the PWA to mid-1934. Edward A. Williams, *Federal Aid for Relief* (New York, 1939) is a workmanlike review of both Hoover and New Deal relief. Two good "revisionist" histories sympathetic to Hoover are Albert U. Romasco, *The Poverty of Abundance* (New York, 1965) and Harris Gaylord Warren, *Herbert Hoover and the Great Depression* (New York, 1959).

J. Woodford Howard, *Mr. Justice Murphy* (Princeton, 1968) describes Murphy's Detroit career in taut, lively prose, while Richard D. Lunt's account in *The High Ministry of Government* (Detroit, 1965) is adequate but plodding. Useful on some points is Robert M. Kvasnicka, "City in Crisis: The Impact of Depression on Detroit, Michigan as Reflected in Records of the Federal Relief Agencies," a preliminary paper prepared for the 1970 Conference on the National Archives and Urban Research.

The best narrative and interpretive account of the New Deal is William E. Leuchtenburg's *Franklin D. Roosevelt and the New Deal,*

1932–1940 (New York, 1963). *The Coming of the New Deal* (Boston, 1959) by Arthur M. Schlesinger, Jr., is standard but does not discuss the WPA. In the spirit of more recent writing that stresses the limits rather than the accomplishments of the New Deal is Paul K. Conkin, *FDR and the Origins of the Welfare State* (New York, 1967). Searle F. Charles' account of Harry Hopkins, *Minister of Relief* (Syracuse, New York, 1963) is conventional and state-oriented, content with fleshing out earlier accounts of Hopkins' activities. Jane De Hart Mathews writes a scholarly and sympathetic study about a New Deal agency producing major plays for urban audiences in *The Federal Theatre, 1935–1939* (Princeton, 1967). An important modification of the "new left" view that the New Deal did nothing special for blacks is in *Negroes and the Great Depression* (Westport, Connecticut, 1970) by Raymond Wolters. For some of the adverse impacts on Cleveland blacks of New Deal housing and hiring, see Christopher G. Wye, "The New Deal and the Negro Community: Toward a Broader Conceptualization," *Journal of American History* (December, 1972), pp. 621–639.

Two essential studies of the New Deal's impact on urban machines are Lyle W. Dorsett, *The Pendergast Machine* (New York, 1968) and Bruce M. Stave, *The New Deal and the Last Hurrah: Pittsburgh Machine Politics* (Pittsburgh, 1970). Both studies reject the "Last Hurrah" thesis.

A good background chapter on New Deal and pre-New Deal housing is in Richard O. Davies, *Housing Reform During the Truman Administration* (Columbia, Missouri, 1966). J. Joseph Huthmacher's *Senator Robert F. Wagner and the Rise of Urban Liberalism* (New York, 1968) is an exceptionally rich, superbly executed study of Wagner and his urban-oriented allies in the Senate. Timothy L. McDonnell, *The Wagner Housing Act* (Chicago, 1957) examines the passage of the 1937 Housing Act in minute detail and leaden prose. For a brief but informative section on national housing policy prior to World War II, see Paul F. Wendt, *Housing Policy—The Search for Solutions* (Berkeley, California, 1963).

The urban vote has been recently analyzed in many ways. John M. Allswang's, *A House for All Peoples: Ethnic Politics in Chicago, 1890–1936* (Lexington, Kentucky, 1971) is an intelligent blend of qualitative and quantitative data on ethnic voting in local, state, and national elections. The bibliographical essay is essential. Useful articles include Carl N. Degler, "American Political Parties and the Rise of the City," *Journal of American History* (June, 1964), pp. 41–59; Samuel J. Eldersveld, "The Influence of Metropolitan Party Pluralities in Presidential Elections Since 1920," *American Political*

Science Review (December, 1949), pp. 669–683; John L. Shover, "Was 1928 a Critical Election in California," *Pacific Northwest Quarterly* (October, 1967), pp. 196–204; and Ruth Werner Gordon, "The Change in the Political Alignment of Chicago's Negroes During the New Deal," *Journal of American History* (December, 1969), pp. 584–603. Robert K. Murray provides a good glimpse of public exasperation with the Woodrow Wilson administration in *The Harding Era* (Minneapolis, 1969).

Urban racial violence and black militance during World War II is probed in two articles by Harvard Sitkoff, "The Detroit Race Riot of 1943," *Michigan History* (Fall, 1968), pp. 183–206 and "Racial Militancy and Interracial Violence in the Second World War," *Journal of American History* (December, 1971), pp. 661–681. Both articles should be consulted for the bibliographic references in the footnotes. The second article is quick to blame F. D. R.'s caution and his alliance with the Southern Democratic Congressional bloc for federal failures in race relations. The wartime psychology is underplayed, and growing white conservatism (as distinguished from prejudice) in the United States is unmentioned. Lowell J. Carr and James E. Stermer, *Willow Run* (New York, 1952) is an excellent picture of the situation despite the authors' determination to date the book by straining for immediacy and relevance. Keith Sward in *The Legend of Henry Ford* (paperback ed., New York, 1968) discusses the Willow Run housing situation.

Index

Abbott, Robert S.
 black businessman, 13
 Chicago *Defender* and, 13
Adams, Thomas
 director of RPNY, 136–137
 Outline of Town and City Planning and,
  138–139
 planning and, 133
 response to Lewis Mumford's criticisms
  of RPNY, 138
Addams, Jane, 7
American City, 125, 164
American Institute of Architects, 167
American Institute of Planners, 163
American Society of Planning Officials,
  163–164
 purposes of, 164
American Tragedy, An, Theodore Dreiser,
  120–121
Americanization
 Inter-Racial Council, 29
 "Jewish problem," 29–32
 Kellor, Frances, 29
 settlement houses and, 28, 29
Auto suburbs
 benefits of, 45–46
 Country Club district, 42–43, 44
 critics of, 36 (*see* Mumford, Lewis)
 growth of, 34–35
 growth of cities and, 39
 house styles in, 35, 37–38
 Huntington Palisades, 44
 Palos Verdes Estates, 44
 reasons for growth, 35–36
 restrictive covenants, 38
 working-class suburbs, 44–45
 zoning and, 38

Automobiles
 advantages of, 47–48
 increase in, 2, 49
 mass transit and, 52–54
 necessity of, 49
 Pacific Electric and, 55–57
 street railways and, 54–55
 urban costs and, 49–52

Babbitt, Sinclair Lewis, 122
Bassett, Edward M.
 chairman of zoning advisory committee,
  131
 chairman of Heights of Buildings Com-
  mittee, 128–129
 Standard State Zoning Enabling Act and,
  132
Bettman, Alfred
 Euclid versus Ambler and, 132–133
 planning and, 133
Bigger, Frederick, 157–158
"Boston–1915," 125–125
Broadacre City, 152–155
Brown Decades, The, Lewis Mumford, 147
Brownlow, Louis
 American Society of Planning Officials,
  163–164
 National Resources Planning Board, 195
 Public Administration Clearing House, 163
Burgess, Ernest W.
 attacks on concentric theory of, 107–108
 background and career, 94–95
 concentric theory of urban expansion, 95,
  105–108
 teaching and, 96
Business-in-government
 council-manager system and, 60

215